A Grand Army of Black Men

A Grand Army
of Black Men

Letters from African-American Soldiers
in the Union Army, 1861–1865

Edited by EDWIN S. REDKEY

CAMBRIDGE
UNIVERSITY PRESS

Published by the Press Syndicate of the University of Cambridge
The Pitt Building, Trumpington Street, Cambridge CB2 1RP
40 West 20th Street, New York, NY 10011-4211, USA
10 Stamford Road, Oakleigh, Victoria 3166, Australia

© Cambridge University Press 1992

First published 1992
Reprinted 1993

Printed in the United States of America

Library of Congress Cataloging-in-Publication Data

A Grand army of Black men: letters from African-American soldiers in
the Union Army, 1861–1865 / edited by Edwin S. Redkey.
p.   cm. – (Cambridge studies in American literature and
culture: 63)
ISBN 0-521-43400-9. – ISBN 0-521-43998-1 (pbk.)
1. United States – History – Civil War, 1861–1865 – Participation,
Afro-American.   2. United States – History – Civil War, 1861–1865
– Personal narratives.   3. Afro-American soldiers – Correspondence.
I. Redkey, Edwin S.   II. Series.
E540.N3G74   1993
973.7'415'0922 – dc20   92-14632
CIP

A catalog record for this book is available from the British Library

ISBN 0-521-43400-9 hardback
ISBN 0-521-43998-1 paperback

For Nancy

Contents

Preface

W HEN, in 1978, the late Bell Irvin Wiley wrote a new introduction to his book *The Life of Billy Yank: The Common Soldier of the Union,* he sadly noted "a dearth of letters written by the 200,000 blacks who donned the blue. A careful search has turned up less than a score of these sources."[1] Wiley's book gives an excellent picture of the daily lives, routines, thoughts, and concerns of Yankee soldiers, and part of a chapter is on the black troops. But without the breadth and depth of documents written by the black soldiers themselves, neither Wiley nor any other historian has been able fully to document the roles played by African Americans in the Civil War.

Private letters of black soldiers may have vanished, but others have now reappeared. A massive quantity of official correspon-

1. Bell Irvin Wiley, *The Life of Billy Yank; The Common Soldier of the Union,* second edition (Baton Rouge, Louisiana State University Press, 1978) 16.

dence by and about black soldiers has been found in the National Archives. And many soldiers wrote "letters to the editors" of black and abolitionist newspapers, to tell their friends at home about their experiences, their fears, and their hopes. This book is a selection of such letters by black soldiers published in newspapers during the war years.

THE NEWSPAPERS

During the Civil War, two nationally read newspapers were published by black Americans: the *Christian Recorder,* of Philadelphia, and the *Weekly Anglo-African,* of New York City. The *Recorder* was the official organ of the African Methodist Episcopal (AME) Church. The Church had been established in 1816 by several congregations of black Methodists who had withdrawn from white-dominated churches because of racial discrimination. By 1860 the Church had spread across the Northern states and into portions of the South where free black communities existed. It established the *Christian Recorder* in 1853 to help unite the denomination and to provide a forum where black writers could discuss their views. Most of the content of the paper focused on church affairs; but in 1863, with the enlistment of many Northern blacks into the army, the editor, the Reverend Elisha Weaver, began to include letters and articles about current affairs. From 1863 through 1865 the *Christian Recorder* each week published several letters from black soldiers. Many of those issues have survived, and most of the letters in this collection come from those pages.

The second major black newspaper of the Civil War years was the *Weekly Anglo-African.* Founded in 1859 by editors Thomas and Robert Hamilton, the *"Anglo"* reported the affairs of the black community throughout the Northeast. It printed religious news from all denominations, but it was not a church newspaper as such, and from the beginning it carried letters and articles of broader concern. It vigorously opposed slavery, and it sponsored an educational group called the "African Civilization Society." Early in the war years it also gave limited endorsement to the idea of emigration to Haiti as a solution to the race issue in the United States. But after the Emancipation Proclamation it urged black men to enlist in the army to fight for the Union, and when they began writing letters from the training camps and battlefields, the *Anglo* published many of them. Robert Hamilton died in 1865, and his newspaper also died at the end of that year. Relatively few issues of the *Weekly Anglo-African* have survived, especially from 1863 through the end of the war. But the rich content of those surviving issues suggests that the *Anglo* was the main voice of the black soldiers of the North.

For four months, from May to August of 1862, the *Weekly Anglo-African* stopped publication and yielded the ground to another weekly, the *Pine and Palm*, published in Boston. This paper was the official organ of the "Haytien Emigration Bureau," headed by a white man, James Redpath, and was sponsored by the government of Haiti. During those early months of the war, the *Pine and Palm* also became the official paper of the African Civilization Society. Before it stopped publishing, after the Emancipation Proclamation, it carried a series of letters from a black man who had joined a white regiment from Connecticut and fought in some of the early battles of the war.

Most of the letters in this volume are drawn from these three newspapers. *Frederick Douglass's Monthly* stopped publishing just when blacks began enlisting, and Douglass himself became an active recruiter. Occasionally letters from black soldiers appeared in other newspapers, including white-edited abolitionist papers such as *The Liberator.* From time to time the general press would publish a letter from a black soldier, and undoubtedly more letters lie undiscovered in the pages of small-town newspapers across the North. This was true of the letters of Corporal James H. Gooding of the 54th Massachusetts Volunteer Infantry, who wrote weekly reports to the *New Bedford* (Massachusetts) *Mercury.* But the *Christian Recorder,* the *Weekly Anglo-African,* and the *Pine and Palm* provided a sympathetic audience and assured publication, so most black soldiers of the Civil War wrote to them, leaving a rich vein of firsthand accounts to be mined by future historians.

PRINCIPLES OF SELECTION AND EDITING

This collection of letters from black soldiers contains 129 items selected and edited to give the reader a broad sample of the experiences and concerns of those men. In over a dozen years of searching, the editor has found almost four hundred such letters. Those in this book have been chosen because they are articulate statements on significant issues or experiences.

Every effort has been made to identify the author of each letter. Many writers signed their letters with their full name, rank, and unit, along with the date and place of writing. Others signed with just initials or a *nom de guerre;* this was especially likely when a letter contained strong criticism of whites, or officers, or of the government. (Sergeant Joseph H. Barquet of the 54th Massachusetts Volunteer Infantry was court-martialed and reprimanded for writing a letter to the *Weekly Anglo-African* complaining about the quantity and quality of army food.) In every case, the editor tried to make positive identification of the writer by searching of service records, by comparison with other letters, and by use of other internal evidence.

The texts of these letters stand essentially as they were originally published in the newspapers. It is clear that the newspaper editors made changes in the letters before publication; grammar, spelling, capitalization, and punctuation were standardized, and letters may have been shortened to fit available space. Occasionally, in reading the handwritten letters, the newspaper editor or typesetter made errors that are obvious, such as misspelling of names or incorrect identification of military units; but we must assume that what actually appeared in print was reasonably close to what the original author scratched by hand under conditions of war. In this collection, minor changes have been made where the original newspaper spelling, capitalization, or punctuation might confuse or distract the modern reader from the content of the letters. Where the print in the newspaper was mutilated, the editor has so indicated and, where possible, made a reasonable guess about the missing words; those guesses are placed in brackets. Also in brackets are the missing ranks and portions of names of people mentioned in the letters, whenever they can be positively identified. Some letters contain references to terms, people, or events that need further identification or explanation; the editor has added footnotes to provide such background information.

Few newspaper letters from black soldiers have been reprinted since the Civil War. Herbert Aptheker, in the first volume of his *Documentary History of the Negro People in the United States* (New York, Citadel, 1951), included three such letters. James M. McPherson, in *The Negro's Civil War* (New York, Vintage, 1965), quoted parts of eight letters. Virginia M. Adams discovered the uniquely valuable series of forty-eight weekly letters from Corporal James Henry Gooding of the 54th Massachusetts Volunteer Infantry written to the *New Bedford Mercury.* She edited and published them in *On the Altar of Freedom* (Amherst, University of Massachusetts Press, 1991).

Ira Berlin and his colleagues assembled a monumental collection of official letters by and about black soldiers. These documents, published in *The Black Military Experience,* Series II, Volume I of *Freedom: A Documentary History of Emancipation, 1861–1867* (Cambridge, Cambridge University Press, 1982), were found in the National Archives. They include letters from the soldiers and their officers, and the editors provide extensive scholarly apparatus for each document. Although that volume does not include the "letters to the editors" that compose this book, a number of the letter writers appear in both collections. Many black soldiers who wrote to army officials, politicians, and government offices also wrote to newspapers.

ORGANIZATION

The letters collected here are arranged in chapters that focus on broad topics. Most of the letters, of course, discuss more than one subject; but usually each soldier had one major reason for writing. In all of the letters there is a clear consciousness that the writer is an African American. This means that the soldiers considered themselves representatives of their race and pioneers in the struggle for equal rights. They were acutely conscious of the discrimination they faced, both nationally and in the army. This perspective appears throughout these letters, no matter what people, events, or ideas the writer focuses on. Therefore, any subdivision of the letters will reflect this social perspective.

The letters fall into two main categories: those that focus on the events of army life and those that focus on issues. The letters in most chapters of the first half of the book are arranged by locale and tell about combat and daily life. Within each chapter, letters are largely arranged chronologically. The first chapter contains letters from black soldiers who served with white units before Lincoln decided to recruit black regiments. The official status of some of these men is not clear; some were not legally soldiers, but they participated fully in combat with their white colleagues. Chapters 2 through 4 deal with the war in different parts of the South. Black troops served in most theaters of the war, but most of those who wrote letters served in the eastern part of the country and along the Gulf Coast. Many were concentrated on the coastline from Charleston to Jacksonville, what the army called the "Department of the South." Others fought in the many battles around Richmond and Petersburg, Virginia. A smaller number served along the Gulf Coast, from Pensacola to Louisiana. Two-thirds of the black soldiers in the Union Army were newly emancipated slaves, generally men who could not read or write, and who may not have known that black newspapers existed. As a result, almost all of these collected letters were written by men from the North, who had been free before the war. Consequently, war zones such as Tennessee and the Mississippi Valley, where many black soldiers served, are not represented in this book.

Chapter 5 has letters from troops on occupation duty. Starting early in 1865, black troops began occupying towns and rural areas that had just been liberated by Union armies. Occupation duty for the black soldiers extended through most of the year, and it included Texas, where a large contingent went as soon as the fighting ended in the East.

In the second part of the book, the letters focus on the issues that concerned the African-American troops. Foremost was their desire for civil rights. The letters in Chapter 6 show that these men clearly believed that the primary reason they had joined the army was to win citizenship and voting privileges for themselves and their people. Chapter 7 contains only a small portion of the many letters written about the issue of equal pay. Closely reasoned, articulate letters came from the men, many of whom refused to accept lower pay. Black soldiers wrote more letters about this particular grievance than any other. Chapter 8 contains letters focused on the other complaints about racism, including the restrictions on having black officers, atrocities against black prisoners by the Confederates, and harsh treatment by their own, supposedly sympathetic white officers.

Few of the thousands of black sailors in the Union Navy wrote letters to the newspapers, and of course they were not part of the "grand army of black men." Five letters from sailors have come to light, however, and they add significant detail to the story of African Americans in the Civil War, so Chapter 9 contains all five of those letters. The book ends with a chapter of letters from black veterans who had returned home. Their war experiences had changed them, and they boldly spoke out for their rights. By the end of 1865, the newspapers carried no more letters from black soldiers.

Acknowledgments

I N collecting, copying, and editing these letters I received help
from many people and institutions. I gratefully acknowledge
the generous aid of the professional staffs of the Library of the
State University of New York College at Purchase, the National
Archives, the Library of Congress, the Moorland-Springarn Research Center of Howard University, the Massachusetts Historical
Society, the Archives of the Commonwealth of Massachusetts, the
Boston Public Library, the American Antiquarian Society, the Ar-
chives of the State of Connecticut, Sterling Memorial Library and
the Beineke Rare Book and Manuscript Library of Yale University,
the Schomburg Center for Research in Black Culture of the New
York Public Library, the Library Company of Philadelphia, the
Ohio Historical Society, and the Library of the University of Ver-
mont. I am particularly indebted to the Massachusetts Historical
Society, the American Literature Collection of the Beineke Rare
Book and Manuscript Library of Yale University, and *Civil War*

Times Illustrated for permission to publish material in their possession. David Swift shared his knowledge and a particular letter with me. Rosalie Reutershan and Sydney Gura spent many hours transcribing letters from blurred microfilm. Travel grants from the Faculty Support Fund of the State University of New York College at Purchase made it possible for me to research the backgrounds of the men who wrote these letters. Without the help, understanding, tolerance, and support of my wife, Nancy Jenks Redkey, this book would never have been written; it is dedicated to her.

Abbreviations

CR   *Christian Recorder*
P&P   *Pine and Palm*
USCHA   United States Colored Heavy Artillery
USCI   United States Colored Infantry
USCT   United States Colored Troops
WAA   *Weekly Anglo-African*

Introduction:
For Freedom and
Equality

FOR A CENTURY after the Civil War, most Americans thought that blacks had done little or nothing to win their freedom from slavery. During the Civil Rights Movement of the 1950s and 1960s, renewed study of African-American history corrected that old ignorance and showed that almost 200,000 black soldiers (and thousands of black sailors) had served the Union. But most interested people thought that those soldiers were newly freed slaves, capable only of labor, afraid of battle, illiterate, and ignorant of the more complex issues of the war.

Forgotten were the thousands of free black men from the Northern states who had fought not only to free the slaves and preserve the Union but also to show the world that they, as much as any other men, deserved to be full partners in the United States. From Vermont and Maryland, from Massachusetts and Iowa, from every one of the Union states, they had put on blue uniforms to show their patriotism and manhood. From 1863 to 1865 they had marched and fought, suffered and died from rebel bullets and army diseases, just as the white troops had done. Whites did not know or care that these Northern black soldiers were different from the slaves, that they could read and write as well as most whites, that they were prepared to struggle not only against rebellion in the South but against racism everywhere.

These brave, free black men let the nation know how they felt about the war. A few were college-trained, many had a public school education, and some were just learning to read and write. They wrote to their friends and families, but few of those letters have survived. They also wrote to army and government officials; many of those official letters were saved in the National Archives. They wrote most often to black and abolitionist newspapers to tell their friends at home about their experiences, their fears, and their hopes. This book is a selection of such letters published by newspapers during the war years.

The writers of these "letters to the editors" told about the many sides of army life. They began by telling about the training days in camp; they proceeded to the marching, digging, raiding, and fighting that made their war. They wrote about comrades, mostly brave, some dead; about officers, mostly white, some gallant, others racist; about Southerners, black and white. They told of the diseases that killed so many soldiers. They described in detail their raids behind Confederate lines, their charges against rebel trenches, and their wounds from Southern guns. And they told of their triumphal marches into Charleston, Wilmington, and Richmond, capital of the defeated Confederacy.

The newspaper letters also told why the black troops were fighting; more than anything else, they wanted to earn their rights as Americans. For many years free blacks had been denied the equality proclaimed in the Declaration of Independence. By joining the army, by fighting willingly and dying bravely, African Americans wanted to earn both respect and citizenship.

Their letters told of the many racist insults they suffered and what they did to endure them. They complained of bad treatment by white officers, soldiers, and civilians, both South and North. The worst of those insults was the government's decision to give black soldiers reduced pay. Instead of the thirteen dollars paid whites, blacks got only seven dollars each month. Thousands of them protested and refused to accept any pay at all until they could get the same pay as whites. Letter after letter told why they took no pay; despite the suffering of their families at home, they would take no government money until they got equality. Despite criticism from their white officers, from civilian leaders, and from some of their black comrades, they kept up their boycott of the paymaster until Congress finally voted them equal pay.

Through all their letters flows a current of dignity and pride. There is an unmistakable note of achievement and self-confidence. They could join with Private Charles T. Brown when he wrote soon after the valiant attack by black troops against Petersburg, Virginia, "What a glorious prospect it is to behold this grand army of black men, as they march at the head of their column over the sacred soil of Virginia. They cause what few inhabitants yet remain to look and wonder."[1]

The United States government was slow to enlist blacks in the war effort. The war had been under way for a year when, in the summer of 1862, Congress authorized President Abraham Lincoln to use black soldiers at his discretion. He and most other whites doubted that blacks could or would fight as well as whites. Furthermore, he had to consider the prejudices of the border states – slave states that remained in the Union and feared that enlisting blacks would undermine their "peculiar institution." As a result, Lincoln refused at first to use his new authority. But as the war dragged on and Union victories seemed to come too seldom, the President risked using black troops. They would serve in all-black regiments

1. Charles T. Brown to Editor, *Christian Recorder*, 9 July 1864.

led by white officers, and they would face the hardships of racism as well as the hazards of war. But they would have the chance to show that they were men equal to any and patriots worthy of citizenship in the nation of their birth.

The first black regiments were raised in the fall of 1862, after Lincoln announced the Emancipation Proclamation. Around the edges of the Confederacy, Federal forces had established important bases that served to harass the rebels and to squeeze the Southern lifeline of supplies from abroad. Especially strong bases had been built on the islands near Charleston, South Carolina, and in Louisiana. The first three black regiments were mustered in New Orleans by November. They were composed mostly of free blacks who had a long tradition of militia training, and who originally had their own black officers. A fourth regiment was formed in Kansas, on the border of a slave state, Missouri; it was mustered into Federal service in January 1863. Also mustered that same month was the fifth black regiment, recruited in the Sea Islands of South Carolina. This was the regiment of ex-slaves described in the classic book *Army Life in a Black Regiment*, written by its white colonel, Thomas Wentworth Higginson.

Lincoln's Emancipation Proclamation, which took effect in January 1863, announced his intention to use black soldiers more actively, and he soon authorized state governors in New England to enlist new black regiments. Massachusetts, led by abolitionist Governor John Andrew, quickly created three such units; they were soon matched by Rhode Island and Connecticut. Because the black population of New England was small, men for these regiments came from free black communities all across the North, from as far west as Illinois and Iowa.

These communities had been founded during the era of the Revolutionary War. Starting with Massachusetts, the Northern states had gradually abolished slavery by 1804. The Northwest Ordinance of 1787 guaranteed that the new states north of the Ohio River would also be free. By 1860 about 210,000 free persons of color lived in the Northern states, mostly in eastern cities and in the parts of other states closest to the slave states, such as the southern portions of Pennsylvania, Ohio, Indiana, and Illinois. Some of the people had been born in slavery but had been given their freedom or run away to the North. Many young men from those black settlements joined the Union Army.

Although they were legally free, blacks in the North suffered much discrimination. Most could only work as unskilled laborers or farmers. Only in New England and New York could they vote, and they could not serve on juries or in the state militias – duties required of white citizens. Public schools spread rapidly across the North in the years before the Civil War, but most of them refused to admit blacks. Despite these handicaps, a small but growing number of free African Americans found ways to get an education, usually at their own expense. Those were the men who would write the letters collected in this book.

The 1850s were difficult years for Northern blacks. A new, harsh Fugitive Slave Law went into effect in 1850. It allowed "slave chasers" to accuse any black of being a runaway slave and would not allow the accused to testify in his or her own defense. As a result an unknown number of free people were taken away to the South. For fear of being kidnapped and sent to the South, many others thought about leaving the United States for Canada, Haiti, or Liberia. This fear grew after 1857, when the Supreme Court ruled in the Dred Scott case that "blacks had no rights that whites were bound to respect," and that they had no rights to be citizens of the United States.

Black leaders spoke out against these injustices. Besides vigorously campaigning to abolish slavery, they organized conventions and wrote petitions to get citizenship and civil rights. But with powerful political forces supporting slavery, it seemed by 1861 that there was little hope for change. Even Frederick Douglass, the bold speaker and writer for black freedom and equality, began to despair for his people. When finally the Federal government started enlisting black soldiers, he immediately began traveling across the North as a recruiter, urging, "Men of Color: To Arms!" By fighting for the Union, blacks could strike a blow against slavery and, at the same time, demonstrate their worthiness to be citizens. Many of the men who wrote the letters in this book joined the army because of Douglass and other black leaders, such as Martin R. Delany, John M. Langston, and many clergymen, who recruited in almost every black settlement in the North.

The first Northern black regiments were raised by Massachusetts, Connecticut, and Rhode Island. But in order to deal more effectively with the training and leadership of black units, the Federal government in May 1863 established the Bureau of Colored Troops. Northern agents began energetically recruiting recently freed slaves in Southern areas held by Union troops. The War Department decreed that henceforth all new black regiments, even though they might be recruited and sponsored by Northern states, would be administered together and labeled "United States Colored Troops" (USCT). Eventually, all black regiments with the exception of those from Massachusetts and Connecticut were designated "USCT." Most were infantry regiments (USCI), some were in the cavalry (USCC), and a few were in the heavy artillery (USCHA).

The army's use of black troops, especially those from the Northern states, varied from region to region, from commander to commander. Some, such as General William T. Sherman, virtually refused to employ them at all. Others used them for garrison and rear-guard duty, for construction details, or in labor battalions. But some generals, especially Benjamin Butler, came to believe firmly in the military abilities of black soldiers and used them in combat. Butler late in 1862 mustered black militia regiments in Louisiana and later used black troops in Virginia and North Carolina during the attacks on Petersburg, Richmond, and Wilmington. In addition to serving in the Gulf Coast and Tidewater regions, Northern black soldiers were used extensively in combat in the Department of the South – coastal South Carolina, Georgia, and Florida – where union forces worked to close the ports and inlets against Confederate blockade runners.

Most whites doubted that blacks would make good soldiers. They reasoned that blacks could not be relied on to fight their "superiors," the white troops of the Confederacy. This belief was put to rest in the spring and summer of 1863, however, when African-American troops began to prove their skill and courage in battle. Black regiments fought and died bravely on May 27 at Port Hudson, Louisiana, a rebel fortress in the swamps near the Mississippi River. A few days later Confederates tried to overwhelm a Union base where black troops were being trained at Milliken's Bend, Louisiana. In hand-to-hand combat those fresh recruits drove off their attackers and won the praise of generals and the press. In July a black regiment helped rout Confederate troops at Honey Springs in the Indian Territory. The next day, July 18, 1863, the 54th Massachusetts Infantry led the bold but futile assault on Fort Wagner, near Charleston, South Carolina. Other major battles in which colored troops acquitted themselves well included the first attack on Petersburg, Virginia, on June 15, 1864, and the engagement at Nashville, Tennessee, on December 14–15, 1864.

When the Union began using African-American troops in combat, the Confederates announced that they would consider any black soldier they could capture not as a prisoner of war but as a fugitive slave. Furthermore, many Southerners announced unofficially that they would execute any black soldier they captured. With this threat hanging over them, the Union's black troops understood what their fate might be if they surrendered. Confederate General Nathan B. Forrest made this threat very real on April 12, 1864, when his cavalry attacked a Union base at Fort Pillow, Tennessee. Both white and black defenders surrendered to Forrest's men, but the Confederates proceeded to shoot their prisoners, especially the blacks. After that, whenever black soldiers went into combat they understood that surrender might mean death. So they were determined to fight all the harder, and their battle cry was "Remember Fort Pillow!"

But even the rebels were impressed by the courage of black soldiers. In desperation during the last weeks of the war, the Con-

federate government authorized the South's state governors to enlist their own black troops. Nothing much came of the decision; the
war was virtually lost by then, and Southerners feared what might
happen if they armed their slaves. Union soldiers often reported
seeing black soldiers in Confederate units, but there is no solid
evidence to confirm these sightings. Probably what they saw was
black servants of rebel officers; even though technically civilians,
such servants sometimes joined in the fighting to defend their
masters. But racism deprived the South of possible further help
from blacks who might have fought for the Confederacy in return
for their freedom.

Racism was also strong in the Union Army. Black soldiers endured a variety of insults and hardships at the hands of white
soldiers and officers. Officers of the early regiments from Louisiana were black, but they were soon pressured to resign. Only at
the end of the war did the Federal government decide that African
Americans could lead troops in combat. This meant that almost all
black soldiers served under white officers. The men resented this;
they knew that some of their own number were as skilled and
experienced as many of the whites promoted over them.

As soon as the war ended, several African-American regiments
were transferred from Virginia to Texas to establish Federal control there and to guard against trouble from Mexico, which was
then under French domination. Elsewhere, black soldiers served as
occupation troops in various communities and for varying lengths
of time. By the end of 1865 most of the Northern black troops had
been discharged and had returned to civilian life.

The letters collected here tell in the black soldiers' own words
what they experienced and what they hoped for. Their words reveal
the texture of their struggles: struggles against an armed enemy
and struggles against ever present racism. Bravery, fear, boredom,
exhilaration, piety, despair, danger, triumph – all these and more
fill the letters, which are an eloquent window on an important
chapter of the past.

I

Black Soldiers in White Regiments

NICHOLAS BIDDLE, a black man from Pottsville, Pennsylvania, marched through Baltimore with the "Washington Artillerists," on April 18, 1861, on his way to help defend the Capitol in Washington, D.C. The people of Baltimore strongly sympathized with the Confederacy, which had attacked Fort Sumter that week. They were outraged that Northern soldiers – with a black man among them – should go through their streets. Shouts and jeers were soon accompanied by stones and bricks; Nicholas Biddle, a special target, was hit full in the face by a stone. Blood spilling on his uniform, he stumbled but was helped by one of his officers. When his unit reached Washington that night, it camped in the Capitol itself, and it was reported that President Abraham Lincoln came in person to thank the men for their help, and especially to console Biddle, one of the first soldiers to shed his blood for the Union.[1]

There would be another year and a half of hard fighting before the Union would begin systematically to enlist African Americans into the army. But from the very start of the Civil War, many blacks wanted to help preserve the Union, hit at slavery, and prove that they deserved full citizenship. Like Nicholas Biddle, some of those men joined regiments that were otherwise all white. Many went as servants of white officers; others went as teamsters to drive the supply wagons; some actually enlisted as soldiers, either in spite of their race or by passing as white.

William Henry Johnson was one such man. When the war broke out, he lived in Norwich, Connecticut. Because he was quite black, he was not allowed to enlist in the local regiment that responded to President Lincoln's call for state troops to come to Washington for ninety days. Nevertheless, Johnson joined the 2nd Connecticut Volunteer Infantry as an "independent man," a status that was not clearly defined. After his "ninety days" expired, he joined the 8th Connecticut Volunteer Infantry. He fought in the First Battle of Bull Run (July 1861) and the "Burnside Expedition" that captured Roanoke Island and New Bern, North Carolina (February and March 1862). He wrote nine letters to the *Pine and Palm* before his health forced him to leave the army in June 1862.[2]

LETTER I

(William H. Johnson, 2nd Connecticut Infantry, Washington, D.C., July 24, 1861; *P&P* (August 3, 1861) The First Battle of Bull Run (or Manassas), Virginia, was fought on July 21, 1861. It was the first fight between major forces of the Union and the Confederacy.

1. Benjamin Quarles, *The Negro in the Civil War* (New York, Russell & Russell, 1968) 24–26.
2. William H. Johnson, *Autobiography of Dr. William Henry Johnson* (Albany, N.Y., 1900) 17.

The Southern troops won, and the Northern troops fled back to Washington in disorder. Johnson mistakenly believed that slaves had helped the Confederate soldiers and said that only when the Union gave them civil rights would black soldiers join the army in large numbers.

We have met the enemy in this pro-slavery war – we have fought two great battles – one the longest and most sanguinary ever fought in America. The first, on the 18th, lasted from 11 1/2 A.M. until 5 P.M., and our loss was great. The second, on Sunday the 21st, was commenced at 8 in the morning, and we were defeated, routed and driven from the field before 1 P.M. We lost everything – *life, ammunition, and honor.* We were driven like so many sheep into Washington, disgraced and humiliated. One week ago we marched into Virginia with the Stars and Stripes proudly floating in the breeze, and our bands playing Yankee Doodle! We had but one thought, and that was of success.

What! 50,000 brave and Union-loving men get beaten? No, it could not be. No one would have believed it for a moment, who saw the firm and soldierly tread of Uncle Sam's men, and the glittering of their bayonets as they moved onward and passed through Fairfax Court House, and tore down the Secession flag, and hoisted the Stars and Stripes in its place. No one would have believed it who saw the burning of Germantown, and the general havoc made along the line of march, and saw the backs of the fleeing rebels, as they went pell mell before our advance guards. But we were all disappointed and the under-rated enemy proved too much for us.

It was not alone the white man's victory for it was won by slaves.[3] Yes, the Confederates had three regiments of blacks in the field,

---

3. There is no objective evidence that the Confederates used black soldiers at the First Battle of Bull Run.

and they manoeuvered like veterans, and beat the Union men back. This is not guessing, but it is a fact. It has angered our men, and they say there must be retaliation. There is much talk in high places and by leading men, of a call being made for the blacks of the North; for Africa to stretch forth her dusky arms, and to enter the army against the Southern slaves, and by opposing, free them. Shall we do it? Not until our rights as men are acknowledged by the government in good faith. We desire to free the slaves, and to build up a negro Nationality in Hayti; but we must bide our own time, and choose the manner by which it shall be accomplished.

LETTER 2

(William H. Johnson, 8th Connecticut Infantry, Annapolis, Maryland, November 11, 1861; *P&P*, November 23, 1861) Johnson reenlisted in the 8th Connecticut Infantry and went with it to Annapolis, Maryland, to prepare for an attack on the coast of North Carolina. He told about the "defensive organization" formed by blacks in the regiment to prepare for military action.

I am again at the seat of war, and again preparing for active service. Our regiment (the 8th C.V.) is in General [Ambrose E.] Burnside's Division, and our destination is said to be South Carolina, and we shall in all probability reinforce General [Thomas W.] Sherman. Annapolis has been chosen as a place of rendezvous, because it is a first class shipping port; it is located on the banks of the Chesapeake Bay, and its facilities for camping purposes most complete. There are now at this port, and attached to this Division, the 21st, 25th, 27th Massachusetts, 51st New York, and the 8th and 10th Connecticut regiments, numbering about 6000 men. There are to be six other regiments joined to the Division, which will augment the number to 12,000 or 13,000. We expect to sail from here about the 25th inst.

The election here last week, whilst it resulted in a Union victory, demonstrated the fact that Annapolis is not quite free from secesh yet, and the process of purging it must still go on.

The proscribed Americans, (and there are many), attached to this regiment have since their encampment here, formed themselves into a defensive association. They propose to cultivate a correct knowledge of the manual of arms and military evolutions, with a view to self-protection. The association is based upon the principles of military discipline, morality and literature; and they hope by a strict observance of the rules and regulations they have adopted, to do credit to their people, and honor to themselves. The name of the association is *Self-Defenders of Connecticut,* and their officers are: – Wm. H. Johnson, Norwich, Conn., first officer; Frederick C. Cross, Hartford, second officer; Prince Robinson, Norwalk, third officer. In forming this association, we have been actuated by the conviction that the time is not far distant when the black man of this country will be summoned to show his hand in this struggle for liberty.

LETTER 3

("Governor" [William H. Johnson], 8th Connecticut Infantry, Annapolis, Maryland, December 29, 1861; *P&P*, January 9, 1862) The "Burnside Expedition" to North Carolina was still preparing to sail when one of the black men in the unit was accidentally killed by a friend.

We are still here, but we expect to embark and sail out of this port, on the 1st of January. The fleet attached to this Expedition will number about one hundred vessels of different kinds – some are ships of war, gunboats, and transports. The army rank and file numbers between 25,000 and 30,000 men. The officers and men are well disciplined, armed, and equipped, and are ready for a fight.

We are going down to Dixie's Land, to carry the sword and the constitution; you will hear from us before long. We expect to take Secesh, box him up, label him "dead," and send him to Bunker Hill, on or before the Fourth of July. Then the banner of liberty will go up.

Our government has surrendered Messrs Mason and Slidell,[4] but we will not give up the South, for it has cost us too much, and her vast territory can and must be converted into free soil for free men, irrespective of color. All went well with the proscribed Americans here, up to the 25th inst., when an accident painful to relate happened to one of our number. He was a young man possessing fine qualities, both of head and heart. He was beloved by all who knew him. His name was John Thompson, and he was attached to the 24th Regiment Mass. Volunteers, and when at home, resided with his mother, at 11 Myrtle street, Boston; he was accidentally shot with a pistol bullet, which passed completely through his body, and he died the same afternoon. The young man who shot him was one of his comrades, and this fact rendered the fact more painful. His funeral took place on the morning of the 27th. It was largely attended by delegates from the several regiments attached to the divisions, and the burial service, which was conducted by the chaplain of the 24th Regiment, was very imposing.

The weather here has been, and is now delightful. It is with us now, as it is generally with you in the months of September and October.

LETTER 4

(William H. Johnson, 8th Connecticut Infantry, Pamlico Sound, North Carolina, February 2, 1862; *P&P*, February 13, 1862) The

4. James M. Mason and John Slidell, Confederate envoys to Europe, were captured by the Union Navy aboard a British ship. The British protested, and the Federal government released the two men to avoid war with Britain.

"Burnside Expedition" arrived in North Carolina waters after a month at sea.

We have not yet struck that decisive blow in this State which it is our intention to strike. . . . Our 20,000 troops are in a very satisfactory condition, all things considered, having been rather closely quartered on shipboard for twenty-six days. We expect to advance tomorrow, and still further "pollute the sacred soil of North Carolina, with the tread of Northern mudsills," and with our advance, will, of course, have achieved another glorious victory, to be added to those already won, and another link in the decaying chain of despotism will be broken. For the which we will give God the praise.

Respectfully yours, W. H. J., 8th R.C.V. P.S. . . . There is an average of one death in each regiment per day, – of the prevailing disease, – the measles. Otherwise, all is well.

LETTER 5

(William H. Johnson, 8th Connecticut Infantry, Pamlico Sound, North Carolina, [ca. February 9, 1862;] *P&P*, February 27, 1862) This letter and the next describe the attack on Roanoke Island, North Carolina. The Federal troops easily defeated the rebel defenders on February 7 and 8, 1862, making General Ambrose Burnside a hero and giving the North an important boost in morale.

The Burnside Expedition has been gloriously successful. The rebels have been defeated, and driven from Roanoke Island. On Friday, our fleet came to anchor at Albemarle Sound, at ten o'clock AM. The rebels fired into the fleet from a battery on the shore.

The gunboats responded with vigor. 4PM – The bombardment is progressing with great fury. 5PM – We are gaining upon the rebels; our troops are being landed in small boats, in the face of the enemy's batteries. 9PM – We are on the Island; the enemy is held in check; hostilities have ceased for the night. Saturday, 10AM – The battle has been resumed; the rebel land battery is being engaged by our troops; the bombardment is still going on. 1:30PM – The rebels have been driven from the batteries at the point of the bayonet. The field is ours; and we are pursuing the rebels. 11PM – Two thousand rebels have unconditionally surrendered. It is the end of one of the bloodiest battles of the campaign.

Our victory has indeed been brilliant, but we have paid dearly for it. Our loss is about thirty killed, among whom is a Colonel and a Lieutenant-Colonel, and a number of line officers. We have in the hospital between 75 and 80 wounded; they are all doing well. The enemy's loss I have not ascertained, but it has been considerable. I counted ten dead in one battery, myself. O. Jennings Wise, son of Gen. [Henry A.] Wise is one of our prisoners, and he is mortally wounded.

LETTER 6

(William H. Johnson, 8th Connecticut Infantry, Roanoke Island, North Carolina, February 10, 1862; *P&P*, February 27, 1862)

Since Saturday, everybody here has been in a perfect state of excitement, and up to this morning I have not had an opportunity to examine the field of battle, and its surroundings; but now that I have done so, I will endeavor to give you a faint idea of things as they are here, and then you will be able to appreciate the importance of our victory. The enemy was attacked at two different points at the same time. The gunboats engaged the enemy's Fort No. 1, which is situated on a point of land commanding the main channel, and mounts twelve 32-pound guns, whilst our forces drove, at the point of the bayonet, the rebels from their inland battery No. 1, which is situated about one mile from the southern extremity of the Island, and commands the main and only road across it. This battery mounts 3 12-pounders.

When the rebels were beaten out of these fortifications, they unconditionally surrendered themselves, and gave up two other forts, and one other battery, without discharging their guns; also, very extensive barracks, capable of accommodating 20,000 troops, together with forage sufficient for their accommodation for thirty days. This is a valuable acquisition. The Island is twelve miles in length, and two miles wide. Its natural defenses are almost complete, and it is the key to all the most important points in the State, and enables us to place a strong Union force behind the rebels at Richmond. The rebels had a force here of 35,000, consisting of Infantry and Artillery. They commanded three forts with twenty-eight 32-pound guns, and two inland batteries of five 12-pound guns, making a grand total of thirty-three guns, of the most approved style. These forts and batteries [were built] by the blacks, who have been brought here in large numbers, and are now jubilant at the success of the Stars and Stripes. They have informed us, (and their statements have been confirmed by the native whites,) that the rebels did not intend to give us any quarter, had their arms proved victorious. Feb. 11. – The victory is complete. Elizabeth City, twelve miles above here, was attacked by our fleet yesterday, and after a sharp and bloody engagement, the rebels burned the city, and ingloriously fled, leaving us in full possession of the burnt city, some heavy guns, three gunboats, and two schooners. The Captain of the rebel Navy, and sixteen soldiers, surrendered. Guns are now being fired, in honor of the victory.

LETTER 7

(William H. Johnson, 8th Connecticut Infantry, Albemarle Sound, North Carolina, March 9, 1862; *P&P*, March 27, 1862) As General Burnside's army expanded its hold on the North Carolina coast, many slaves were liberated or escaped to Union lines. Federal policy about these "contrabands" was not yet clear, but Johnson saw Union victory as freedom for the slaves.

My last letter to you was written after our first victory, and I had just overlooked the field of our operations. We had, in two days, reduced the enemy's fortifications, beaten him in a land engagement, 2,000 of his best troops were ours, and we were masters of Roanoke Island.

You can estimate something of the importance of our victory, by a recent speech made by the rebel President, Jeff. Davis, in which he said that if he was defeated at Manassas, at Richmond, and elsewhere, he would fall back upon Roanoke Island, and hold it, against the combined forces of the world. And well might he say so, for it was a strong position, and determined troops, in a good cause, would have baffled us for weeks – yes, I may say for months; but their cause was that of the *Devil*, and they themselves were cowards – hence, our success is not to be marvelled at.

We are now on the eve of departure for new conquests; we hope to meet the enemy again, fight, conquer him, end the rebellion, and then come home to our Northern people, to freemen who look South with joyous hearts, and behold not a single Slave State – but only free territory, from Maryland to Texas. Our armies will defeat the rebels, and hang slavery; a just Administration will execute the monster, and the good news and glad tidings will be borne by the many gallant ones to all parts of the Christian world; but the glory will belong to God!

The abolition of slavery is rapidly progressing, South – it is in the natural course of events, and must be; for wherever the Federal Army goes, the so-called master dies, and the slaves, once chattels, are transformed into men! We have especial cause to be pleased with our commander – Gen. Burnside. In answer to a Union pretender (and all who are beaten immediately profess to become lovers of this glorious Union, when they have anything to gain by coming into our lines,) who came to the Island the other day, and demanded the General to surrender to him several slaves who had sought safety under the Stars and Stripes, the General looked the fellow full in the face, and delivered himself thus: "Sir, you misunderstand my mission – I am not here to bag slaves for their owners. No, sir! I am here to teach rebels their duty to their Government, and, with the help of God, I will do it!" The fellow *seceded*, and the scene closed.

This is just what we want; let commanders of Divisions look out for traitors, and the slaves will take care of themselves, to be cared for by their friends.

Quite a large number of contrabands have already congregated on the Island, who are free to go or stay – no one being authorized to hinder them. Many go North, in every Northern-bound vessel, whilst others prefer to follow the Army.

The sanitary condition of this Division is good, notwithstanding the hardships we are subjected to, in being exposed to the inclement weather, night after night, with no covering save the canopy of heaven. It rains on the Island, as a general thing, four days in the week, and during the other three, the sun refuses to shine upon [us].

LETTER 8

(William H. Johnson, 8th Connecticut Infantry, Roanoke Island and New Bern, North Carolina, March 11–14, 1862; *P&P*, April 3, 1862) From Roanoke Island, General Burnside attacked the North Carolina mainland. Johnson helped fight a two-day battle that drove the rebels from the town of New Bern, which soon became a major Union base and a magnet for runaway slaves.

Confederate States of America. Gunboat Sentinel, Roanoke Island, March 11, 1862 – 7 o'clock A.M.

Everything being ready our fleet sailed. Ten o'clock P.M., anchored for the night. March 12. Seven o'clock A.M.; made sail. We are on Pamlico Sound, headed for the Neuse river, four o'clock P.M., entered the mouth of the river; eight o'clock, let our anchor go. We have had a fine sail today.

March 13. Ten o'clock A.M., disembarked with safety in Hallow's Creek, our landing being covered by the guns of the gunboats. Eleven o'clock, we succeeded in driving in the enemy's pickets. We are moving on to New Bern. The rebels retreated from their first battery, without discharging a gun. We are in hot pursuit of them; the roads are very muddy; it is raining. Seven and a half o'clock; a halt has been made for the night; we are exposed to a drenching rain. We expect hard work tomorrow.

March 14. Seven o'clock A.M. – We are engaging the rebels. They are behind water and sand batteries. The fight is waxing warm. Many brave souls have been sent to their last account; and a larger number of traitors have been made to bite the dust. I forbear to name the locality. The fleet is also engaged.

Nine o'clock A.M. – The rebels are fighting like devils; they do not give an inch; *their slaves are working their guns.* I cannot stand that. This may be the last line from me; for now I go into the field armed with a revolver, and a sure rifle; and shall take my post to defend the colors of my regiment. We *must* win the day, though half our number are slain.

One o'clock P.M. – Thank God! the battle is ended; blood has ceased to flow. Victory perches on our banners, but we have paid dearly for it. At eleven o'clock we broke the enemy's ranks; their right wing gave way. The Eighth, with the Fourth and Fifth Rhode Island, and the Eleventh C[onnecticut] V[olunteers] drove their left. They retreated to a third battery which they held till twelve o'clock, when they were again driven from their position. Their flag came down, and the Stars and Stripes were run up in its place, amid the almost deafening shouts of our brave and victorious army.

We have, for two days, fought them in their well constructed batteries and rifle pits covering a space of twelve miles in a dense forest of tall pines and obstinate underbrush, on a poorly constructed railroad, and a turnpike which was covered with a slippery mud, and raining all the time. If it does not satisfy them that Uncle Sam is in earnest, and that *Old Abe* does not mean to split them like *rails*, we will give them another turn, and this time near *Richmond*.

While the army was doing their duty so nobly, the invincible [Louis M.] Goldsborough with the fleet, had bombarded the city, and set it on fire and our gunboats are at its wharves. This is glory enough for this time, don't you think so?

Four o'clock P.M. – The railroad bridge is ablaze, and everything is in ruins.

LETTER 9

(William H. Johnson, Albany, New York, June 2, 1862; *P&P*, June 19, 1862) Disease proved a worse killer than all the Civil War battles. But Johnson survived and settled in Albany, New York, where he later became an active recruiter of black soldiers for the Union Army. In this letter he endorses the black nationalism proclaimed by Dr. Martin R. Delany, who had just returned from Africa. In 1865 Delany himself was commissioned a major in the Union Army and recruited soldiers in South Carolina.

I write to inform you that whilst I am not at the seat of war I am in the land of the living. I am still afflicted with the rheumatism – not badly; but so as to render it unsafe for me to return to the field again for the present. . . . Dr. M[artin] R. Delany has been lecturing here with good effect. His subject has been *Africa*. He has very ably set forth the advantages to be derived by us, as a people, in emigrating. The doctor is liberal. I think that he is right. He is for Africa first, "but any country," says he, "where a *negro* nationality can be established is far better than remaining here." So say I.

When the proposition is fully endorsed by our people, and I

think that it will shortly be, I hesitate not to say that the good
people of Albany will turn their steps to Hayti.

(G. E. S., 26th Pennsylvania Infantry, Union Mills, Virginia,
November 20, 1862; *WAA*, December 5, 1862) This letter was
probably written by George E. Stephens, a cabinetmaker from
Philadelphia. Stephens later joined the 54th Massachusetts regiment and rose to the rank of first lieutenant. But first he served as a
cook for the colonel of a white Pennsylvania regiment in the Army
of the Potomac. After the Battle of Antietam in September 1862,
the army slowly followed Robert E. Lee's Army of Northern Virginia south toward Fredericksburg. Stephens was too optimistic
about the skills of his generals, but he was quite sensitive to the
plight of the fugitive slaves who followed the Federal troops, seeking freedom.

A sudden, unexpected and brilliant change of direction has been
given to the grand Union Army, now in full advance on the Rebel
Capital. . . . Our troops commenced falling back to the line of Bull
Run Creek last night, destroying bridges and culverts and rendering the road utterly useless for rebel purposes. The rebels occupy
various points as we evacuate them.

The Excelsior Brigade, and the New Jersey Brigade fell to the
rear this morning. The rain is now falling in torrents, and we are
guarding the front against surprise. The base of operations is the
City of Fredericksburg. The Union Generals are too wily to allow
the rebels to draw them into a fox and goose chase up and down
the Shenandoah Valley.

As is ever the case when our troops fall back from the enemy's
country, large numbers of contrabands or fugitive slaves follow in
our wake. At the last battle of Bull Run [August 26–31, 1862], this
whole region was depopulated of its slaves. None remain but the
aged, infirm, young, and a few of that class of treacherous, pam-

pered, and petted slaves, known as house servants. Large numbers are flocking around us here; they come from Fauquier Co. Women and children are walking, as if for dear life, to reach Washington, which is considered by every negro within the boundaries of the Old Dominion as his city of refuge. There is one case which may be worthy of notice. George and Kitty Washington and four remaining children belonged, with seventy others, to a man named Joe Weaver, living near Warrenton Junction. Our forces evacuated that place yesterday morning. Weaver had carried off to Richmond two other children of Washington, but our troops came on him before he could get the rest away. Kitty knew as soon as the Union soldiers left that she and her children would be carried down South, so she took as many of her things as she and her husband could conveniently carry and turned her steps northward. Her little children walked so slow that the rebel cavalry watching the movements of our troops came near to capturing them; but they struck the woods, and reached here in the drenching rain about 12 o'clock. They say they saw a great many others on the way. They also stated that all negroes caught attempting to escape are ordered to be shot.

A rebel deserter has just come in. He says he belongs to Stewart's [J. E. B. Stuart's] Flying Artillery. Stewart left Culpeper last Monday morning with his whole command, cavalry and artillery, for some point in the vicinity of Fredericksburg. He says [he] don't know the force of the cavalry – Stewart always takes his whole command to make his raids. The deserter, who is a Prussian by birth, states that he has been in the army since last May one year, and is now tired of fighting, has no objections to fighting if he can get enough to eat. Stewart's battery consists of a new breech-loading Whitworth gun, two Parrotts, and two Napoleons. I have no doubt that Stewart is hovering around our flank between here and Fredericksburg to harass us with bold and unexpected raids on any undefended points. The deserter states that the rebels curse old [General] Joe Hooker just as they do [General Benjamin] Butler at New Orleans and pronounce [General Franz] Sigel a devil.

(H. Ford Douglas, [Co. G,] 95th Illinois Infantry, Colliersville, Tennessee, January 8, 1863; *Frederick Douglass's Monthly*, February 1863) Hezekiah Ford Douglas, a preacher from Chicago, joined a white regiment in July 1862. His unit fought in Tennessee and Louisiana. Later, he would be sent to recruit a black regiment in Louisiana, and eventually he was promoted to be captain of an artillery battery from Kansas. In this letter he praised the Emancipation Proclamation, which had just become official on January 1, 1863. He urged editor Frederick Douglass to raise a regiment of black soldiers to show the world that they could and would fight for their rights.

My wife sent me this morning the Monthly for December containing your appeal to England to *"hands off"* in this fearful conflict for freedom. It was indeed gratifying to me who have always felt more than a friendly interest in you and yours to read your eloquent and manly words of admonition to the Old Saxon mother States to give no moral or legal countenance to the claims of the impious Confederate States of America in their attempt to set up a Government established upon the idea of the perpetual bondage of the Negro. England has wisely withstood every temptation to do so – Abraham Lincoln has crossed the Rubicon and by one simple act of Justice to the slave links his memory with immortality.

The slaves are *free!* How can I write these precious words? And yet it is so unless twenty millions of people cradled in Christianity and civilization for a thousand years commit the foulest perjury that ever blackened the pages of history. In anticipation of this result I enlisted six months ago in order to be better prepared to play my part in the great drama of the Negro's redemption. I wanted its drill, its practical details, for mere theory does not make a good soldier. I have learned something of war, for I have seen war in its brightest as well as its bloodiest phase, and yet I have nothing to regret. For since the stern necessities of this struggle have laid bare the naked issue of freedom on one side and slavery on the other – freedom shall have, in the future of this conflict if necessary, my blood as it has had in the past my earnest and best words. It seems to me that you can have no good reason for withholding from the government your hearty cooperation. This war will educate Mr. Lincoln out of his idea of the deportation of the Negro quite as fast as it has some of his other pro-slavery ideas with respect to employing them as soldiers.[5]

Hitherto they have been socially and politically ignored by this government, but now by the fortunes of war they are cast morally and mentally helpless (so to speak) into the broad sunlight of our Republican civilization there to be educated and lifted to a higher and nobler life. National duties and responsibilities are not to be colonized, they must be heroically met and religiously performed. This mighty waste of manhood resulting from the dehumanizing character of slave institutions of America is now to be given back to the world through the patient toil and self-denial of this proud and haughty race. They must now pay back the negro in Spiritual culture in opportunities for self-improvement what they have taken from him for two hundred years by the constant over-taxing of his physical nature. This law of supply and demand regulates itself. And so this question of the colonization of the negro; it will be settled by laws over which war has no control. Now is the time for you to finish the crowning work of your life. Go to work at once and raise a Regiment and offer your services to the government, and I am confident they will be accepted. They say we will not fight. I want to see it tried on. You are the one to me of all others, to demonstrate this fact.

I belong to company G, 95th Regiment Illinois volunteers – Captain Eliot N. Bush – a Christian and a gentleman. . . .

5. Lincoln advocated settling free blacks outside the United States. In 1863 he tried to set up a colony of African Americans on Ile-à-Vache, near Haiti; the colony quickly failed.

2

South Carolina, Georgia, and Florida

S ERGEANT ROBERT J. SIMMONS of the 54th
Massachusetts Infantry collapsed with fatigue onto the sand
of Morris Island, South Carolina. It was July 18, 1863, a
date that would bring glory to his regiment, the first one made up
of African Americans from the free states. Simmons and his men
had fought their first brief but bloody battle on nearby James Island
two days before. It had been intended merely to divert the attention
of the Confederate troops from a Union buildup on Morris Island.
The 54th Massachusetts had lost fourteen men killed and thirty
wounded or missing in that first fight; then they had marched
several miles through swamps by night and sand by day. Now they
had crossed over to Morris Island, which guarded the entrance to
the harbor of Charleston, South Carolina. Exhausted from fighting
and marching for two days without sleep, Simmons and his men
took what rest they could while artillery and ships bombarded Fort
Wagner.

Simmons did not know it, but three days earlier, his home in New York City had been burned by angry rioters, upset at being drafted to fight to free the slaves. They had taken out their anger on blacks living in the city, lynching and burning; Simmons's seven-year-old nephew had been killed by stones from the mob. But here, near Fort Wagner, Simmons wrote in a brief letter to his mother; "We are on the march to Fort Wagner, to storm it." Soon Colonel Robert Gould Shaw roused his men – they were to lead the charge.[1]

The story of that "one gallant rush" led by Shaw, who died with many of his men on the wall of the sand-and-log fort, has been told in poetry, sculptures, and film. Of the 600 men from the 54th Massachusetts who fought at Fort Wagner, 259 were killed, wounded, or missing. Sergeant Simmons was wounded and captured; he died a month later in a jail cell in Charleston. Lieutenant Colonel Edward N. Hallowell, second in command of the regiment, cited four men for distinguished bravery in the attack: Sergeant Simmons's name headed the list. The attack, however, failed; Fort Wagner remained in rebel hands for another six weeks. But the bravery of the black soldiers demonstrated to their white colleagues, and to a doubtful nation, that African-American soldiers could and would fight. For a time, all eyes were focused on these sandy, swampy islands off the coasts of South Carolina, Georgia, and Florida – the Department of the South.[2]

The southeastern coastline was held by Union forces mainly to keep Confederates from using the rivers and ports for smuggling. Blockade-running ships brought weapons, supplies, and medicines

---

1. *New York Tribune*, December 23, 1863.
2. Ira Berlin, Joseph P. Reidy, and Leslie Rowland, *The Black Military Experience*, series II, Volume I of *Freedom: A Documentary History of Emancipation, 1861–1867* (Cambridge, Cambridge University Press, 1982) 534–538. Peter Burchard, *One Gallant Rush* (New York, St. Martins Press, 1965) 130–131. Luis Emilio, *History of the Fifty-fourth Regiment of Massachusetts Volunteer Infantry, 1863–1865*, second edition (Boston, Boston Book Co., 1894) passim. William Wells Brown, *The Negro in the American Rebellion* (Boston, Lee & Shepard, 1867) 209.

from Europe, and they took cotton out to earn money for the rebel cause. Federal ships tried to seal off the coastline, but the job was difficult; to make the task possible, blockading ships needed bases where they could get fuel and food. On November 7, 1861, a joint army-navy force captured Port Royal, South Carolina, and soon controlled many of the nearby islands. Roanoke Island and New Bern, North Carolina, fell in February 1862. Fernandina, Florida, fell in March, and the approaches to Savannah, Georgia, were taken in April. These bases helped support the Federal blockade, but the major ports of Charleston, South Carolina, and Wilmington, North Carolina, remained in Confederate hands; throughout the war, of every five trying to enter or leave these ports, the Union Navy caught only one blockade runner.

The coastal islands were heavily populated by slaves. General David Hunter, an ardent abolitionist, tried to organize the 1st South Carolina Volunteer Infantry (Colored) in the spring of 1862. His successor, General Rufus Saxton, completed the job that winter. The regiment was commanded by Thomas Wentworth Higginson, who described his experiences in the classic book *Army Life in a Black Regiment.* By the summer of 1863, a second "contraband" regiment had joined the first. Based near Port Royal and Beaufort, these units carried out raids along the rivers and islands of South Carolina, Georgia, and northern Florida.

Charleston lay about fifty miles northeast of Beaufort. It had powerful symbolic value because it was the original home of secession. It also was a major smuggling port. Its harbor was guarded by several islands: Fort Sumter sat in the middle of the harbor; Sullivan's Island guarded the northern approach; James Island defended the inner harbor; Morris Island protected the main channel to the sea. The Confederates built a ring of forts on the islands to fight off attacks by navy ships. One of the most important was Fort Wagner, a large pile of sand and logs that aimed many guns at both the main channel and the narrow, swampy sand of Morris Island.

After attacks by sea failed to capture Charleston, Union generals and admirals set about taking Morris Island in July 1863. On July

16, the army made a diversion at James Island while the main force massed on the southern end of Morris Island. The 54th Massachusetts Regiment fought at James Island, its first combat. Then, on July 18 at sundown, the Federal troops attacked Fort Wagner. The black soldiers from Massachusetts, after two days' march, without much rest or food, led the attack. But Fort Wagner was too strong. Despite the brave charge by the 54th and the subsequent attacks by white units, the fort held. For the next six weeks the Federal troops, with black soldiers doing much of the work, built trenches and tunnels toward Fort Wagner, and navy ships shelled the place furiously. On September 6, the Confederate defenders evacuated the fort and left Morris Island, and the mouth of Charleston harbor, in the control of the Yankees.[3]

Early in February 1864, Major General Quincy Gillmore, new commander of the Department of the South, led his troops to Florida. The purpose was twofold: to keep food and cotton from reaching the other Confederate states and to get Florida quickly "reconstructed" under President Lincoln's "ten-per-cent plan" in time for the November presidential election. After occupying Jacksonville on February 7, the Union troops quickly pushed westward along the railroad toward Lake City. They took an important rail junction at Baldwin on February 9. Gillmore put Brigadier General Truman Seymour in command of local operations, ordering him to fortify Baldwin against an expected rebel attack, and not to advance any farther until more troops and supplies arrived. Gillmore then returned to South Carolina to expedite reinforcements.

Seymour, however, was eager for a fight, and he disobeyed

---

3. Shelby Foote, *The Civil War: A Narrative;* Volume II: *Fredericksburg to Meridian* (New York, Random House, 1963) 695–701. Herman Hattaway and Archer Jones, *How the North Won: A Military History of the Civil War* (Urbana, University of Illinois Press, 1983) 426–427. Richard E. Beringer, Herman Hattaway, Archer Jones, and William N. Still, Jr., *Why the South Lost the Civil War* (Athens, University of Georgia Press, 1986) 192–194. Willie Lee Rose, *Rehearsal for Reconstruction* (Indianapolis, Bobbs-Merrill, 1964) 242–263.

Gillmore's orders. On February 20, he marched his 5,500 men toward Lake City, expecting to be opposed only by a smaller number of Florida militiamen commanded by Brigadier General Joseph Finegan. But Finegan had known of the Union advance and had received reinforcements from Georgia. He had set a trap for the Federal troops near a railway station called "Olustee." When the Yankees arrived, they were surprised by Rebels who had picked the battlefield for their own advantage. The fighting started about noon and lasted until after six o'clock. The Confederate troops decisively defeated the Union Army, which withdrew to the east, reaching Jacksonville two days later. General Seymour, who had disobeyed orders by challenging the enemy, and who had then managed the battle badly, was removed from command. The army fortified Jacksonville and Palatka on the St. Johns River and settled in for the rest of the war.

Of the eight Union regiments engaged at the Battle of Olustee, three were black. The 8th USCI was at the focus of the first Rebel attack, and although everyone said it fought well, it lost heavily and had to retreat. The 54th Massachusetts replaced the 8th on the firing line and helped prevent a complete collapse of the Union forces. The 1st North Carolina (Colored) Regiment (35th USCI) also fought well but in vain. Other African-American regiments, especially the 55th Massachusetts and the 3rd USCI, arrived in Jacksonville too late to get into the fight. The men who wrote letters to the newspapers criticized the generals for the disastrous battle, but took pride in their own courageous performance. Even though they had received no pay, they had fought as well as the whites and had earned equality.[4]

After the Battle of Olustee, the generals decided not to push farther into Florida but to hold Jacksonville, Palatka, St. Augustine, and Fernandina to prevent smuggling. The 3rd USCI remained in

4. Richard McMurry, "The President's Tenth and the Battle of Olustee," *Civil War Times Illustrated*, 16:9 (January 1978) 12–24. Shelby Foote, *The Civil War: A Narrative;* Volume II: *Fredericksburg to Meridian* (New York, Random House, 1963) 898–906.

Jacksonville while other black regiments were transferred to Virginia or South Carolina. Back on the islands near Charleston, the Union troops continued their harassment of Fort Sumter and the city itself. During the summer of 1864, the black soldiers raided Confederate installations, built up Federal positions, and waited impatiently for equal pay.

In mid-November, General William T. Sherman started his march across Georgia, from Atlanta to Savannah. To prevent Confederate reinforcements from getting to Savannah before Sherman, troops from the islands off South Carolina launched a poorly planned attack on the railroad that led from Charleston to Savannah. On November 30, they fought a bitter engagement with rebel militia troops who were well entrenched at Honey Hill. Both black and white Union troops suffered heavy casualties, and the rebels still held the railroad. Nevertheless, Sherman took Savannah and presented it as a "Christmas present" to President Lincoln.

Although General Sherman would not allow black units in his own army, African-American regiments from the Department of the South did help take and hold the outlying forts and islands around Savannah. When Sherman turned north and started marching through South Carolina, the Confederates realized that they could no longer hold Charleston. It formally surrendered on February 18, 1865, and black soldiers were among the first to enter and occupy the city.

Although Charleston had fallen, Confederate troops still roamed the countryside. They attacked Federal soldiers on the outskirts of Charleston and harassed slaves who were fleeing their plantations for the city. Union troops made several expeditions into the interior of South Carolina. The most extensive of those raids began at Georgetown on April 1, 1865; for three weeks a force of black and white regiments pursued rebel soldiers and guerrillas more than a hundred miles inland to Sumter and Camden, which Sherman's army had already passed. They captured prisoners, freed slaves, burned railroads, and asserted Federal authority in the state that had started the Civil War.

Soldiers' letters from the Department of the South, in addition to arguing for equal pay and civil rights, told of battles, both victories and defeats. They also told of life in camp, of the endless packing up and moving to new bivouacs, and of the black and white people they met. The letters give a detailed picture of how the black soldiers fought the war on the coasts of South Carolina, Georgia, and Florida.[5]

SOUTH CAROLINA: I

LETTER 12

(R. J. Simmons, 1st Sergeant, Co. B, 54th Massachusetts Infantry, Folly Island, South Carolina, July 18, 1863; *New York Tribune*, December 23, 1863) The famous attack on Fort Wagner took place on Saturday, July 18, 1863. Sergeant Robert J. Simmons, who had served in the British Army and emigrated from Bermuda, wrote a letter on that same day. He told about the fighting on nearby James Island two days before. He survived Thursday's fight but was wounded and captured in the charge on Fort Wagner, the same day he wrote this letter, probably to his wife. He died in a Charleston prison on August 23.

We are on the march to Fort Wagner, to storm it. We have just completed our successful retreat from James Island; we fought a desperate battle there Thursday morning. Three companies of us, B, H, and K, were out on picket about a good mile in advance of

5. Luis F. Emilio, *History of the Fifty-fourth Regiment of Massachusetts Volunteer Infantry, 1863–1865*, passim. [Charles B. Fox], *Record of the Service of the Fifty-fifth Regiment of Massachusetts Volunteer Infantry* (Cambridge, Mass., Wilson, 1868) 1–84. Virginia M. Adams, ed., *On the Altar of Freedom* (Amherst, University of Massachusetts Press, 1991) passim.

the regiment. We were attacked early in the morning. Our company was in the reserve, when the outposts were attacked by rebel infantry and cavalry. I was sent out by our Captain in command of a squad of men to support the left flank. The bullets fairly rained around us; when I got there the poor fellows were falling down around me, with pitiful groans. Our pickets only numbered about 250 men, attacked by about 900. It is supposed by the line of battle in the distance, that they were supported by reserve of 3,000 men. We had to fire and retreat toward our own encampment. One poor Sergeant of ours was shot down along side of me; several others were wounded near me.

God has protected me through this, my first fiery, leaden trial, and I do give Him the glory, and render my praises unto His holy name. My poor friend [Sergeant Peter] Vogelsang is shot through the lungs; his case is critical, but the doctor says he may probably live. His company suffered very much. Poor good and brave Sergeant [Joseph D.] Wilson of his company [H], after killing four rebels with his bayonet, was shot through the head by the fifth one. Poor fellow! May his noble spirit rest in peace. The General has complimented the Colonel on the galantry and bravery of his regiment.

LETTER 13

(Henry S. Harmon [Herman?], Corporal, Co. B, 3rd USCI, Morris Island, South Carolina, October 23, 1863; *CR,* November 7, 1863) Fort Wagner finally fell to Union troops seven weeks after the famous charge of the 54th Massachusetts. Corporal Henry Harmon wrote that his Pennsylvania regiment, for digging trenches under intense enemy fire, deserved as much credit as the other regiments, such as the 54th Massachusetts Infantry, which had tried to storm the fort.

. . . If our friends of the city of Philadelphia could but look into our hospital and see the wasted frame of those who were but yesterday noble specimens of manhood, the fear that we were forgotten would never again enter our mind, and if those persons could but receive a few cheering words from friends at home how their spirit would be elevated, their hopes revived. But instead they receive nothing but the rough sympathies from the rougher hands of their comrades in arms. How many careful housewives of our city have their many jars of preserves? I would ask you if they could not spare one to the care-worn and poor unfortunate soldiers in our hospitals. Now I would say to the male friends of our city, could they not spare some books and papers, and pipes or smoking tobacco, or something to cheer the heart of the poor unfortunate soldier, with soft hands to soothe his aching head, and food to satisfy his appetite. Hark! What sound is that we hear? It is the mournful sound of the muffled drum, and the slow tread of the soldiers as they carry some comrade in arms to his last resting place. His blue uniform is his shroud, and a rough pine coffin is the last we see of what was once our companion in arms. But I am proud to say that these are men who in the early part of their career, before sickness laid its heavy hands upon them, upheld the banner of the colored man in Pennsylvania.

Dear sir, we have taken Forts Wagner and Gregg, and you would ask how and by whom was it taken? By the soldiers of the gallant 3d Regiment of United States Colored Troops, backed by the 54th Massachusetts Volunteers, and the 2nd South Carolina Volunteers [Colored], with spades and shovels dug up to the very parapet of the rebel fort under a heavy fire of grape and canister shell from rebel batteries Gregg, Wagner, Sumter, and James Island, Fort Johnson, and other batteries. In those trenches our men distinguished themselves for bravery and coolness, which required more nerve than the exciting bayonet charge. And, sir, I am proud to say that I am a member of the 3d United States Colored Troops, and I hope that I am not considered boasting when I say so. Our career has not been unmarked by loss of human life. We have had ten of our number killed and I cannot say exactly how many wounded; but it amounted to over twenty. When you hear of a white family that has lost father, husband, or brother, you can say of the colored man, we too have borne our share of the burden. We too have suffered and died in defense of that starry banner which floats only over free men. . . . With our duties before us, and with a good leader such as we have in the gallant Colonel [Benjamin C.] Tilghman, formerly of the 26th Pennsylvania, who has left his luxurious home to aid in elevating our race; with a firm confidence in his abilities as a commander, we are ready to follow wherever he may lead us. He has three noble traits as a commander: justice, humanity, and firmness in all his orders to both officers and men. We expect some warm work here before long, but with the help of the God of battles, who knows the justice of our cause, we hope to go through without wavering, and though many of us must find graves in this land, I feel assured that the name of the colored soldier will stand out in bold relief among the heroes of this war. . . .

LETTER 14

(Henry S. Harmon [Herman?], Sergeant, Co. B, 3rd USCI, Morris Island, South Carolina, December 3, 1863; *CR*, December 26, 1863) For their bravery before Fort Wagner, the men of the 3rd USCI were awarded medals. Sergeant Harmon told in this letter how the men themselves chose the ones to get the awards.

. . . Our duties as diggers and sappers and miners have been considerably lessened, so that we now have time to receive instructions in drilling; while one portion are working on the forts and batteries, the other is in camp under instructions, and all have an opportunity of displaying their courage, for the enemy is determined we shall not work in peace – and by the way, I may as well tell you that General [Quincy] Gillmore, commanding this department, promised a medal of honor to two men of every company in this regiment for bravery shown before Fort Wagner, and it was left to the company officers to make a selection, but they left it to the men to decide by a vote, and I expected to have seen some wrangling among the younger portion of our men. On the contrary, everyone seemed to vie with the other in giving honor to his neighbor, and in all the companies the selections were readily, and I think, justly made. I can only name the recipients in our company. They were Privates George Reed and William Roberts, both Lancaster County boys.

FLORIDA

LETTER 15

(R. W. W., [Sergeant,] 55th Massachusetts Infantry, Palatka, Florida, March 14, 1864; *CR*, April 2, 1864) Commissary Sergeant Richard W. White, of Salem, Ohio, probably wrote this letter. His regiment followed the 54th Massachusetts to Jacksonville, and his letter told how the 55th Massachusetts departed from South Carolina, leaving behind its dead.

. . . It was on the 12th inst. our Col. received orders for the 55th to break up our then very pleasant camp on Folly Island. We were not in the least sorry, I assure you; for the ever memorable 54th Reg. Mass. Infantry, had left some time before for the same place; and as we are so much alike in disposition, and both being from the same state, it is natural to suppose we would hail with joy the time when we should join them. The camp was soon broken up, and everything scattered hither and thither, resembling the western country after one of those awful storms that sometimes recur. This was not all; there not being transportation enough for all the regiment, everyone was anxious to know if he or some one else was to go. But that matter was soon settled by a small man, generally known as the Colonel, who ordered three companies, A, C, and I, under the gallant leadership of Lt. Col. [Charles B.] Fox, to get ready to embark on the U.S. transport, Peconic, then at Pawnee Landing, these, with our brigade commander, J[ames] C. Beecher, Col. of the 1st N[orth] C[arolina] Reg., and his staff officers, composed the cargo on board of the above named transport.

After we were all safe on board, we expected to be off, when we received the sad news from the captain of the boat that we would not leave before the next morning; so we made up our minds to spend the time as agreeably as possible by engaging in the following amusements; some playing cards, and some telling stories, &c., &c.

Before we bid adieu to Folly Island, there is one thing more worthy of a place in my story. While we were waiting with patience for the long looked for morning to dawn, some of the men got to rambling about, as is common among all soldiers, when one of them happened either by chance or otherwise, to get a little too near one of those men, contemptible scamps, notable for no greater crime than having burned the colored Orphan Asylum, in the city of New York, less than a year ago,[6] who took on himself the prerogative of calling one of our men a nigger: this not going down well with the soldier, he was for using the stock of his gun over Pat's head. But Pat, being very sensible of his danger, soon found his way to the hull of a ship that lay near the dock. The soldier, having one more way by which he could get justice, lost no time in resorting to it. He well knew that if he reported the case to Col. Fox, that he would see that he got justice, for Col. Fox is not one of those men who let his men be run over by a lot of mobocrats, who better deserve to die than live. As soon as the news reached Col. Fox, he hurried to the place where the men were gathered in groups discussing the impropriety of such a man calling a soldier a

6. In a riot against the draft, working-class people in New York, many of them Irish immigrants, released their anger by lynching blacks and burning the Colored Orphan Asylum. See Iver Bernstein, *The New York City Draft Riots* (New York, Oxford University Press, 1990) 21, 27.

nigger, but when the Colonel commanded silence, and assured them that he would have the scamp attended to, they soon all became quiet. Col. Fox ordered Pat to come out and give a reason why he should call a soldier a nigger, but, not being able to satisfy the Col., he ordered him under arrest, and sent him, accompanied by at least two files of good brave colored soldiers, to report to the Provost guard. A few cases like this will teach these fellows to attend to their own business and let other folks alone.

At daylight the order was given for all to come on board, and we were off. As we steamed down the river, I could see the many forts and batteries our men had helped to build since they had been on the island. There was one thing more I saw, as the boat glided down that beautiful stream, which caused me to take a hurried glance over the past. I think I hear someone asking, what was that? I will tell you. As I passed near the place of the regimental grave-yard, I could not help thinking how many of our number we were leaving behind, whom we would never more see on this earth; those who had left their homes and home comforts at the same time that I did, the young, the noble, and the brave, to fight for their country, and to avenge the country's wrongs. . . .

LETTER 16

(Rufus S. Jones, Sergeant-Major, 8th USCI, Jacksonville, Florida, March 20, 1864; *CR,* April 16, 1864) The 8th USCI suffered heavily in the Battle of Olustee: More than three hundred men were killed, wounded, or missing, including its slain commanding officer. Sergeant-Major Jones, of Pittsburgh, Pennsylvania, told in this letter how the battle went and how Jacksonville was then for-tified against an expected Confederate counterattack.

In my last letter I stated that the Federal forces were on their way to Lake City, about sixty miles west of Jacksonville. The eighth, which had been left at Ten-Mile Station, formed a line of march on the fifteenth of February, for Baldwin, some ten miles from Ten-Mile Station, or Pickett's house.

Baldwin is one of the towns of which so much is said at Jacksonville, that one would naturally suppose it would justify itself in appearance, and show that it wanted to be a town, at least. In general appearance, a person would not take it for a town in the North, nor even disgrace the name of town by applying it. Notwithstanding the contempt which Northern people have for such excuses for towns, the Floridians have made Baldwin a depot of more than ordinary importance to the Rebel Government. The railroad, which runs from Jacksonville direct to Lake City, passes through Baldwin, and one railroad leads to Fernandina, and another to Tampa, on the Atlantic Ocean. The Rebels had stored a quantity of cotton in the warehouses which was seized by the Federal forces and shipped to Jacksonville for re-shipment North. Also large quantities of grain were seized. At noon on the 15th the Eighth halted, and a camp was laid out, after some difficulty had been experienced trying to select a dry place. The ground was very marshy, and so unfit for a camp that the tents were all obliged to be raised two feet from the ground, and board floors put under them. The troops at this point were the Third United States Colored Troops, a detachment of the Fifth [54th?] Massachusetts (Colored), and a detachment of Engineers (New York Volunteers), who were engaged in constructing rifle-pits and stockades. A post having been established here, in command of Colonel Tilghman, of the Third United States Colored Troops, the Eighth reported to him, and was kept constantly on picket duty till the 19th. Baldwin having been tolerably well fortified against attack from the enemy, the Eighth was ordered to strike tents at ten o'clock, A.M. on Friday, February 19th, and advance eleven miles to Barbour.

Barbour is about one and a half miles north-west of the railroad. This place has been a slave plantation, and was owned by one Moses Barbour, whose slaves, numbering one hundred, were driven to the front by the enemy on his retreat to Lake City. The

Barbours are noted slave-holders, and own several plantations in Florida. We halted here at four o'clock P.M., the same day. All the troops were bivouacked here for the night, and at six o'clock A.M. on Saturday, February 20th, again formed lines to advance on Lake City. Our force was five thousand troops, composed of artillery, cavalry, and infantry. The Eighth and Seventh Connecticut and Seventh New Hampshire Volunteers are brigaded together. No interruption was had during the day till [3] o'clock P.M. Musket firing was heard in front, the Federals having driven in the Rebel pickets. Heavy firing was soon heard, and the troops were moved forward rapidly. The Eighth, having been on the railroad for a short distance, was ordered to change direction to the right, and received orders to go into the fight without unslinging knapsacks, or the sergeants taking off their sashes, which caused nearly all the first sergeants to be killed or wounded. Only one-half the regiment was loaded, so harmless had been the estimate placed upon the enemy, that he was not looked for short of Lake City, and not there, if any place was left open for retreat. The Battle of Olustee, or Ocean Pond, on the 20th of February, will be long remembered by the Eighth, which suffered terribly in the conflict. No expectation of meeting the enemy is apparent, when not sufficient ammunition was brought along to fire over sixty rounds of musketry. Colonel Charles Fribley, of the Eighth, fell, mortally wounded, a short time after going into the engagement. Major Loren Darret [Burritt] then took command, and fell, badly wounded, and was borne to the rear. Both field officers now being taken from the regiment, Captain R. C. Bailey, of Company B, being the Senior Captain, took command of the regiment, and knowing that the ammunition was exhausted, ordered the regiment to the rear of the Fifty-Fourth Massachusetts, which was now engaging the enemy successfully, and, had one more regiment come to its assistance the occupation of Jacksonville by so large a force as is now here would be useless. The battle lasted from three o'clock P.M. till dark, when a retreat was ordered by the Commanding General. The wounded, both white and colored, were placed in ambulances and wagons of all

kinds, and hurried to Baldwin or to Barbour. I cannot but speak of
the conduct of Dr. Alex. P. Heickhold, Surgeon of the Eighth, who
was particular in collecting the colored troops who were wounded,
and placed them in his ambulance and pushed on for a place of
safety. Some one thought the white troops should be brought away
also; but Dr. H. said: "I know what will become of the white troops
who fall into the enemy's possession, but I am not certain as to the
fate of the colored troops," and pushed with alacrity towards Baldwin. He also dressed the wounds of all the Eighth that came into
camp at Barbour, and a great many others belonging to white
regiments. It looked sad to see men wounded coming into camp
with their arms and equipments on, so great was their endurance
and so determined were they to defend themselves till the death. I
saw white troops that were not badly wounded, that had thrown
away everything.

We arrived at Barbour at two o'clock A.M. on Sunday, rested
there until eight o'clock A.M., and continued the retreat to Jacksonville, which place was being fortified (on the return of the
advance) by the detachments that were in possession of the town.
Jacksonville is encamped upon the extreme left, in a beautiful grove
on the premises of Mrs. Fort, overlooking Jacksonville and giving a
fine view of the St. John's River. Vessels from the North can be
seen one and a half miles before landing at the dock at Jacksonville.
This point is very important to the Union forces. The Rebel pickets being only three miles distant from our camp, eighty men from
the Eighth are put on picket daily, and set out to the front of the
fortifications which have been thrown up by the Eighth since encamping here. One fort, mounting three heavy guns and one Parrot
gun, which can do execution at seven miles, are in readiness at any
time the Rebels feel disposed to advance on this point. This preparation is independent of extensive works in the centre and extreme
right. One fort on the right is called Redoubt Fribley, in honor of
the late Colonel of the Eighth. The Eighth, in command of Captain R. C. Bailey, and a detachment of the Third United States
Colored Troops, in command of a Hungarian artillery captain, are

the troops here. The order from the War Department, giving authority in this department to enroll and draft all male colored persons, is to be put into effect in a few days. It creates some excitement among those who prefer to be servants instead of soldiers. They are not very numerous here, as the Rebels have sent them away.

An expedition from the "Florida Expedition" has grown up recently. The little town of Palatka, on the left bank of the St. John's River, about seventy miles from the mouth, and fifty miles from Jacksonville, was occupied by our forces, under Colonel Barton, on Thursday morning last, the 10th inst., at daylight. It was taken without a gun being fired on either side. On the 23rd inst., two steamboats were brought down at seven o'clock A.M., which had been captured up the St. John's, in the vicinity of Palatka. One, in appearance looked like an Allegheny steamboat. This boat was built by Northern mechanics last March and was guarded nightly, at the Jacksonville wharf, by a prisoner who is now at Jacksonville.

The gunboat *Pawnee,* which has been lying at the port of Jacksonville for some time, has been ordered to Boston, Massachusetts. It has been replaced by another gunboat of equal size. It is rumored that a vessel laden with oranges from near Palatka, was brought to the wharf today. Oranges are the only fruit which grows in Florida in abundance. Apples are not seen, except they are brought from the North, and sell readily at five cents a-piece, and not large nor sound at the price.

LETTER 17

(G. E. S., [Sergeant,] 54th Massachusetts Infantry, [Jacksonville, Florida,] March 10, 1864; *CR,* April 9, 1864) Sergeant George E. Stephens described the Battle of Olustee (or Alucia, or Ocean Pond), which took place on February 20, 1864. In that fight, Confederate troops surprised and defeated a Union expedition about 60 miles from Jacksonville. Several black regiments were involved;

the 54th Massachusetts helped defend the retreating Federal troops, preventing the defeat from becoming a complete rout.

I suppose the Battle of "Olustee" has been fully chronicled, in which the Fifty-fourth took so conspicuous a part. Olustee, or Alucia, was the first battle in which the colored soldiers in this department met the rebels on equal terms. In the battle on James Island, July 16, a long, alternated picket line fought against a close, compact line of battle. In the assault on Fort Wagner, July 18, the colored troops engaged were pitted against a work which, if fully garrisoned, could boldly defy the assaults of ten thousand of the bravest men. But at Alucia, they stood face to face and fought them with a more undaunted courage than their white comrades. I fear the rebels, in the Battle of Alucia, have out-generaled us. They chose the battle-ground, and intrenched it and managed it so adroitly that no man in the Union Army knew anything about it. Their plan was an admirable one. They could have fortified Barbour, a beautiful spot near the north fork of the St. Mary's River; but this was too near our base of supplies, and too remote from theirs. A simple reverse or check to our progress, fifty miles from our base of supplies and our reinforcements, they well knew, must result in a falling back.

Reverses are terrible affairs to the army, and the soldier is always dreading flank and rear movements. After a reverse, all that would be necessary to create an uncontrollable panic would be to send a battalion of cavalry to some point in the rear.

After our army had got twenty miles beyond Baldwin, the men commenced to inquire whether there was any danger of the rebels getting into our rear. If our General could have done as the matchless Grant, plunge into the interior, destroy communications with the rear, burning bridges, &c., we might have startled them, and had thrown on us the alternatives of annihilation or victory.[7] But there seems to have been a strange ignorance of the number, position, and plans of the rebels. I think that the most essential thing to the success of any General is his knowledge of the number and purpose of his antagonist. There is not a shadow of a doubt that the enemy knew our numbers and purposes perfectly well, and calmly awaited our approach, and whipped us completely. And how can they help frustrating any movement we may undertake, if so much criminal leniency is extended to them? There have been several hundred prisoners fallen into our hands since the re-occupation of Jacksonville, and I am almost certain that the greater part of them are returned within the rebel lines. The plan, as adopted with reference to prisoners of war, is this: the prisoners are captured and brought in. A day or two after their arrival, they are invited to take the oath of allegiance to the United States. If they refuse to do this, they are sent to [Hilton] Head. Now, these rebels are, in most instances (as the history of this war has shown) men who have but little regard for the sanctity of an oath. In the present instance, there are more than the ordinary incentives to take the oath of allegiance to a Government they certainly hate. Their families are living in this vicinity, and they naturally desire to be with them, and, by taking the oath, they are immediately released and relieved from danger of enrollment in our army, and, as long as they remain in our lines, from service in the rebel army. If they can furnish intelligence to the enemy, they are regarded as spies by the rebel officers, and whatever is reprehensible in regard to the oath is disregarded and forgiven. I believe they are urged to take the oath. They are granted passes by the Provost Marshal to pass outside our lines to their families. How can we know but that a regular system of communication is kept up by those scoundrels with the enemy? How easy for a rebel to come in, give himself up, take the oath, and get a pass to go home, twelve

7. General Ulysses S. Grant had captured Vicksburg, Mississippi, by means of such a bold move.

or fifteen miles off, and transmit information which might be fatal to us!

There are a great many men, who were rebel soldiers, employed in the various departments here, and our Commissary furnishes hundreds of rations to the poor. They pretend to be in the most destitute condition, and there are some drawing rations from the Government who are well to do and fully able to provide for themselves.

I cannot fail to contrast this treatment which rebels receive at the hands of our authorities with that meted out to the negro soldiers by the rebel authorities. A flag of truce was sent out to the rebels the other day, and when asked about the negro prisoners and [their] officers, the reply was: "We will hang every d——d negro officer we catch."

We can learn nothing of the colored prisoners. It is reported that they were killed on the field. When shall this weakness and folly on the part of our authorities cease? and when shall these atrocities be met with that vengeance and retaliation they so justly merit? Where are the colored prisoners captured on James Island, July 16th, 1863, and those captured at Fort Wagner, July 18th? And lastly, where are those captured at the Battle of "Olustee," February 20th, 1864?[8] Can any escaped prisoner answer? Can any man answer this question? If, while we are pampering and petting rebel prisoners, Federal prisoners are hung and enslaved, we are exchanging smiles for kicks – paying gold and honor for dross and dishonor.

There are comparatively few contrabands coming into our lines. The rebels had been expecting our force here in Jacksonville a fortnight before its arrival, and ran all their negroes off to Georgia. As soon as the male contrabands reach here, they are put into the army, and the females are sent to Hilton Head, or permitted to go to Fernandina. Poor creatures! They are the most wo-be-gone set – no shoes, hats or clothing, and, what the most impoverished

8. Most were sent to the Confederate prison at Andersonville, Georgia.

slave-woman seldom fails to possess, turbans. I have noticed a strange peculiarity among the people here. They are all the most outrageous stutterers. If you meet one and say, "How are you?" as you pass, you could walk a whole block before he could sputter out the Southern, "Right smart, I thank-ee."

There have been four inflictions of the death penalty on colored soldiers since the landing of the expedition, February 7th, 1864. Is this not strange?[9]

LETTER 18

(E. D. W., [Private,] Co. B, 54th Massachusetts Infantry, Jacksonville, Florida, March 13, 1864; *CR*, April 2, 1864) This letter was probably written by Edward D. Washington of Philadelphia, who had been wounded at Fort Wagner. His view of the Battle of Olustee was that of a private in the firing line. After watching both blacks and whites fall to rebel bullets, he could not understand why whites got higher pay.

It is with pleasure that I now seat myself to inform you concerning our last battle: thus we were in Co. B, on the 20th of Feb. Mr. Editor, I am not sitting down to inform you about this battle without knowing something about it.

The battle took place in a grove called Olustee, with the different regiments as follows: First was the 8th U.S. [C.I.]; they were cut up badly, and they were the first colored regiment in the battle. The next was the 54th Mass., which I belong to; the next were the 1st N[orth] C[arolina]. In they went and fired a few rounds, but they soon cleared out; things were too warm for them. The firing was very warm, and it continued for about three hours and a half.

9. Four soldiers were convicted of rape and executed at Jacksonville on February 17, 1864.

The 54th was the last off the field. When the 1st N.C. found out it was so warm they soon left, and then there were none left to cover the retreat. But Captain J[ames M.] Walton, of the 54th, of our company, with shouts and cheers, cried, "Give it to them, my brave boys! Give it to them!" As I turned around, I observed Col. E[d-ward] N. Hallowell standing with a smile upon his countenance, as though the boys were playing a small game of ball.

There was none left but the above named, and Lieut. Col. [Henry N.] Hooper, and Col. [James] Montgomery; those were the only officers left with us. If we had been like those regiments that were ahead, I think not only in my own mind, but in the minds of the field officers, such as Col. Hooper and Col. Montgomery, that we would have suffered much less, is plain to be seen, for the enemy had taken three or four of their [artillery] pieces.

When we got there we rushed in double-quick, with a command from the General, "Right into line." We commenced with a severe firing, and the enemy soon gave way for some two hundred yards. Our forces were light, and we were compelled to fall back with much dissatisfaction.

Now it seems strange to me that we do not receive the same pay and rations as the white soldiers. Do we not fill the same ranks? Do we not cover the same space of ground? Do we not take up the same length of ground in a grave-yard that others do? The ball does not miss the black man and strike the white, nor the white and strike the black. But, sir, at that time there is no distinction made; they strike one as much as another. The black men have to go through the same hurling of musketry, and the same belching of cannonading as white soldiers do.

LETTER 19

(Rufus Sibb Jones, Sergeant-Major, 8th USCI, Jacksonville, Flor-ida, April 13, 1864; *CR*, May 7, 1864) After the Battle of Olustee, black regiments helped fortify Jacksonville, and soon they were the main garrison there. In this letter, Sergeant-Major Jones describes the work and thoughts of the men.

My last letter, dated March 24th, was written on the premises of Mrs. Fort, on the bank of the beautiful river St. John's. The camp was just beginning to look handsome, when the 8th was ordered to exchange camps with the 7th Conn., one of the regiments with which the 8th was brigaded. The 8th having suffered in the late battle of Olustee, and their strength being thereby greatly diminished, were not considered sufficiently strong to hold as important a position, though strong enough to perform the labor of intrenching, fortifying, and beautifying that point. Details for fatigue were very heavy, and the work pushed forward with rapidity for the first eight or ten days after encamping there.

The exchange of camps was reluctantly made by the men of both regiments; having just completed their camps to suit their eccentric tastes. The exchange, on the part of the 8th, was rather profitable than otherwise, as to convenience of water facilities. Water in the camp of the 7th Conn. is obtained with little or no labor. Barrels had been sunk at the front of nearly all the company streets.

These improvements were appreciated by the 8th, with the exception of the view of the St. John's river.

Soldiers, as well as farmers, have their signs, and can tell pretty truthfully when the moving-camp day comes, though they do not use the horn; but the preparing and decorating of a camp are signs that orders for moving will soon follow, and no one is surprised when the order comes. Although such irregularities occur, the soldier is not reluctant in trying to make another camp to please him as well as the one he left behind. . . .

The rebel Gen. Patten Anderson, commanding the rebel forces in Florida, has furnished the commanding General of the federal forces this place, with a list of the names of those taken prisoners at the battle of "Olustee". It may possibly be that they will be treated as prisoners of war; yet it is uncertain what disposition will be made of the colored troops in their possession, eventually.

It is hoped that the authorities at Washington will give special attention to the selection of officers to command colored regiments. Such officers as Isiah E. Richardson, Adjutant of the 8th, and 1st Lieut. Elijah Lewis, possess qualities as officers of colored soldiers, I truly admire. These officers are kind and respectful to those whom they command, and feel interested in the welfare of the common soldier; and at the same time demand that respect which is due to an officer. These good qualities are appreciated by the men; and if the promotion of these officers were in the power of the men of the regiment, they would soon occupy the most prominent positions in the regiment.

The sick and wounded colored troops of the department, in the hospital at Jacksonville, are treated with the utmost attention and kindness.

Hospital No. 5, occupied by the colored troops, is pleasantly located. The building, probably, once belonged to one of the prominent citizens of Jacksonville, from the appearance of the construction of it, and the beautiful shade trees and flowers with which it is surrounded.

It must be humiliating to those who once lived in style and owned slaves, to see their property and that of others occupied as hospitals by Negro soldiers from the North. It often happens here that the mistress and servant eat together in Sutler stores.

I have seen beautiful bouquets here in the month of March. Florida, for pleasantness of climate and beauty of country, is almost a "Paradise." With the exception of the prospective crop of the Alligator family, and flourishing condition of the reptile kingdom, I should prefer making Florida my future home.

It seems the farther South the 8th advances, the farther "payday" gets away from it. Just think of the colored troops not receiving any pay for nine months! Every vessel which lands at Jacksonville from the North is expected to bring the Paymaster; but I have begun to think none has been sent; and that the privilege of fighting and getting killed is the only pay given.

The 54th Mass. has had one of their sergeants [Stephen A. Swails] recently promoted to a 2d Lieutenancy, on recommendation of Col. E[dward] N. Hallowell, of the 54th (now acting Brig. General of the 3d Brigade, composed of the 54th, 55th Mass, and 8th U.S.C.T.) and by Gov. Andrew of Massachusetts; and no doubt the appointment of one of "African descent" to that position will create a little flutter among those officers (of the 54th and other regiments) who are not favorable to promoting black soldiers.

The Government probably places some estimate of value on the services of the [newly] organized army, which it has put into the field to combat with slave catchers.

The freedom given to the rebels in Jacksonville, who were taken prisoners by the federal forces on advance to the front and sent to Jacksonville, really surprises me. It seems that they can obtain permission to open stores, restaurants, and engage in business generally, in preference to citizens from the North.

In appearance, one would think that all the rebels about Jacksonville were millers (by occupation) going or returning from their meals. The clothing worn by them is of a grayish color, and made after the fashion of tights, showing that cloth is scarce, or too many men for the supply of cloth.

Captain Anderson (the instructor of the band) of Philadelphia, is with the regiment and gives the band his undivided attention, having already taught it some twenty pieces of music. The band is highly prized by the regiment, being the only one belonging to a colored regiment, except the 55th Mass., in the department.

"Lion," the old white dog which has been with the 8th ever since its organization (at Camp "Wm. Penn," Pa.) is with it yet, and has no objection to being among black soldiers. He was in many battles in the army of Virginia previous to enlisting in the 8th, and lastly took part in the battle of "Olustee," and was wounded in the fore-leg, from the effects of which he has not yet recovered but is ready to march at any moment the regiment is; if going on board of a vessel, he is the first one on board. He is a soldier, and has no respect for citizens who may visit the camp and does not hesitate to bite. He attends "Dress parade," has musical taste, and shows that he has not been brought up a savage.

("Bay State," 55th Massachusetts Infantry, Palatka, Florida, April 10, 1864; *WAA*, May 14, 1864) "Bay State" may well have been Sergeant Joseph H. Walker of Company B, whose adventures on patrol are related in this letter. With a small group of men, he found himself in a tight spot. Afterward, he wondered about the fate of black soldiers taken prisoner at Olustee; most had been taken to Andersonville, Georgia, the worst of the Confederate prisons.

. . . I understand Sergt. [Joseph H.] Walker, Co B, was out scouting last Friday, Saturday, and Sunday, and went within ten miles of Jacksonville. He got into the rebs lines. This was, certainly, a bold, saucy, daring adventure, to go so far with only three men and himself, 22 miles from his camp, through a strange country and new roads; but it showed of what material he was made. He went to a house where he was sure secesh were in the habit of coming. Madam Brewer met him at the door. Sergt. Walker (bringing his musket down to arm), "Good day, madam." "Good day, sir." Walker (looking savage enough to eat a man, let alone a weaker vessel!) – "Whose place is this madam?" "It belongs to me." (looking very shy and timid, trying to affect modesty). Sergt. Walker – "Can you inform us where Dun's Creek is?" (he knew). Mrs. B. (pointing her finger to the left) – "About three miles." Sergt. Walker – "What creek is this?" (a stream that he and his men had just forded.) Madam B. – "Cedar Creek." Sergt. Walker – "How far is it to Jacksonville?" Madam B. – "Ten miles." Sergt. Walker – "Whose quarters are those over the road?" (meaning the slaves). Madam B. – "They belong to me." Sergt. Walker – "Where are your slaves?"

Madam B. – "I don't know." (Lie No. 1) Sergt. Walker – "Do you live inside the Union or rebel lines?" Madam B. – "Well, I am here." Sergt. Walker (angrily) – "I know you are here. I did not ask you that. I ask you again, do you live in the Federal lines or not?" Madam B (woman-like drawing herself out large. Southern blood could not stand such questions.) – "I claim the protection of your commander." Sergt. Walker – "If you are a Union woman you do not need protection." Sergt. Walker, happening to see a fair saddle, and an oil-cloth blanket and a set of equipments, asked "Whose equipments are these?" Madam B. – "They belong to my old colored man." (I do not think the old chivalry ever said "colored" before in her life.) Sergt. Walker – "Where is your colored man?" Madam B. – "I do not know." (Lie No. 2.) Sergt. Walker – "Where are all the male members of your family?" Madam B. – "I do not know." (Lie No. 3. She has two sons in the rebel ranks.) Sergt. Walker – "Where is your husband?" Madam B. – "He is old and sick and is in the interior." (It was known that he was in the woods, so I had to put that down as lie No. 4.) At this time the old woman thought it her time to ask a few questions: Madam B. – "Where did you come from?" Sergt. Walker (sharp enough to detect she wanted information) – "I came from camp." Madam B. – "Where are you going?" Sergt. Walker – "I am lost and want to find my way back to Dun's Creek; then I can get where I intend to go." Madam B. – "Are you going to Jacksonville?" Sergt. Walker – "I shall go to my regiment when I leave your house." You ought to have seen her eyes. They lost their glad eagerness when he said "regiment." He thought she had some company to Sunday dinner.

While this conversation was going on in front, two of his men went in search of articles contraband of war. The search revealed lard, butter, sweet potatoes, cotton cloths, cotton gins, to gin cotton by hand, and leather looms – everything to make a man happy. The things I have just mentioned were in houses outside of the mansion. The boys then went into the dining-room. Lo and behold! six plates, cups and saucers on the table; the coffee was warm, the eggs were warm, and the day was warm (March 27), and to tell the truth, Sergt. Walker found himself in a close place. He had only seen the female; but there were six rebel cavalry men in the house. He smelt danger; now then, to get out of it. He told his men to fall in and get down to the company, and not keep them waiting in the woods all day. By the way, the company he meant was 24 miles away from him at Yellow Bluff. The scouts that went out after Walker came in said that besides the six men there were three females in the house. He is a large man, but had to back out that time; but he done well, not having orders to take prisoners, and not force enough. I think he showed his bravery by retreating with his men, which he did, coming safe and sound with his small force.

The exchange of colored prisoners. Will the government fulfill its promise made us that we shall be exchanged if captured? As far as this regiment is concerned we will ask no quarter, and rest satisfied that we will give none. Where is the wounded that fell into the enemy's hand at the battle of Olustee? Echo answers, "where?" We will never forget the cry of "Kill the G——d d——n s——s of b——s," when the 54th Massachusetts Volunteers went into the fight, neither the well-aimed shot that made a rebel officer bite the dust before he had time to draw his sword. We are compelled to take this in our own hands. The Johnny Reb will find out that niggers won't die so fast. . . .

LETTER 21

(Rufus, 7th USCI, Jacksonville, Florida, May 17, 1864; *CR*, May 28, 1864) "Rufus" arrived in Jacksonville to find conditions better than reported by others. He and his regiment came from Maryland, a slave state. He did not like the people of Florida, and he wanted a different general, but he claimed that his black regiment was as well equipped and supplied as the white regiments.

. . . I was agreeably surprised on coming here to find that even Florida – geographically proverbial for its marshes and alligators – is yet a "garden spot" in the "sunny South." The people here are less a people than any I have seen; they do not seem to understand anything but that they are the most God-forsaken looking animals on earth, and all miserable accordingly. They look *mean;* they live *meanly,* act *meanly,* and they don't *mean* to be anything but *mean;* and it is safe to assert that they are *very mean.* To think that these fellows voted Florida out of the Union without the aid of the primitive inhabitants – alligators – is simply preposterous.

I was agreeably surprised to find that we are not suffocated by the intense heat of this torrid climate; the weather is warm – the sun is powerful, yet withal it is pleasant. We have fine land and sea breezes daily, and while I write I feel as pleasant as though in the enjoyment of a stroll on the beach at Cape May, and that at ten o'clock A.M.

Upon the whole, I like Florida very well, and if we but get the right men to command us here we will teach these "ginger-colored gentlemen" their duty to civilization and Christianity. In the short time we have been here we have had four commanding generals. The first, [Gen. Truman] *Seymour,* was removed for good reasons; the "battle of Olustee" proved that he was not the man to command colored troops; and we do not desire to see any more of his experiments. The next was removed to give place to Brig. Genl. [William] Birney; and he, after thoroughly organizing the district, and capturing $2,000,000 worth of property for the government, was removed because of seniority of Genl. Gordon, who is now in command.

I do not desire to detract from the military worth of the commanders in this department, or show a want of confidence in them; but I am certain that there is but one man that can make the "Florida Expedition" a perfect success with the forces composed chiefly of colored troops, and that man is Genl. Birney. The men of this regiment would follow him anywhere, and our confidence in him is unbounded.

It is my fond hope that he may be returned to us. He is a stern soldier, but his heart is in the right place; and he feels that is a part of his mission on earth to elevate our race. . . .

In your issue of April 23d, I noticed a communication from a soldier of the 8th U.S.C.T. I felt sad to peruse his article, for there are assertions therein that are seriously exaggerated; there is no duty imposed upon colored soldiers here that is not shared by their white brothers in arms, and our camp equipage and other necessaries are just the same as those furnished to white troops, and in better condition than theirs. With regard to rations, I most flatly contradict the soldier's assertion: after an experience of eight months in this regiment and extensive observation in others, I have come to the conclusion that these troops are the best fed men in the service; and if there is any fault, it should fall upon the regimental Q[uarter] M[aster's] department, and not upon the General Government.

LETTER 22

(H. S. H., Sergeant, Co. B, 3d USCI, Jacksonville, Florida, April 3, 1865; *CR*, April 22, 1865) Although blacks generally were not given command of soldiers, on at least one occasion the sergeant-major of the 3rd USCI led a group of thirty African Americans on a raid deep into the interior of Florida. This letter, probably written by Sergeant Henry S. Herman, told the story of that daring raid, for which Sergeant-Major Henry James received an official commendation from the commanding general.

. . . I take the liberty of your columns to present for their perusal an account of an expedition which left Jacksonville under the command of Sergeant-Major Henry James, 3d U.S.C.T., on the night of the 7th of March, consisting of sixteen (16) of the 3d U.S.C.T., six men of the 34th U.S.C.T., and seven colored citizens, and one (1) of the 107th O[hio] V[olunteer] I[fantry], thirty (30) men in all. After waiting some time for darkness to throw her pall over the scene, the commander gave the order to push off. The party then moved up the St. John's River in pontoon boats to Orange Mills, where he landed with ten men and skirmished the country to a point near Palatka, where the boats met them, and seeing all well, he again skirmished to what is called Horse Shoe Landing, said to be 100 miles from Jacksonville, which brought them well up in the day; having fatigued themselves considerably, they remained in the swamp until the boats came up about nine o'clock in the evening, when he embarked again and came up to what is called Fort Gates. He then ordered the boats pulled close into shore under cover of the dense swamps, and proceeded with the whole force across the country to the Oclawaha River, to what is known as Marshall's plantation. Here was one of the objects of the expedition reached without serious opposition, and almost in the heart of the enemy's country, and as yet quite unknown to him. Here the expedition captured some 25 horses and mules, burnt a sugar mill with 85 barrels of sugar, about 300 barrels of syrup, a whiskey distillery, with a large amount of whiskey and rice, and started on their return, bringing along 95 colored persons, men, women and children, re-crossed the Oclawaha River, burning the bridge. Six men then were detached from the command and sent under charge of Sergeant Joel Benn, of Co. B, 3d U.S.C.T., with Israel Hall, scout, to Hawley plantation, where they were attacked by a small body of rebels, and Sergt. Benn was killed, shot through the heart. Henry Brown, scout, wounded, and Israel Hall, chief scout, captured, as was another citizen named Ben Gant, the others being compelled to return to the main body.

Their troubles had now commenced in earnest, this being the second fight of the day, for having to charge the bridge in going to Marshall's, and killing three rebels had only stirred them up, but they pushed on, for much of their success depended on their speed, but when within about twenty miles of the St. John's River, the enemy, numbering about fifty men well mounted, came down on them, calling on them to surrender or suffer themselves to be hanged. But there was another alternative which he, the enemy, did not think of, and which the Sergeant-Major, who by the way is not a surrendering man, resolved to take, which was to fight them a while first. Seeing this, the enemy prepared himself to make it warm for the little band of colored men. Breaking to the right and to the left under cover of a hill, they dismounted and formed their line of attack, and came over the crest of the hill, in quite an imposing array to find the little band of seventeen men (the balance being left to guard some prisoners and the avenues of retreat) deployed as skirmishers to meet them, covered as much as possible by the trees.

But on they came. And every man selecting his man, when they were near enough for every man to make sure and waste no ammunition, Sergt. James gave the command to commence firing, and for a while nothing was heard but the sharp crack of the soldier's rifle and the louder roar of the citizens' fowling-piece, blended with the yells of their wounded and dying. The firing on the part of our men was good, as was shortly proved, for the enemy suddenly broke for their horses, when our men, leaving their cover, dashed in among them with the bayonet and clubbed guns, scattering them in every direction, leaving some 20 of their men dead and a few wounded. Finding the way clear again, Sergt. James, on summing up, found the woods had afforded them such good covering that he had only two men wounded, after taking possession of the best of their horses, (although the enemy suffered so severely, he showed himself to be no mean marksman, as numerous holes in our men's clothing amply testified, among which, a hole through the commander's cap, caused him to withdraw his head from a dangerous position) he again took up the line of march for the St. John's, having to abandon one wagon on the way, and soon reached the river and commenced crossing it at twelve o'clock on the night of the 10th, and at daylight on the 11th, had all across except 9 horses, when the enemy coming up made it impossible to recross, consequently had to leave them. They then destroyed the three boats which they had used, and pushed on towards St. Augustine, and by the time they had got one day's start, Dickerson's guerrilla cavalry were in full pursuit, and when within seven miles of St.

Augustine, the enemy overtook some of the colored people, who were unable to keep up. The remainder of the party reached St. Augustine on the 12th inst. in safety with the wounded, 4 prisoners, 74 liberated slaves, 1 wagon, 6 horses, and 9 mules having traveled over 200 miles of our own country, in five days and nights, reaching Jacksonville, last evening, the 19th inst., with all their booty.

The expedition reflects great credit on Sergt. Major James, for the masterly manner in which it was commanded, and gives further proof that a colored man with proper training can command among his fellows and succeed where others have failed. And a great deal is due to the men for their good behavior, and steadiness, and obedience, and if it were not for occupying too much of your space, which I fear I have done already, I would give their names, but that at some other time.

I am still an ardent lover of my race, and a soldier.

LETTER 23

(W. B. Johnson, [Private,] Co. A, 3d USCI, Jacksonville, Florida, April 28, 1865; *CR,* May 20, 1865) Conditions for prisoners of war were bad throughout the Confederacy. The worst of all the prisons was at Andersonville, Georgia, where thousands of Union men, including many black soldiers, died from disease and malnutrition. When the fighting stopped, those prisoners were released to Federal forces. Some of them went to Jacksonville, Florida, for transportation by sea back to the North. William B. Johnson told in this letter how the prisoners were received by his regiment.

About half past four o'clock this P.M., I heard cheer after cheer break from the lips of the quiet inhabitants of Jacksonville, and all running towards Battery Myrick, and I there saw over 500 Union prisoners making their way from Rebeldom. It would have done you good to have seen them look at the old flag. Some of them had been prisoners for eighteen months. Fancy you can see 500 men clad in the poorest garment, coming into our lines, crying, "God save the flag."

The 3d U.S.C.T., with the assistance of the 34th, soon had camp-fires made, and in half an hour many were partaking of U.S. salt beef and hard bread. They continued to come in during the night, and as I now write, they are singing:

> "My country, 'tis of thee,
> Sweet land of Liberty."

April 20. – This morning as I was going to my boarding house for breakfast, I met a crowd of exchanged prisoners: having a pitcher of sweet milk, they asked me if I could get them some. I told them to follow me, and I assure you I felt proud to see them gather around, and drink to their hearts' content. One told me that there are 250 acres of land, filled with our Union dead, that died completely from starvation. – Another said he subsisted on the coarsest of meal, and was glad to grind up the cob with the corn. I call on God to judge such treatment. May God speed on the time when peace shall reign throughout the land.

We have received the sad news of the death of our President. The churches are all in mourning. But I shed not a tear for him. He has done the work that was given him, and today sings the song of redeeming love. I shed tears for our country. May we humble ourselves and cry aloud, "God save the State." Yes, Abraham Lincoln has done his work, and

> Sleeps in Jesus, blessed sleep,
> From which none ever wake to weep:
> A calm and undisturbed repose,
> Unbroken by the last of foes.

SOUTH CAROLINA: II

LETTER 24

(John H. W. N. Collins, Sergeant, Co. H, 54th Massachusetts Infantry, Fort Green, Folly Island, South Carolina, [May 1864]; *CR*, June 4, 1864) Sergeant Collins tells of the movements of the 54th Massachusetts Regiment from Jacksonville to the islands near Charleston. The continual transfers from place to place made life hard, especially with no pay.

Wishing at all times for our friends to hear from us, and knowing of no other mode, only through and by your paper – the Recorder – I therefore hope that you will, if you have a spare column, be kind enough to let our friends and the community at large, know that we are yet alive, as it is a very hard matter for us to get our mail out here, and we are all anxious to hear from home, and that our friends should also hear from us.

Mr. Editor, since my last letter to you, there has been a great change made in this department. On Sunday, the 16th of April, we were to take up our march; but owing the delay of the transports, we had to remain over night, and on Monday morning, the 17th, at an early hour, the regimental line was formed, and the regiment took up the march for the city of Jacksonville. We marched by the right flank until we had passed all obstacles, and then we received the orders to break into platoons, which was done in good order; and never did a regiment of soldiers march better than did the 54th, escorted by the regimental band, which rent the air with its martial music. Onward we went, with light step and bounding hearts, and in a few more moments we halted in front of General [Adelbert] Ames' Head Quarters. The regiment halted, came to the front and saluted; and after being acknowledged by the general, we came by; the right of platoons to the rear, and then by the right flank and onward we went, and a few moments more brought us to the Head Quarters of General [John P.] Hatch. We came by inversion to the left, in front, saluted, and took our final leave of the general. We came by the left of platoons to the rear, and then by the left flank, and onward we went towards the transport, which was waiting for us at the wharf. What sound is that we hear? Why, the sound of our comrades in arms, who are bidding us God speed. Then came the order, by the left flank file left, which was done in good style by the 54th. In a few moments we were at the wharf. Then the inquiry was made as to what boat it was that was to leave us at the point of destination. Why, it is the Cosmopolitan. Can she take all of us? says one. Why, yes, and another besides. We embarked with everything that belonged to the 54th, and it was just as much as we could do to get aboard. The 55th left before us, on board the transport Neptune.

The band struck up as the boat pushed off from the landing. There were three cheers given, and then all was as silent as death for awhile. Onward glided the steamer; we passed Yellow Bluff, where a detachment of the 8th U.S. Colored Troops went to relieve a detachment of the 55th; they gave us three hearty cheers, and we passed by leaving the solitary state of Florida behind us. The night on the water passed off very pleasantly. Here and there lay the brave members of the 54th, scattered all over the decks of the steamer – some dreaming of those at home, some humming a hymn of praise, some reading the Testament – thus we passed the solitary night on the water. On Tuesday afternoon, at 4 or 6 o'clock, we landed at Stono Inlet. We received orders to move down to the Pawnee Landing, which we started to do, but the steamer, being heavily laden, got aground, and there we lay until another steamer came to our assistance. Three companies disembarked from the Cosmopolitan and embarked aboard of the other steamer. She was trying to assist us off, but finding that she could do no good, she left us by ourselves on the bar. The rain began to fall in torrents, and the river began to rise, and we worked ourselves off the bar, and a few moments brought us to the Pawnee Landing, and there we disembarked in the rain, and after all were off, we took up our march for our old stand, which we thought we had now left never to behold again while we wore the blue uniform of Uncle Sam. The rain fell in torrents upon us, and we all got wet through to the skin. We received orders to come by company into line; all this was done in the rain storm on the beach. After a while we landed at the dock, and part of the regiment went over to Morris Island, while the other half waited in the rain for the steamer to return. When we got over we marched to the old campground, and took up our quarters for the night (as we supposed) but after we had got a few fires going, and were getting some beef soup, orders came for three companies to repair to Black Island and relieve the 11th Maine. Cos. H, E, and C formed the detachment, and we went to our post like men. We were wet through; we went up in small boats, and after staying there a fortnight, Co. H was ordered to garrison Fort Green, and tonight we received orders (after having been here ten days) to report to Black Island again. This is the way we have been dragged from post to pillow since we have been in the service, and yet we don't receive our pay for all that. . . .

LETTER 25

("Sergeant," 55th Massachusetts Infantry, Folly Island, South Carolina, May 29, 1864; *CR*, July 9, 1864) A regular part of army life was heavy labor at building fortifications, trenches, and roads – fatigue duty. In this letter, "Sergeant" complains that his regiment has done nothing but fatigue duty since arriving in the South, and this while being underpaid.

. . . A soldier's life, take it what way you will, is a hard one. I have seen a good bit of it. Being the steward of an officer on the Potomac, I had a chance of seeing and learning a great deal of how a soldier ought to be treated. Now I am going to address myself to the public, and shall endeavor to be as brief as possible. I shall not add, but rather diminish.

The 54th, our brother regiment, came to this department last summer, and made that gallant charge on Fort Wagner on Morris Island, where many a brave man fell; I will not say soldiers, for in these two regiments we are only soldiers for the time being.

Shortly after this charge we landed on Folly Island, and soon after fatiguing duties began. We went to the front every night and day for six or eight weeks in a stretch, mounting cannon, pulling cannon, throwing up batteries, when I would much rather have taken my position in line of battle; for the seizing of Morris Island, preparatory to the siege of Charleston, was anything but a pleasant undertaking; so we fatigued from that time until the 13th of February, when we embarked for Florida. The 54th being several days in advance from Jacksonville, we marched out to Barber's Station, en route to assist in making the attack at Olustee. Arriving at Barber's Station, and finding our troops on the retreat, we concluded to encamp there for the night.

The next morning found us retreating back on Jacksonville, where we were immediately set to work throwing up entrenchments and erecting batteries, building forts, and so on, which were all successfully completed. After remaining there a few days we were detached, part going to Palatka and part to Yellow Bluff, where fatigue duty commenced. When we got through there, we were ordered to South Carolina, leaving the 8th [USCI] Pennsylvania regiment to enjoy the fruits of our labor, as we had done for other regiments.

So we entered South Carolina once more, and it was intimated by some prominent officers that by promising to do double duty we would be allowed to land, but not otherwise. However, we landed and commenced picket duty, each man coming off and going on the next day. This kept up for some time. We were then taken off that duty and put on fatigue duty on Saturday – all this going on, and we not receiving a cent of remuneration, after having been in the service for one year. . . .

LETTER 26

("A Colored Private," 54th Massachusetts Infantry, Morris Island, South Carolina, June 26, 1864; *The Liberator,* July 15, 1864) Abolitionist William Lloyd Garrison received this letter from "A Colored Private," who describes some of the shelling around Charleston. Most of the white gun crew of a giant cannon shared the antislavery principles of "Private" and Garrison.

I thought you might be pleased to know that your principles were strongly represented in the department that loaded the 100-pounder gun that threw the first three shells at Charleston city, S.C. No. 1 is a strong abolitionist and has worked well among the soldiers. This man puts the loads into the gun. No. 2 is now in favor of emancipation, though he don't think the negro is his equal. No. 3 was an old emancipationist years ago, and always took your paper. And the gunner is a Republican. The other members seem to go with the strongest party, but believe in extirpating slavery from the land at the present time.

Some of the Boston papers say that Fort Sumter has guns which annoy the fleet and the camps on this island. This is a mistake. It has not sent a shot from its shattered walls since last August, with the exception of a few grape and canister thrown at the picket boats and storming party, from a 12-pounder Howitzer. It cannot reach Fort Putnam with this, which is the nearest point.

The rebels have some thirty batteries on James' and Sullivan's Islands, mounting about 75 guns. From these they throw shot and shell at us, now and then, but not very often, as our men are by far the best gunners, notwithstanding they are mudsills, and send them back with interest. Charleston might be taken without great

loss of life at the present time. I don't think there are more than
one thousand men on James' Island just now.

O! for some men who have not been brought up under the
enervating influence of slavery and rum, and who have not
breathed the pestilential air of Washington too long to be honest, to
lead our army and navy in this department now!

I have been in this State almost three years, during which time I
have seen many a golden moment slip away, I think, and many a
blunder made. Cause – rum and lack of principle.

I am a private, and have no right to express an opinion, or to
think; therefore you will excuse this if you think it impertinent; and
believe me your friend, while you demand freedom for all throughout the land.

LETTER 27

(Samuel A. Valentine, Sergeant, Co. B, 54th Massachusetts Infantry, Morris Island, South Carolina, July 25, 1864; *CR*, August 27,
1864) The fighting on the islands near Charleston was a drawn-
out struggle to capture land nearer the city so that heavy artillery
could shell it. Confederate forces yielded that ground reluctantly,
frequently bombarding the black soldiers who manned the Union
positions. Sergeant Valentine, a shoemaker from Boston, told here
of the hazards of living and working close to the rebel guns.

. . . I have been in the United States' service almost seventeen
months, and I have never yet had a furlough to go home to see my
family. But as to a furlough, I would not care for that, if they would
deal justly with us. There are men in this regiment who have
respectable families that have been torn to pieces and driven to
beggary. It is hard to bear. But the only and best way that I can see
is to look to God for help; for he has promised to help in time of

trouble. I hope the time will come soon that we shall have justice done to us all.

On the 1st day of July, we crossed the creek from Morris Island to Folly Island, and, marching to Stono Landing, we took the boat again and landed on Cole's Island at day-light. We then started at almost double quick for James Island, where the 55th Massachusetts regiment had charged upon the rebel works and taken two small guns; but with all our hurrying, we did not get there in time. Companies B and F were sent to strengthen the skirmishing line; but when we got in line, the enemy was not to be seen. We lay there about two hours, the sun beaming down hotter than I ever felt in my life; there were a great many men sun-struck, and one man in the 54th died from the effect of the heat. Our loss was very light, only one man killed, Cornelius Price, of company A; he was struck with a shell from the rebel guns. So we cannot complain of our loss.

But our loss since has been very shocking. Last Wednesday two weeks, while everything was quiet, the enemy opened fire on our camp from Sullivan's Island, and the second shell killed two men in my company while eating their dinner. A piece of shell, weighing about a pound, struck the tent, cutting a hole through, and struck John Tanner in the left temple, passing through his head, and scattering his brains about the tent; the same piece struck Samuel Suffay [Sufshay] in the breast, passing through his body, causing instant death to both of them. Since I have been in the army, I have seen a number of killed and wounded, but I have never had anything to rest on me so much in my life. It was an awful sight.

LETTER 28

("Sergeant," 55th Massachusetts Infantry, Folly Island, South Carolina, July 26, 1864; *The Liberator*, October 4, 1864) James Island was the scene of frequent skirmishes between Union troops and the defenders of Charleston. On July 2, 1864, in a costly attack, the

55th Massachusetts Regiment captured a rebel artillery position. "Sergeant" told in this letter about the rewards of victory.

I have seen considerable service, one way or another, both in the infantry tactics and also in artillery practice, both light and heavy. It was my privilege to be the first non-commissioned officer that reached the enemy's guns in the fight we had on James Island, on the 1st of July. I found one of them loaded, and fired it; afterwards, loaded it with another charge which the rebels failed to take away, and fired that also. The two guns were afterwards given in my charge (two twelve-pounders, Napoleon guns, manufactured in Richmond, Va.) by the Colonel of our regiment, who commanded the successful charge.

I selected from our company (F) two gun detachments, and during our stay on James Island used the guns pretty effectually on the Rebs. I also covered the retreat of our forces from James to Cole's Island with them. The guns are now in front of the quarters of our colonel; the General having granted the Colonel the privilege of keeping them, in consideration of the valor of the 55th.

For services of myself and the men under my charge, I received, through our Colonel, the thanks of the chief of artillery.

Today I can say, without depreciating any other regiment, that none stand higher than the old 55th in the estimation of our Commanding General.

Could you have been on the battle-field on the morning of July 1st, and seen them under a shower of shot and shell deploy into line of battle when it seemed as though the day was lost by the giving way of two regiments – (one white, and the other colored, both rushing back discomforted) – I say, could you have seen the old 55th rush in, with the shout of "Remember Fort Pillow!" you would have thought that nothing human could have withstood their impetuosity. We know no defeat. The guns we were bent on having, and there they are, near my tent door. . . .

Sept. 11th: – Two large tents have been erected and floored

adjoining each other, making a room some 45 by 25 feet, with suitable desks and benches for its furniture. Evening schools have been established. The valuable accessions to the reading matter of the regiment, recently received from Massachusetts, have given us quite a library. God bless the noble friends at home for their philanthropic efforts in behalf of the soldiers in the field! The appreciation of their effort is attested in the interest manifested by the large numbers in attendance every evening. I find there are not a few in the regiment, who, although never having been slaves, are unable to write their names, and many are unable to read. A year's experience in the army has shown most of them the disadvantage of being dependent upon others to do their writing and reading of letters; and they are now applying themselves assiduously with spelling book, pen, ink, and paper. Another class are equally, if not more desirous of improving their mental faculties. I allude to those whom the withering, blighting, cursed system of slavery has robbed of the golden moment of youth and the maturer hours of manhood. Many of these are destined to make their marks bright ornaments [*missing*] to their homes.

LETTER 29

(J. H. W. N. C., [Sergeant,] Co. H, 54th Massachusetts Infantry, Deveaux Neck, South Carolina, January 24, 1865; *CR*, February 25, 1865) Sergeant John Collins complains that the men in his regiment, especially himself, received little mail from the folks at home. To let his friends know where he was and what he was doing, he has written this letter describing the advance of the 54th Massachusetts on Charleston by way of Deveaux Neck, South Carolina.

Sitting under the bright canopy of heaven, and looking back at the past events of my spent life that have passed and forever gone into an endless eternity, never to return again, and looking at the future to see what nature has in store for me, and for all that love and fear the Almighty; looking around and seeing my fellow soldiers-in-arms standing in groups, and some looking with a wishful eye and palpitating heart for the mail, to see what our people north are doing, and to see if any news comes from the loved ones at home, but after the mail is distributed and they are told there is nothing for them, you can just imagine how they feel, when finding no news from home, from mothers, sisters, wives, nor friends, they exclaim, "Well, I'm forgotten." Some will say, "Perhaps death, that grim monster, has called them from time to eternity, and I will see them no more until the day of reckoning."

Since your humble servant has returned to his company, he has not heard from home nor friends, and he thinks that he must be forgotten by those at home, and wanting them and the friends of the regiment to know of our whereabouts, he avails himself of the columns of the *Recorder,* which has a wide circulation amongst the colored people, both north and south.

You will see by my letter that we left camp to start upon an expedition to strike terror to this rebellion. We have thus far been successful, and the armies of Generals [William T.] Sherman and [John G.] Foster have met at last. On the 14th of this month we left camp to join the Seventeenth Army Corps of General Sherman, commanded by General [Francis P.] Blair. After marching some three miles, companies H and I were sent in advance. Company H deployed as skirmishers; the column advanced slowly, wending our way through the woods and high grass towards the enemy, expecting every moment to encounter them; but onward we went fearing nothing. After advancing about five miles, we came to the spot where only a few weeks before, Captain [Charles E.] Tucker of Company H, and a detachment of Company C, encountered the rebel pickets, and a skirmish ensued, resulting in the loss of one of the rebels, whom Corporal Clifford brought to the ground never to rise again, and our forces being rather small, we returned. But not so on the 14th, for the 54th was on hand, and also the 33d U.S.C.T., and a company of the 3d Rhode Island light artillery. We intended to strike a blow and try to carry the works by storm, but finding no impediment in our way, onward we went, and a few moments brought our skirmish line in sight of the rebel line of intrenchments. The column halted, and Captain Tucker went forward to ascertain the whereabouts of the enemy, and as fate would have it, they had fled the same morning, about three o'clock, to parts best known to themselves, leaving nothing but an aged colored man and wife, and two small children. I must confess that in all my travels through South Carolina, I never saw such a beautiful section of country before; but it shows plainly that desolation had long since visited it, and that its lord had left, perhaps never to return again. The stately dwelling will no more be inhabited by its cruel owners, nor the blood of poor slaves dampen its soil. We could plainly see that no federal soldiers had trod upon that ground before the black warriors of 1865. Onward we went till our ears caught the sound of the cannon, but we heeded that not, for the sweet breeze and the warbling voices of the birds told us that victory awaited us, and in a few minutes we were in sight of the works which they had skedaddled from, and to our surprise we met General Blair, with the Nineteenth Army Corps. After resting we took up our march and returned to camp, having fulfilled our mission; but had the rebels been there we would have tried them one time at any rate, but they "smelt a rat," and left beforehand. As I write it rains quite hard, and has done so for four days. The mud is quite deep, and our shelter very poor, and it is very hard living at this time. We are all destitute of clothes, and some have not as much as a shoe upon their feet, but when we look at the suffering condition of the poor slaves, we can stand all: only give us our liberty and freedom, and we will give our lives for liberty, for we love that well-known sound.

LETTER 30

(William Waring, Chaplain, 102d USCI, Beaufort, South Carolina, February 15, 1865; *WAA*, March 4, 1865) After General

William T. Sherman and his army marched to the sea at Savannah, they turned northward in January 1865 and started through the Carolinas. Chaplain William Waring (or Warring), an African American from Oberlin, Ohio, served in a black regiment from Michigan. It was stationed in Beaufort, South Carolina, where one wing of Sherman's army stopped for a time. In this letter, he describes in detail his impressions of Sherman's all-white troops.

As you have any amount of correspondence describing the appearance and character of colored soldiers, the thought struck me that my observation of "Sherman's Army" would not be out of place in your columns, and, if nothing more, would at least lend variety to the entertainment.

[The world] has looked on with admiration and wonder at the boldness and daring of this victorious host, and men of science have held their breath as they have seen it apparently set at defiance all military law, and stake such important interests upon movements that scarcely had a precedent in the annals of warfare. But whether our fears were excited when we thought of his long and narrow line of communication from Chattanooga to Atlanta, or the entire absence of communication during his march through Georgia, they were alike dispelled when Sherman announced to his anxious countrymen that "Atlanta is ours," and again, "I have this day carried Fort McAllister by storm, and established perfect communication with the fleet." By us who have been cooped up on these Sea Islands with scarcely force enough to make secure our frontier picket-line, the movements of Sherman were looked upon with anxiety as intense, to say the least of it, as any portion of loyal Americans; and when our forces operating against the Charleston and Savannah R.R. received the news that he had been signalled by Gen. Foster, one long and wild shout of joy swelled on the midnight air.

But as we were anxious to know of his success, so we were

anxious to see and look upon those men of whom so much had been said – with the full expectation that, as the brilliancy of their exploits had exceeded all contemporaries, so they would surpass all others in their soldierly appearance and bearing.

In them we expected to see "heels on a line," "toes turned out," "head erect," "eyes front." Here, according to our anticipations, would be displayed a stately martial tread and a graceful carriage of arms that could not be boasted of by soldiers ordinarily.

But a glimpse of Sherman's Army will convince any one at all acquainted with military attainments that as their great leader – like Bonaparte – acknowledges no criterion but success, and adopts means only to secure that end, so his men in their movements and bearing consult their personal comfort, even if in so doing they treat with infinite contempt the most approved "School of the Soldier" extant. In fact, contrary to all his previously elevated expectations, a Western man is at once struck with the fact that he sees before him a material with which he was perfectly well acquainted at home, and in the passing crowd recognizes the counterpart of some "Bill Smith" or "Joe Brown" that he saw at some shooting-match or house-raising in Ohio, Indiana, Michigan, or Illinois. That reckless free and go easy air of Western country life is everywhere conspicuous, and is a characteristic that they take pains in cultivating, rather than in restraining.

But let us stand upon the sidewalk and notice them as they pass along.

Here comes one. His pantaloons leg is split half way up to the knee; his face is unshaven and his hair unshorn; the crown of his hat, too, is gone, but he is perfectly oblivious to the eyes that are upon him, or the remarks that are made about him, and with his gun swung carelessly over his shoulder, the whole appearance of the man says, "I can hold all the ground that I cover." You have seen the same character in the Western wilds, bent on getting a crack at some fine old "buck," the difference being only in his object – he is after a "Johnny" now.

Here comes a six mule team! The wagon is loaded with bales of hay as high as they will lie on. Perched on the topmost bale is a soldier crowing like a rooster. That crowing is suggestive! A fellow-soldier on the street says that means chicken to-night. This proneness to disturb the nocturnal soliloquies of chickens I am not willing to admit is necessarily a Western characteristic (being myself a Western man), but when we reflect that those men have been so long in the "enemy's country," and have been so accustomed to look upon everything they see as the property of rebels, and feeling that they had a perfect right to take it wherever they found it, it is not surprising that they should become so addicted to the habit as to regard it as a matter of course.

But they like turkey as well as chicken, as our surgeon [Dr. Wesley Vincent] can well attest. The Doctor has had a fine old gobbler perambulating the camp at pleasure for some weeks past, and was looking forward to the time when he should enjoy a nice roast; but, unfortunately for his expected feast, some of Sherman's men reconnoitered during the day. The gobbler was discovered and marked for a victim. About midnight, as the Doctor lies upon his peaceful couch, he heard his fattening bird cry, "quit! quit!" The Doctor, who is a true Western Yankee, at once established an intimate connection between Sherman's army and his fowl, but having too much good sense to rush out in his night clothes and expose himself to ridicule in addition to his loss (knowing that they had the start of him), quietly submitted to the outrage; but next morning expressed the feeling that he cared not so much for the gobbler as for the idea of having them beat him while he was almost looking at them.

But let us look again on the street. Here comes [one] not with a "regulation hat" or an "army cap," but an old fashioned helmet with a prodigious horse tail streaming down his back, feeling particularly glorious that he has contributed so much in overthrowing the doctrine that soldiers should be dressed in uniform.

Over the way, there is a squad building a fire, getting ready to cook. A strange officer orders them to put it out; one of the number turns around and promptly invites him to go to that region which all men should seek to avoid, and quietly goes on with his cooking.

Up the street a little farther the negro-hating element shows itself.

One of them takes a colored woman's pies and then slaps her over because she complained. Another one inflicts a wound on an already wounded colored soldier. Two more go up to the quarters of the Post Band, who are colored men, and raise a disturbance there. But here they unexpectedly meet with resistance; for one of the Bandmen unceremoniously knocks them down stairs.

Around the corner another one interferes with a colored woman in her own yard, and she, like a true South Carolinian, falls back on her "reserved rights" and cuts his head with an axe.

Again, however, the other side of the negro question presents itself.

Here comes a soldier full of fun, and meeting an old contraband lady of fresh arrival, throws his arms around her, with a "hurrah, old woman, bully for you!" – and here is another, with four or five loaves of bread in his arms, gnawing industriously away. A recent contraband lady asks him for one. "Oh! yes, Aunty, we will fight for you, and feed you, too." and with that shares his commissaries with her. But here is another, and though he is plainly one of Sherman's men, yet he entertains an idea different from his comrades that we have seen. He is inquiring after the Christian Commission's agent to obtain something to read; and after a few minutes conversation very unreservedly declares his preference for the things that pertain to religion, by saying that he hoped while the army was receiving supplies that it would, above all things, get a good supply of Gospel Grace. And in this he is not alone. On the sabbath, I noticed quite a sprinkling of them in the Baptist Church, who were all orderly and seemed to be well-disposed. But while the services were going on my attention was arrested by seeing a number of them pass the door and halting for a moment, look in with that curious stare that a man assumes when he is not quite certain whether he understands the thing or not. They probably thought that they had seen something similar to what was going on in there, and paused a moment to be perfectly sure.

Taken altogether, Sherman's army certainly does not come up to the common idea of a well-appointed body of troops; and to the mind of a person who has been accustomed to think that armies are effective in proportion to their discipline and soldierly attainments, the question will present itself, in what lies the effectiveness of this army? This question can be partially, if not fully, answered.

They have been filled with an idea that to some extent supplies the lack of what we are accustomed to call military discipline, and that is, that they are *invincible.*

Every man seems to have unlimited confidence in himself, and an implicit faith in the fidelity of his comrades, together with an unbounded belief in the ability of their leader.

Hence, when called upon to carry a fortification or climb a mountain in the face of bristling cannon – they think that it can be done or Sherman never would have attempted it; and if its accomplishment is within the range of human possibilities, that they, of all other men, can accomplish it. Each man feels, too, that no matter how hot may be the place in which he may get, he will not be left alone as long as there is a comrade alive – consequently there are no doubts, no misgivings, no hesitation but, when "forward" is the word, forward they go like an irresistible avalanche.

I was told by an officer that in the assault on Fort McAllister [near Savannah] that the line was actually formed after they had reached the outside works. Men must have full reliance on the courage and fidelity of their comrades who will charge singly and in squads in the teeth of belching artillery up to such a stronghold.

Another feature in the character of this army that contributes to its success is its highly cultivated talent of destroying everything within its reach.

The practice of traipsing through the enemy's country with an army so carefully that an experienced Indian would be puzzled to discover its trail – like I have seen and heard tell of before now – is held in ineffable contempt by these men.

It is the common boast with them, that there is no need of policing the country through which they have passed, and now they declare that when they pass through South Carolina, that they will strip it so clean that a "crow when it flies over it will have to carry its own rations."

In their trip through Georgia the exercise of this talent made them almost secure from any danger at the hands of [Confederate General John B.] Hood; for had he followed them he would have found himself in a country without supplies or railroads, and would have been as effectually from home as Sherman.

Armies are disciplined and drilled for the purpose of acquiring the greatest possible amount of destructive power, and whether Sherman's army shows that it has been taken through the usual course of instruction or not, it *possesses* that power in a preeminent degree. It seems to have become part of their nature, and it is irksome to them to be restrained, as they are here, among loyal people.

One of their Captains remarked that he hoped they would leave here soon, "for," said he, "we have to behave them too well." In expressing this sentiment, he was the truthful deponent of the whole army.

If God, in his infinite wisdom, as we believe, is visiting these Southern people for their wickedness, surely in Sherman's army he has provided an effectual scourge, and to one who thinks ever of the moral features of this great conflict, the thought will suggest itself, as he looks upon this host, how great and heaven-daring must have been the crimes of the people that a merciful God would prepare so terrible a retribution! And involuntarily he will breathe a prayer that the day may speedily come when the loud clang of battle will have hushed, and in its stead the hum of peaceful industry and the songs of a free people float on the morning zephyr.

LETTER 31

(J. H. W. N. Collins [Sergeant,] Co. H, 54th Massachusetts Infantry, Savannah, Georgia, March 19, 1865; *CR*, April 15, 1865) Late in February 1865, Federal troops, including the 54th Massachusetts, marched into Charleston. Two weeks later the regiment was sent by sea to Savannah, Georgia, which had been taken by Sherman's army in December. In this letter, Sergeant John Collins describes the reaction of the black people of Savannah and Charleston when they saw the men of the 54th.

. . . Whilst we are doing our utmost in the far South, the Head of Government is doing something for our race. I noticed, not long since, a column in the *Anglo-African,* stating that Dr. Martin R. Delany had been commissioned as Major in the army of the United States. I am happy to see that our people are beginning to be something more than mere chattels, and that we have got rights that the white man is bound to respect, and I hope and pray that the day is not far distant when not only Dr. M. R. Delany, but all those who are competent enough to become more than privates and non-commissioned officers in the service of the United States will be promoted. I fancy before the suppression of this rebellion that the colored man will not only wear the plain straps, but the spread eagle.

I must say something about our regiment to let our friends know that we are on hand yet, and ready for any call that can be made. Although we were not allowed to remain in the city of Charleston, yet we claim the largest share in capturing it. On the day we entered that rebellious city, the streets were thronged with women and children of all sizes, colors and grades – the young, the old, the halt, the maimed, and the blind. I saw an old colored woman with a crutch – for she could not walk without one, having served all her life in bondage – who, on seeing us, got so happy that she threw down her crutch and shouted that the year of jubilee had come. The city is a little better than a mass of ruins, but ere long it will be repaired by Uncle Sam.

Now that we are encamped at Savannah, Ga., I must say something about it. It is quite a fine city in appearance, but there are a few rebels left here yet, who will however, change their tune before long. There are a nice set of colored people here. Though some of them seem to be afraid of the colored soldiers, others are very friendly. . . .

LETTER 32

(John H. W. N. Collins, Orderly Sergeant, Company H, 54th Massachusetts Infantry, Georgetown, South Carolina, April 30, 1865; *CR* May 20, 1865) After the fall of Charleston, the 54th Massachusetts joined other regiments in a major raid inland from Georgetown, South Carolina. Sergeant John Collins told in this letter about the excitement and achievement of that raid. By the time he wrote, however, Confederate General Robert E. Lee had surrendered in Virginia and President Abraham Lincoln had been killed. Fighting had formally ended in the Carolinas on April 21.

. . . Well, we arrived at Georgetown, S.C., on the 31st, and went into camp. On the 1st of April we started upon our errand through the State, and had nothing to molest us for three days. We saw nothing of the "Johnnies," and on Friday the 8th of April, at Epp's Ferry, Cos. H and A were detached from the regiment to go and destroy the said Ferry. Myself, one corporal and fifteen privates were in the advance. On we went, neither hearing nor seeing any thing in particular.

After advancing about two miles, and wading through water and mud, we spied a Johnny sitting upon his horse as a picket. He left his post and secreted himself. Halting my men for further orders, I received instructions to proceed forward with the utmost caution, and screen my men as much as possible in the woods. The swamp through which we had to pass was waist-deep.

Onward we went, and after getting through the swamp, not over seventy-five yards from Johnny, he saw that we were getting too close to him; and at that time the Second-Lieutenant of Co. A came along, and I told him that Johnny was getting ready to fire; and at that moment, Johnny's balls began to fall thick and fast around us.

The Lieutenant got wounded in the right arm. I had two men wounded – one in the right leg, the other in both shoulders; and it appeared to us that the Johnnies had nothing much but *bird-shot* to fire at us, which whizzed about our ears in perfect showers. The writer got stung slightly in the left hand by one of these diminutive missiles from Johnny's shot-gun. They saw that we were determined to complete the job, and they destroyed the levee and fled. So we returned to our command on the 8th. We entered Manningville with a loss of but one man killed, who belonged to the 4th Massachusetts Regiment.

On the 10th we left Manningville, and arrived at Sumterville on Sabbath, the 11th; and after a short and sharp fight, we took the place, captured three pieces of artillery complete, killed five rebels, wounded some more, and also captured a few.

We encamped in the city that night, and destroyed the depot, together with three locomotives and a train of thirty-five cars. We left on the 13th, after destroying every thing that fire would burn, and went to Manchester, and there destroyed one locomotive and a train of twenty cars.

The 54th was detailed to go seven miles from the place for the purpose of destroying some trestle-work. After a considerable amount of delay, the advance guard, which was from Co. F, Sergeant [Frank M.] Welch commanding, pushed forth.[10] They had not gone far when they espied a train of cars, with locomotive

10. Welch was promoted to lieutenant soon after this letter was written.

attached, and a full head of steam on. The column at once halted, and Colonel [Henry N.] Hooper went forward to see for himself, and there, sure enough, was the train. The sharp report of a rifle soon told those on the train that the blood-hounds were on their track. The engineer immediately jumped from the train and ran for his life. Nothing could be seen of him but coat-tails and dust. The command to move forward was given. With a loud yell and tremendous cheer the boys charged over the trestle-work, three miles in length, caught the cars, and ran them ourselves in place of the rebels.

Lieutenant [Stephen A.] Swails got wounded in his right arm.[11]

There are forty cars and six locomotives, and we destroyed them all. Some of the cars were loaded. We then turned the track upside down. Sergeant Major [John H.] Wilson and Private Geo. Jorris, of Co. A, got mashed by the cars. Private Jorris got his collar-bone broken. The Sergeant Major has got partly over the injuries he received.

Leaving there, we encamped at Singleton's plantation, and sent two thousand contrabands to Georgetown in charge of the 32d U.S.C.T. When they returned, we started upon our mission – and from that time, the 14th, we fought every day with the rebels, and drove them before us. But at length they made a stand at Swiss Creek, and fought desperately. We captured nine prisoners. On the 15th we left for the purpose of taking Camden, which we did – capturing all of the rebel sick and wounded there, numbering, at least, from three to four hundred men.

On the 16th we left Camden, and from that we fought until we got to Swiss Creek, where the rebels again made a stand. Cos. F and H were on the skirmish line, the battalion on the reserve, the 102d U.S.C.T. in the centre, and the 32d U.S.C.T. on the left wing. We drove them to their den, when they fought quite desperately for a time. For if they flee from the horsemen, how can they contend with the footmen?

11. Swails was one of the first black soldiers to be made a commissioned officer.

The rebels had a dam constructed all around them, and there was no way of getting at them but to pass over it in single file. The left wing went to extreme right for the purpose of flanking Johnny – and there it was that we lost our noble Lieutenant [Edward L. Stevens]. Who will help us mourn his loss – for he fell in defense of the dear old flag?

Corporal [James P.] Johnson and Corporal [Andrew] Miller of Co. H had six privates wounded. But the 54th stormed the hill and carried it at the point of the bayonet, making themselves masters of the field, as they always do. Just like them! Brave boys they are! Who will say, Three cheers for the 54th Mass. Vols., 32d and 102d U.S.C.T., and for the 25th Ohio Vols., the 107th Ohio Vols., 15th and 56th N.Y. vols., and the 4th Mass., and the 3d New York Artillery, and for General [Edward E.] Potter's brave troops? For we are the ones that destroyed and drove the rebels from the field, totally demoralizing them.

The last fight we had was at Statesburg, and there the rebels stood for the last time; for we slaughtered them in great numbers. They left the field strewn with their dead and wounded. We captured, for the rest, in South Carolina, on our return to Georgetown, fifteen locomotives, and one hundred and forty cars loaded with ammunition, small arms and stores. We destroyed them all. We captured five hundred contrabands, five hundred prisoners, destroyed a vast deal of property, and captured about eighty head of horses.

We are now encamped at Georgetown, and I hope we will soon be home with our friends and relatives.

3

Virginia and
North Carolina

G ARLAND WHITE grew up near Richmond, Virginia, the capital of the Confederacy. He had been a slave there until he had been sold to a politician from Georgia. But he had run away from his owner and gone to Canada, where he had become a Methodist minister. Now, in the summer of 1864, as chaplain of the 28th USCI, he was returning to familiar places. As one of the few African-American officers in the army, he was going there to help defeat the slaveowners and liberate Virginia. But before that, there would be much hard fighting to do. He would see his men die in the futile "Battle of the Crater," victims of Yankee racism and Confederate bullets. They would spend long months digging trenches, dodging rebel shells, and making forced marches by night. Like many black soldiers who had been slaves there, Chaplain White had a personal interest in liberating Virginia. When the final victory came, he would be among the first to enter Richmond. He would make a speech to a mass of citizens proclaiming "for the first time in that city, 'Freedom to all mankind!'" And among the throngs of freed slaves he would meet an old woman whom he had not seen for twenty years: "This is your mother, Garland."[1]

Chaplain White had a special interest in Virginia, but in 1864 it was also the focus of the entire nation. Richmond, the Confederate capital, was just a hundred miles from Washington, the Union capital, and much of the combat in the Civil War took place between those two cities. The Confederacy's ablest and most famous general, Robert E. Lee, defended Richmond from a series of Union generals. In 1864, President Abraham Lincoln made General Ulysses S. Grant the supreme commander of the Union Army, and Grant launched major attacks on Lee. Eventually, Grant would defeat Lee, but it would take another year. And it would take a massive army that included thousands of African Americans.

When black troops first went to Virginia in the summer of 1863, they went to the Tidewater area, where Union troops held Yorktown, Fortress Monroe, Portsmouth, and Norfolk. From there they could raid nearby plantations and into North Carolina to liberate slaves. Liberated slaves might make useful soldiers, so the Federal government launched a drive to recruit them in Virginia and North Carolina. General Edward A. Wild led the drive. He had lost an arm in combat in 1862, and while he recovered from that operation, he had helped recruit the 54th and 55th Massachusetts regiments. He believed strongly that African Americans could and would fight, so he worked hard at recruiting his "African Brigade." He started in coastal North Carolina, and hired some Northern blacks to help recruit. Later, in the winter of 1863–4, regiments of black troops from the North helped Wild

1. Garland H. White, Chaplain, 28th USCI, Richmond, Virginia, April 12, 1865; *CR*, April 22, 1865.

raid the back country of North Carolina to liberate slaves and enlist soldiers.[2]

General Benjamin F. Butler commanded the Union Army's Department of Virginia and North Carolina. Butler was a politician from Massachusetts who had learned to have confidence in black troops. He eagerly accepted black regiments into his Army of the James, and he made sure that they got good officers and training. Almost 40 percent of that army was made up of black soldiers. In the spring of 1864, Butler was ready to attack the Confederates along the James River, which led westward to Richmond.[3]

Richmond was also the goal of General Grant in the spring of 1864. On May 4 the Army of the Potomac launched a massive attack against Lee's Army of Northern Virginia. Even though Union troops outnumbered the Confederates, Lee skillfully blocked their assaults and stayed between Grant and Richmond. In a series of battles at the Wilderness, Spottsylvania, North Anna, and Cold Harbor, Union forces suffered terrible losses. But Grant kept moving south, trying to get around Lee. By early June, Grant had come within ten miles east of Richmond – almost to the James River – but Lee stayed between him and his goal. Several regiments of black soldiers protected the supply routes of the Army of the Potomac during this campaign, but few saw combat.[4]

While Grant attacked from the north, General Butler attacked

2. Edward Longacre, "Brave Radical Wild: The Contentious Career of Brigadier Edward A. Wild," *Civil War Times Illustrated*, 19:3 (June 1980) 9–19. Frank R. Levstik, "The Fifth Regiment, United States Colored Troops, 1863–1865," *Northwest Ohio Quarterly*, 42:4 (Fall 1970) 89–90. Frank R. Levstik, "From Slavery to Freedom," *Civil War Times Illustrated*, 11:7 (November 1972) 10–15.
3. Edward G. Longacre, "Black Troops in the Army of the James," *Military Affairs*, 45:1 (February 1981) 1–8.
4. Shelby Foote, *The Civil War: A Narrative; Volume III: Red River to Appomattox* (New York, Random House, 1974) 146–317. Joseph T. Wilson, *The Black Phalanx* (Hartford, American Publishing, 1890; reprint, New York, Arno, 1968) 377–397. Herman Hattaway and Archer Jones, *How the North Won* (Urbana, University of Illinois Press, 1983) 538–593.

from south of Richmond. He landed his main force at Bermuda Hundred, intending to cut the railroads leading to Richmond. In order to protect that invasion force, Butler seized several beach-heads along the James River and placed them under the command of General Wild. One of those points was Wilson's Landing. Wild put several regiments of African-American soldiers on guard. On May 24, Confederate cavalry attacked the black brigade, hoping to capture them or drive them away. But the Union troops fought bravely and well; it was the rebel cavalry that was driven away with heavy casualties. The African-American soldiers had triumphed in their first battle in Virginia.[5]

Butler's other troops, however, failed to cut the railroads south of Richmond; instead Butler let himself and his army get pinned down on Bermuda Hundred, a peninsula between Richmond and Petersburg. On June 12, Grant surprised Lee by sending his large Army of the Potomac across the James River, southeast of Richmond. If he could combine with Butler's smaller Army of the James, they might cut off Richmond from the rest of the Southern states. The immediate target was Petersburg, a major railroad center about thirty miles south of Richmond. Butler's army attacked Petersburg on June 15, with African-American troops doing much of the fighting. They captured several enemy gun positions and trenches; if their generals had not overestimated the Confederate opposition, those black soldiers might have captured Petersburg that day. Instead, because of Butler's caution, rebel reinforcements arrived, and the Union troops settled down to a nine-month siege, keeping pressure on Lee and the Confederate capital.[6]

---

5. Longacre, "Brave, Radical Wild," 15. Longacre, "Black Soldiers in the Army of the James," 5. Wilson, *The Black Phalanx*, 392–393.
6. Foote, *The Civil War: Red River to Appomattox*, 427–439. Hattaway and Jones, 589–590. Benjamin Quarles, *The Negro in the Civil War*, 298–300. Wilson, *The Black Phalanx*, 397–406. George W. Williams, *A History of the Negro Troops in the War of the Rebellion, 1861–1865* (New York, Harper, 1888; reprint, New York, Negro Universities Press, 1969) 234–243.

During the siege Grant ordered several attacks on the Confederate defenses, and black soldiers participated in most of them. The most infamous of those attacks was the "Battle of the Crater," near Petersburg, on July 30, 1864. The Union and Confederate armies faced each other from trenches that, in some places, were only a hundred yards apart. A regiment of Pennsylvania soldiers from the coal-mining region dug a tunnel under a gun position in the rebel lines. Four tons of blasting powder were to blow up the enemy fort, and several regiments of black soldiers were trained and ready to charge the adjacent lines and break through to Petersburg. Just before the explosion was scheduled, Grant decided to send unprepared, exhausted, but experienced white troops instead of the black troops. He later said he had made the change because he had feared that the public would think he had put the African Americans in front because he did not care about their safety in a bloody battle. When the powder went off, it blew hundreds of rebel soldiers and their guns high into the air, then buried them under tons of dirt and rubble. It left a crater "170 feet long, sixty to eighty feet wide, and thirty feet deep." After some confusion and delay, which rendered surprise impossible, the white soldiers charged; but instead of spreading out into the nearby lines, they stopped in the crater itself to protect themselves from enemy fire. The Confederates rallied quickly and soon put heavy rifle and artillery fire onto the crater. The black troops were ordered to charge through and past the pinned-down white troops. They managed to get past the far rim of the crater, but heavy rebel fire soon drove them back; many were trapped in the crater, and casualties among both whites and blacks were heavy. The general, having decided that the attack had failed, ordered the Union troops back to their own lines. Despite the last-minute shift from prepared black troops to unprepared white troops for the charge, and the disastrous delay in starting the attack, the African Americans had fought well. General Grant later told a congressional committee that if the colored division had been in front as planned, the attack would have succeeded. But failure meant that the siege would continue.[7]

On September 29, 1864, Grant launched his last direct attack against Richmond. He sent Butler's army, with its white and black divisions, north of the James River to capture rebel positions at Fort Harrison, Chaffin's Bluff, and New Market Heights, and to break through Lee's defenses. The fighting was intense for four days, with the Confederate troops defending their well-prepared trenches and forts. In several costly charges against the rebels, Union troops finally won their immediate objectives. But Lee skillfully shifted his troops from place to place, and Richmond's inner defenses held. Many black soldiers won medals for heroism in this operation, and General Butler was greatly pleased; but the siege went on.[8]

One reason why the Confederates could continue to fight around Richmond was that they could still get supplies from states farther south and from overseas. The Federal navy and army had managed to capture or close all the major seaports around the coastline, with the exception of one: Wilmington, North Carolina. Wilmington was still, at the end of 1864, a major port for rebel blockade runners who brought guns, ammunition, and other supplies from foreign countries. The railroad from Wilmington to Richmond still passed safely through Petersburg. General Grant was determined to cut off Lee's imports, so he planned an attack on Fort Fisher, which protected the approaches to Wilmington. Late in December 1864, a massive amphibious attack was launched by the navy and part of Butler's Army of the James, including several black regiments. The ships blasted away at the giant fort made of

7. Hattaway and Jones, *How the North Won*, 613–615. Williams, *A History of the Negro Troops*, 243–250. Berlin, Reidy, and Rowland, *The Black Military Experience*, 549–553. Wilson, *The Black Phalanx*, 411–428. Foote, *The Civil War: From Red River to Appomattox*, 530–538.

8. Richard J. Sommers, *Richmond Redeemed: The Siege at Petersburg* (Garden City, N.Y., Doubleday, 1981) passim. Foote, *The Civil War: From Red River to Appomattox*, 560–563. Wilson, *The Black Phalanx*, 413–441. Levstik, "The Fifth Regiment," 93–94. Williams, *History of the Negro Troops*, 251–256.

logs and sand, and on Christmas Day, Butler sent about six hundred troops ashore to capture it. But without explanation, Butler then pulled his troops off the beach and returned the entire expedition to Virginia, leaving Fort Fisher and Wilmington in rebel hands. Grant was furious; not only had the mission been aborted, but Butler had once again failed to hit the enemy hard. So Grant fired Butler, appointed a new general to lead the expedition, and finally, on January 15, 1865, Fort Fisher surrendered to Union troops. Black regiments protected the invading force from counterattack. Soon Wilmington itself fell, and African-American soldiers occupied the town. In March, they moved northward to join General Sherman, who had marched through Georgia the previous fall and then moved through the Carolinas toward Virginia. With Wilmington lost and railroads cut off, Lee's days in Richmond were numbered.[9]

While part of the Army of the James invaded North Carolina, the siege of Petersburg was relatively quiet. What action there was consisted of Grant's tries at cutting the last remaining railroad into the town. That campaign finally succeeded when General Philip Sheridan broke through on April 1 at the Battle of Five Forks. Several black regiments were in the attack force that cut the railroad, routed the Confederates, and sent them streaming back into Petersburg. General Lee then realized that he could no longer hold Petersburg and Richmond. He thought his only hope would be to escape westward, get around the Union Army, and flee to North Carolina. Before he could do that Sheridan and General Grant caught up with him at Appomattox Court House, where he surrendered. There to help celebrate the surrender were the black troops.

When Lee had left Richmond on April 2, the trenches there suddenly were empty. The Union soldiers who were waiting to begin a new attack found no opposition on the morning of April 3.

9. Hattaway and Jones, *How the North Won*, 658–661. Foote, *The Civil War: From Red River to Appomattox*, 715–721, 740–747. Edwin S. Redkey, ed., "Rocked in the Cradle of Consternation," *American Heritage*, 31:6 (1980) 70–79.

So they started marching, some of them at double time, to capture the city. Among the very first to enter were some of the black regiments that had fought so hard near there for the past year. With Chaplain Garland White, they celebrated on the steps of the Confederate Capitol the sure demise of the rebellion.[10]

The letters selected for this chapter tell of the fighting black soldiers did in the most closely watched theater of the war. The men reveal a pride in their accomplishments, an awareness of what they meant for the nation and for the race. When generals failed, black enlisted men criticized them. Always, they knew they were fighting to prove themselves worthy of citizenship and equality.

LETTER 33

(Joseph E. Williams, Wild's Brigade, New Bern, North Carolina, June 23, 1863; *CR*, July 4, 1863) Joseph E. Williams, an African American from Pennsylvania, was widely known as an antislavery speaker. When the Federal government decided to enlist black soldiers, he went to North Carolina with General Edward A. Wild to recruit soldiers among the freed slaves. He helped Wild raise the 1st North Carolina Infantry, later named the 35th USCI.

. . . We are now determined to hold every step which has been offered to us as citizens of the United States for our elevation, which represent justice, the purity, the truth, and aspiration of heaven. We must learn deeply to realize the duty, the moral and

10. Hattaway and Jones, *How the North Won*, 672–674. Williams, *History of the Negro Troops*, 293–303. Quarles, *The Negro in the Civil War*, 330–335. Wilson, *The Black Phalanx*, 445–460. Berlin, Reidy, and Rowland, *The Black Military Experience*, 565–566. Foote, *The Civil War: From Red River to Appomattox*, 864–956.

political necessity for the benefit of our race. . . . Every consideration of honor, of interest, and of duty to God and man, requires that we should be true to our trust.

The colored women of Newbern have ordered a splendid battle flag to be made in the highest style of that art, no pains or expense to be spared, and to be presented to the First Regiment of North Carolina Colored Volunteers. This regiment is now completed. The flag is to be made of blue silk, with a yellow silk fringe around the border. On one side the Goddess of Liberty is represented with her right foot resting on a copperhead snake. On the reverse side, a large gilt rising sun, with the word "Liberty" in very large letters over the sun. This flag is ordered from Boston, Mass. It will be consecrated in Boston, and Governor [John A.] Andrew will deliver a speech. On the staff there will be a plate with the following inscription – "Presented to the First Regiment of North Carolina Colored Volunteers by the colored women of Newbern, N.C."

General E. A. Wild has surveyed and examined Roanoke Island,[11] and established a colony there for the support of the wives of the soldiers in his brigade, and also homes for the old and young and those who are not fit for service. He will establish and erect churches and schoolhouses for the use of the colony; and also a number of vessels of all sizes, such as schooners and small sail boats that are lying along the island, which have been captured from the rebels, will be turned over for the use of the colony. I was with him at the time he was exploring the island, and I never saw a place that I ever liked better than Roanoke Island. . . .

LETTER 34

(Joseph E. Williams, Wild's African Brigade, New Bern, North Carolina, July 11, 1863; *CR*, July 18, 1863) One way of re-

11. Roanoke Island was captured by Federal troops in February 1862.

cruiting black soldiers was to raid the interior districts. Joseph Williams describes one such successful raid on Warsaw, North Carolina.

I am happy to state that I, with the invading expedition in the enemy's country, safely returned to Newbern. Indeed, we were exceedingly successful in marching ninety miles over the rebel country. . . . We expected to have to fight our way through, but the rebels flew away from our advancing forces as the darkness flies from the rays of light. We made rapid charges, but only caught their pickets. Our destination was Warsaw, and there we tore up and twisted their railroad track so that it can never be used again. But I am somewhat before our march. When we arrived at the town of Duplin, we were informed that there were upwards of thirty colored prisoners in the Duplin Court House prison that were to be tried for their lives for attempting to escape inside the lines of the United States forces. We tried to break down the door with axes. We worked for about an hour. This door seemed to be about as hard as that of any iron safe. Finally the key was sent for, threatening the sheriff with vengeance in case of refusal, in the form of a can of tar and feathers. At the arrival of the key the prison doors were opened and another iron cell opened, and Paul and Silas came walking out. The thirty was a fabulous number, which had diminished to three live colored men; their lives were saved. Two of them came on to Newbern to join Wild's Brigade. With more vigorous determination, we burnt the sabre factory and dashed on to Warsaw. We planted our artillery up and down the railroad to meet the enemy should they come in iron horse. Whilst the Union forces were tearing up the railway, storehouses were sacked and burnt, and also the depot, and slaves came running from every side of the road seeking our protection by coming into our lines. . . .

(Milton M. Holland, Orderly Sergeant, Co. C, 5th USCI, Norfolk, Virginia, January 19, 1864; *Athens (Ohio) Messenger,* February 4, 1864; first reprinted in *Civil War Times Illustrated,* 11:7 [November 1972] 10–15) Sergeant Milton Holland had, on his own initiative, recruited a company of men from Athens, Ohio, to serve in one of the Massachusetts regiments. But he was persuaded by John Mercer Langston, a prominent Ohio African American, to lead his men into the new Ohio regiment, the 5th USCI. Later, he would win the Congressional Medal of Honor for bravery in a battle near Richmond. Here Holland describes the regiment's first action, a raid into North Carolina to liberate slaves and recruit black soldiers.

You will be reminded of the company of colored soldiers raised by myself in the county of Athens, and taken to Camp Delaware, 25 miles north of Columbus, on the Olentangy. It has since been mustered into the service in the 5th Regt. U.S. Colored Troops. The regiment is organized, and has been in active service for three months. Our company is C – the color company – in which you may remember of the flag presentation, made by the kind citizens of Athens, through Mr. Moore, at which Mr. [John Mercer] Langston was present and received it, pledging in behalf of the company, that they would ever be true to the flag, though it might be tattered or torn by hard service, it should never be disgraced. I am happy to say that those colors have been used as the regimental colors for several months, and we had the honor of forming the first line of battle under their floating stars. We now have new regimental colors, and the old ones are laid away in my cabin, and I am sitting now beneath them writing.

The regiment though young, has been in one engagement. The

men stood nobly and faced the cowardly foe when they were hid in the swamp firing upon them. They stood like men, and when ordered to charge, went in with a yell, and came out victorious, losing four killed and several wounded. The rebel loss is large, as compared with ours. As for company C she played her part admirably in the charge. Our 4th sergeant, Charles G. Stark, is said to have killed the picket guard while in the act of running away.

I must say of the 5th, that after twenty days of hard scouting, without overcoats or blankets, they returned home to camp, which the soldiers term their home, making twenty-five and thirty miles per day. Several of the white cavalry told me that no soldiers have ever done as hard marching through swamps and marshes as cheerfully as we did, and that if they had to follow us for any length of time it would kill their horses. During that raid, thousands of slaves belonging to rebel masters were liberated. You are aware that the colored man makes no distinction in regard to persons, so I may say all belonging to slaveholders were liberated. We hung one guerrilla dead, by the neck, by order of Brig. Gen. E. A. Wild, a noble and brave man, commanding colored troops – "the right man in the right place." He has but one arm, having lost his left one at the battle of Antietam, but with his revolver in hand, he was at the head of our regiment cheering us on to victory.

One of the boys belonging to Co. D was captured and hung. He was found by our cavalry pickets yesterday and is to be buried today. We hold one of their "fair daughters," as they term them, for the good behavior of her husband, who is a guerrilla officer, toward our beloved soldiers. The soldier was found with a note pinned to his flesh. Before this war ends we will pin their sentences to them with Uncle Sam's leaden pills.

The boys are generally well, and satisfied that though they are deprived of all the comforts of home, and laboring under great disadvantages as regards pay and having families to support upon less wages than white soldiers, still trust that when they do return they will be crowned with honors, and a happier home prepared for them, when they will be free from the abuses of northern and southern fire-eaters. . . . I will close my letter in the language of the immortal Henry – "Give me liberty, or give me death!"

LETTER 36

(G.W.H., Sergeant, 1st USCI, Wilson's Landing, Virginia, May 10, 1864; *CR*, May 28, 1864) Black troops in southern Virginia were part of the drive to capture Richmond from the south while General U.S. Grant attacked from the north. They set up a base at Wilson's Landing, on the James River, and in this letter Sergeant George W. Hatton tells how the men reacted to the capture of a notorious local slaveowner.

You are aware that Wilson's Landing is on the James River, a few miles above Jamestown, the very spot where the first sons of Africa were landed in the year 1620, if my memory serves me right, and from that day to the breaking out of the rebellion was looked upon as an inferior race by all civilized nations. But behold what has been revealed in the past three or four years; why the colored men have ascended upon a platform of equality, and the slave can now apply the lash to the tender flesh of his master, for this day I am now an eyewitness of the fact. The country being principally inhabited by wealthy farmers, there are a great many men in the regiment who are refugees from this place. While out on a foraging expedition, we captured a Mr. Clayton, a noted reb in this part of the country, and from his appearance, one of the F.F.V.s [First Families of Virginia]; on the day before we captured several colored women that belonged to Mr. C., who had given them a most unmerciful whipping previous to their departure. On the arrival of Mr. C. in camp, the commanding officer determined to let the women have their revenge, and ordered Mr. C. to be tied to a tree in front of head-quarters, and William Harris, a soldier in our regiment, and a member of Co. E, who was acquainted with the gentleman, and who used to belong to him, was called upon to undress him and introduce him to the ladies that I mentioned before. Mr. Harris played his part conspicuously, bringing the blood from his loins at every stroke, and not forgetting to remind the gentleman of the days gone by. After giving him some fifteen or twenty well-directed strokes, the ladies, one after another, came up and gave him a like number, to remind him that they were no longer his, but safely housed in Abraham's bosom, and under the protection of the Star Spangled Banner, and guarded by their own patriotic, though once down-trodden race. Oh, that I had the tongue to express my feelings while standing upon the banks of the James River, on the soil of Virginia, the mother state of slavery, as a witness of such a sudden reverse!

The day is clear, the fields of grain are beautiful, and the birds are singing sweet melodious songs, while poor Mr. C. is crying to his servants for mercy. Let all who sympathize with the South take this narrative for a mirror.

LETTER 37

(Henry M. Turner, Chaplain, 1st USCI, City Point, Virginia, June 18, 1864; *CR*, June 25, 1864) The base at Wilson's Landing worried the Confederates, and on May 24, 1864, General Fitzhugh Lee, nephew of Robert E. Lee, attacked. The Union troops successfully defended their base against the rebel cavalry. Henry M. Turner tells in this letter how the battle went. He was one of only fourteen African American chaplains in the army; in 1880 he would become a bishop in the African Methodist Episcopal Church.

. . . Things, however, moved on quietly until the 24th ult., on which occasion I was retiring from dinner, feeling very jolly over the idea of having eaten quite heartily once more of a fat chicken,

&c., which is generally something special in camp, when my attention was called to the front of our works by a mighty rushing to arms, and shouts that the rebels were coming. I immediately joined the proclaiming host and bellowed out, (I reckon in fearful tones) "The rebels! The Rebels! The Rebels are coming!" At this period the long [drum] roll began to tell that doleful tale that she never tells unless the enemy is about to invade our quarters. Then commenced another rush to arms, fearful in its aspect. Notwithstanding many were at dinner, down fell the plates, knives, forks, and cups, and a few moments only were required to find every man, sick or well, drawn into the line of battle to dispute the advance of twice, if not thrice, their number of rebels. Captains Borden [Stephen A. Boyden?] and [Giles H.] Rich of the 1st U.S. Col'd Troops, with their gallant companies, were at some distance in front, skirmishing with the advance guard of the rebels. And here permit me to say, that this skirmish was the grandest sight I ever beheld. I acknowledge my incapacity to describe it, and thus pass on. By the time our pickets had been driven in, a flag of truce was seen waving in the distance, when General [Edward] Wild gave orders to cease firing. Lieutenant Colonel [Elias] Wright was immediately dispatched to meet it, and found it to be a peremptory demand from Gen. Fitz Hugh Lee for the unconditional surrender of the place, with the promise that we should, upon such compliance, be treated as prisoners of war; but upon a refusal, we would have to abide by the consequences, assuring us at the same time, that he intended to take us, for he could and would do it. Gen Wild told him to try it. In fifteen minutes rebel balls were flying like hail all around our heads; but gallantly was the compliment returned. It would be contraband to tell you our force on that occasion. But this much I must tell you, that the 1st Regiment of United States Colored Troops, with a very small exception, did all the fighting. I am also sorry that it is inexpedient to give you a full description of that terrific battle, which lasted several hours; but the coolness and cheerfulness of the men, the precision with which they shot, and the vast number of rebels they unmercifully slaugh-

tered, won for them the highest regard of both the General and
his staff, and every white soldier that was on the field. And the
universal expression among the white soldiers was, *That it is a
burning shame for the Government to keep these men out of their full
pay.* . . .

Allow me to say that the rebels were handsomely whipped. They
fled before our men, carrying a large number of their dead, and
leaving a great many on the field for us to bury. They declared our
regiment were sharp-shooters. Our loss, considering the ter-
ribleness of this conflict, was incredibly small.

From that place we went to Fort Powhattan, a few days after
which we came here, and will remain here till we receive marching
orders. A few days ago, we went in front of Petersburg, our regiment even went under the guns of the rebels, and laid down while
their bombs were flying over our heads. We would have gone into
the city had we been permitted; but we accomplished all we were
sent to do, and then we returned. . . .

LETTER 38

(Charles Torrey Beman, [Private,] Co. C, 5th Massachusetts Cavalry, Point-of-Rocks, Virginia, June 20, 1864; to Amos Beman, and
published in an unidentified newspaper, probably *Weekly Anglo-
African;* clipping in Amos Beman Scrapbook, Vol. II, p. 36, Yale
Collection of American Literature, Beineke Rare Book and Manuscript Library, Yale University Library, used by permission. Cour-
tesy David Swift.) Federal troops of the Army of the James, commanded by General Benjamin F. Butler, attacked Petersburg,
Virginia, on June 15, 1864. Black soldiers played a prominent role
in the attack. Among them was Charles Beman of New Haven,
Connecticut, who describes the action to his father.

. . . Since I last wrote, almost half of the 5th Massachusetts Cavalry have been in several engagements, and about thirty have been
killed and wounded. The first notice I had of going into the en-

gagement was about 1 o'clock, a.m., Wednesday, the 15th. We heard the bugle, and sprang to our arms, and, with two days rations, we started towards Petersburg, and when about four miles on our way toward that city, at a place called Beatty's House, we came in front of the rebels' works. Here we formed a line of battle, and started for the rebs' works. I was with some thirty of my Company. We had to pass through the woods; but we kept on, while the shell, grape and canister came around us cruelly. Our Major and Col. [Henry F.] Russell were wounded, and several men fell – to advance seemed almost impossible; but we rallied, and after a terrible charge, amidst pieces of barbarous iron, solid shot and shell, we drove the desperate greybacks from their fortifications, and gave three cheers for our victory. But few white troops were with us. Parts of the 1st, 4th, 6th and 22nd [USCI] were engaged.

The colored troops here have received a great deal of praise. The sensations I had in the battle were, coolness and interest in the boys' fighting. They shouted, "Fort Pillow," and the rebs were shown no mercy.[12]

LETTER 39

(John C. Brock, Commissary Sergeant, 43d USCI, Manassas Junction, Virginia, July 3, 1864; *CR*, July 30, 1864) The Army of the Potomac moved south toward Richmond and Petersburg during the summer of 1864. For the first time, African-American regiments served with that army, starting as rear-guard units protecting Union supply lines. Marching through Virginia was a heady experience for Sergeant John C. Brock of Philadelphia.

. . . We are now encamped at a very pleasant place in Virginia, between Manassas Junction and Brandy Station. We have been

---

12. At Fort Pillow, Tennessee, Union troops, especially black soldiers, were shot by Confederate troops while trying to surrender.

moving considerably since I last wrote to you. We were then lying at
Annapolis, Maryland. We left there on the 23d of April, on Saturday. We were delayed a considerable length of time in starting, as
there was a large division. It took a long time for us all to get finally
under way. Well, we marched all day on Saturday, and also on the
Sabbath, (how different that Sabbath to some we have formerly
spent) and on Monday evening we arrived at Alexandria, Va. How
horrible it must have been to the rebels that their "sacred soil"
should have been polluted by the footsteps of colored Union soldiers! We lay at Alexandria all day on Tuesday, and on Wednesday
morning we commenced the march farther into the interior. On
Wednesday evening we reached that historic village named Fairfax
Court House. The inhabitants, what few there were, looked at us
with astonishment, as if we were some great monsters risen up
out of the ground. They looked bewildered, yet it seemed to be
too true and apparent to them that they really beheld nearly 10,000
colored soldiers filing by, armed to the teeth, with bayonets bristling in the sun – and I tell you our boys seemed to fully appreciate
the importance of marching through a secesh town. On, on we
came, regiment after regiment, pouring in, as it seemed to their
bewildered optics, by countless thousands – with colors flying
and the bands playing; and, without intending any disparagement
to other regiments, I must say that the 43d looked truly grand,
with the soldierly and imposing forms of our noble and generous
Colonel ([H. Seymour] Hall) and Adjutant C. Bryan riding at the
head.

The next day, being Thursday, we crossed the memorable
stream known as Bull Run. It had been raining considerably, and
the stream was swollen, so that the men were obliged to roll their
pants up to their knees in order to cross it, which they did amidst
great shouting and cheering from the men.

On the same day we passed by the famous town of Centreville,
which comprises some eight or ten houses, surrounded by fortifications. This is the spot where the gallant (though unjustly
abused) McDowell, sword in hand, vainly endeavored to check the

progress of the panic-stricken and flying army at the time of the first Bull Run fight.[13]

Next day we arrived at the place where I am now writing from. It is a very pleasant grove. We are doing guard duty here on a railroad, the older veterans having been sent to the front on the same day that we arrived to take their place. So you will now see that we have performed considerable marching for a new regiment, and one that was hardly formed. But the boys bore up with great perseverance and fortitude under the task.

We have been regularly detailed for picket duty both day and night since we came here. The boys halt a man very quick, and if he does not answer quick, he gets a ball sent through him. . . .

LETTER 40

(William H. Hunter, Chaplain, 4th USCI, near Petersburg, Virginia, July 9, 1864; *CR*, July 16, 1864) When soldiers wrote to newspapers about their battle experiences, their letters sometimes caused arguments. Each of these accounts was based on the writer's own point of view, experience, and pride. Other soldiers, who fought at a different corner of the battlefield and belonged to a different unit, sometimes disagreed with the letters in the newspapers. In this letter, William H. Hunter, African-American chaplain of a Maryland regiment, criticizes "Africano," probably of the 5th Massachusetts Cavalry, for his description of the fight at Petersburg.

It has been a long time since I have communed with my friends through the columns of your paper. Though often urged to write, I have deferred it from time to time, until now. I believe my silence would have continued, had it not been disturbed by an *infamous*

13. Major battles were fought at Bull Run in July 1861 and August 1862.

falsehood published in the "Anglo-African" under the signature of Africano.

I hardly think it worth while to spend either much time or paper in showing up the willful misrepresentations of the wondrous Africano. The ungarnished and uncalled-for falsehoods with reference to the 4th U.S.C.T. and the deeds of daring performed by the 5th Mass. Cavalry are both stories manufactured, as a general thing, but just such men as the noted correspondent, who, in fact, only heard the bursting of shells thrown by the guns of which he spoke. He claims that the 5th Mass. Cavalry (dismounted) captured two guns, when there was but one taken in that part of the fight, and that was taken by the 22nd U.S.C.T., while the *5th Mass. Cavalry* were not within 600 yards of it. And so little were the commanding officers impressed by the efficiency of the famous Africano and his host, that they were detailed to draw the gun to the rear, and we were not blessed with the privilege of seeing them again that day, though there were *seven forts to be taken, which were captured before our day's work was done.*

Mr. Editor, his letter is an insult to every soldier in our division, and is a production emanating from the brain and pen of a coward of the basest character, who will not dare to answer this communication over his own signature.

As I have but little time, I must not spend it all in speaking of a creature of so little importance. I will now write of our noble soldiers, and of the day which will be held sacred forever in the memory of colored men.

The 15th of June, 1864, is a day long to be remembered by the entire colored race on this continent. It is the day when prejudice died in the entire Army of the U.S. of America. It is the day when it was admitted that colored men were equal to the severest ordeal. It is the day in which was secured to us rights of equality in the Army and service of the Government of the United States.

It is true, it cost us some of the best blood of our race – noble men fell to rise no more. The names of such noble men as Burgee, Shaw, Anderson, Warren, and others will be handed down with reverence to all coming generations.

The gallant 4th suffered dreadfully on that memorable day. We were the first to leave the cover of the woods, thereby suffering more than any regiment in our division. Our loss was estimated at about 150 in that charge, and still we pressed forward until the outer works of Petersburg were ours, and the order was given to halt, which order, like good soldiers, we obeyed; but I assure you we had a great desire to enter that city on the night of the 15th of June, but we were told by those who ought to know, that the work of that day was the greatest of the campaign. When daylight of the 16th made its appearance, it was our lot to look upon works more formidable than those of Missionary Ridge,[14] and those taken by colored soldiers of the 1st, 4th, (5th Ohio), 6th, and 22d Regts.

While I write, the boom of cannon is not far distant. The "Petersburg Express," as the soldiers call one of our heavy guns, is a short distance from where I sit. It speaks forth in tones severe, the hatred of all true men to treason and rebellion, together with their intention to punish and subdue them. . . .

LETTER 41

(Milton M. Holland, Orderly Sergeant, Co. C, 5th USCI, near Petersburg, Virginia, July 24, 1864; *Athens (Ohio) Messenger*, ca. August 1864, as reprinted in *Civil War Times Illustrated*, 11:7 (November 1972) 10–15, and used by permission) The attack on Petersburg made heroes of the black soldiers in the Army of the James. Sergeant Holland (who won a Congressional Medal of Honor for a later battle) writes of his experience in the charge and criticizes the generals for timid leadership.

. . . We have been successful in achieving the object we aimed at. We have also undergone severe marches to Bottom Bridge, within twelve miles of the Confederate Capitol. On some of those

---

14. A major battle fought on November 25, 1863, near Chattanooga, Tennessee.

marches it rained incessantly, making it very fatiguing. I have also seen men sleep while marching. If I should say that I have been guilty of the same art myself it would not be less than the truth. It seemed like imposing on green troops, but the boys bore it admirably with great patience and endurance. Near the latter part of April, we were ordered to Fort Monroe to organize into the 3d division of the 18th Army Corps, commanded by Brigadier Gen. [Edward Ward] Hinks. While at Fort Monroe [the regiment] were reviewed by Maj. Gen. [Benjamin F.] Butler, and was classed among the best grade of white troops. All passed off very nicely until about the 4th day of May, when an order came to break camp, and be ready at moment's warning [to be moved] by transports, which we quietly did in good order, as all good soldiers do. We were then awaiting the orders of the Adjutant to fall in. The Adjutant with a loud voice sang out, "Fall in Fifth"; the companies were formed and moved out on the parade ground and were formed in line of battle under supervision of the Adjutant. We moved off by the right flank to the transports and embarked, shoved in the bay a short distance from the fort, and cast anchor for the night to wait for the fleet to gather. About daybreak on the following morning all was ready, and we set sail for the James River, the fleet of gunboats taking the advance. Immediately in rear were the boats of General Butler and Hinks followed by the Fifth U.S.C.T. Many things attracted our attention along the banks of the James, too numerous to mention. One I might mention particularly was the ruins of Jamestown, the spot where the curse of slavery was first introduced into the United States. A serpent that has inserted its poisonous fangs into the body of this government, causing it to wither in its bloom. Slowly we worked our way up the winding James, until within sight of the City Point celebrated for being the Department where the exchange of prisoners was made. As we neared the shore at that point, Co. C was ordered to take the advance as soon as we landed. Up the hill we marched to where the rebel flag was stationed. Down with it cried the boys, and in a moment more the flag of the glorious free could be seen floating in the breeze. The company banner was the first company flag that waved over the rebel city. Forty prisoners were captured at this place by the provost guard of the division. One platoon of our company was deployed as skirmishers and followed a short distance the retreating foe that escaped.

On the following day we began throwing up fortifications around the city. In less than sixteen days we had completed the works and was ready for some new adventure. The regiment then moved to Point of Rocks, and on the 9th of June a detachment of the 1st, 5th, 6th [USCT] under Gen. [Quincy A.] Gillmore made a demonstration against Petersburg, Va., where we were brought into line of battle, under a most galling fire of the enemies' guns. The 1st U.S.C.T. took the right, the 6th the left, and our detachment supported the artillery. In this order we advanced while Gen [August V.] Kautz with a superior force of cavalry made a flank movement and broke the enemies' left, reaching the town. Had he been supported by General Gillmore the town would have been ours on that day, with slight loss of life. But did he do it? No. He withdrew without a fight, putting the enemy on his guard and consequently allowing him to prepare for an emergency. Suffice it to say that we withdrew and fell back to Point of Rocks. All passed off very quietly until the 14th, when we were summoned to make a second demonstration against the rebel city under the command of Maj. Gen. [William F.] Smith. In a few moments we were out and on the road. We crossed the Appomattox shortly after nightfall, and lay down to rest our weary limbs. On the following morning about daybreak, we dispatched a hardy breakfast of hardtack and coffee. Orders were given then to fall in; of course we made no delay, knowing duty to be before everything else, a moment before and the column was off. About sunrise our advance came in contact with the rebel pickets who, discharging the contents of their pieces into our ranks, fled back to their main force. Skirmishers were then thrown out in front of the different regiments. Companies C and B were deployed in front of the 5th, other skirmishers in front of their respective regiments, forming a skirmish line in front of the line of battle. We moved forward slowly, making our way clear and open, we advanced about a mile in this manner till in sight of the first line of earthworks. We were then in the open field, halted, where we kept up a brisk fire on the skirmish line until the regiments could get through the swamps and form in order again. All this while the enemy poured a galling fire of musketry, grape and canister into the ranks, slaying many. The order was given to forward the skirmish line one hundred paces. This being done we halted, keeping up our fire along the line. One thing that I must mention which attracted the attention of the whole division. It was that brave and daring but strange personage that rides the white charger. We could see him plainly riding up and down the rebel lines, could hear him shouting from the top of his voice to stand, that they had only niggers to contend with. This peculiar personage seems possessed with supernatural talent. He would sometimes ride his horse at lightning speed, up and down his lines amid the most terrific fire of shot and shell. But when the command was given to us, "Charge bayonets! Forward double quick!" the black column rushed forward raising the battle yell, and in a few moments more we mounted the rebel parapets. And to our great surprise, we found that the boasted Southern chivalry had fled. They could not see the nigger part as the man on the white horse presented it. We captured here one gun and caisson. [Our] column moved out to the left in front of the second line of fortifications while the white troops took the right. We moved off in a line of battle, took a position right in range of the enemies' guns, in which position we remained six hours, exposed to an enfilading fire of shot and shell. Just at nightfall after the placing of our guns had been effected, we were ordered to charge a second fort, which we did with as much success as the first. It is useless for me to attempt a description of that evening cannonading. I have never heard anything to equal it before or since; for a while whole batteries discharge[d] their contents into the rebel ranks at once. The result was a complete success.

LETTER 42

(William McCoslin, 1st Sergeant, Co. A, 29th USCI, near Petersburg, Virginia, July 26, 1864; *CR*, August 27, 1864) Sergeant William McCoslin of Bloomington, Illinois, traveled by rail with his regiment to Washington, D.C., by ship to White House Landing, Virginia, and on foot to the trenches near Petersburg. When he wrote this letter, he was tired of digging trenches and eager for combat.

As I have little leisure time, I thought I would give you a short history of our campaign in Virginia. As you are aware, we left Illinois, our glorious state, under the command of Lieutenant-Colonel John A. Bross, formerly of Chicago, but lately of the 88th Ill. Regiment, for the army of the Potomac, with orders to report to Major-General [Ambrose] Burnside. We had a pleasant journey of it, but very tiresome, on account of having to stay on board the cars all the time, until we arrived in the city of Chicago, when we were marched to the Soldiers' Rest, where a fine breakfast was in waiting for us. We charged on it immediately, and captured it without any loss whatever. We rested here all day, and then started for the cars on route for Pittsburgh, where we arrived after a fatiguing ride of thirty hours, but all in good spirits. On our arrival in the Iron City, we were marched to the Soldiers' Rest, where we were served up with a splendid supper; every kindness was shown us that could be shown on so short a notice. At 11 o'clock, P.M., we started en route for the East, tolerably well rested, and in good spirits, feeling proud of the treatment we have received, being the same if not better than some of the white soldiers received. Our trip over the mountains was a new thing to some of our Western boys, who have never been away from home. It seemed to interest them very much; crossing the mountains was quite an undertaking, especially when we went through the tunnels. Nothing of any great importance transpired until we arrived in Baltimore, when we marched up the identical street where the citizens mobbed the first white regiment. There was talk of mobbing the colored regiment. We did not have any arms then; but success ever favors the brave, and so it was with us. We were treated with some respect by all the citizens. We had to remain here over one day. During the time we went about the city, and were not molested by any one. So, when transportation was furnished to us, we started for Washington City, which place we reached on the evening of April 30th, 1864. After disembarking from the cars, we marched to the Soldiers' Rest, where we stopped till the evening of the 1st of May. Our regiment marched over to Alexandria, a distance of five miles, and stopped for one day; then we were ordered back to Camp Casey, near Washington, where we went into camp for instruction. Here we received our arms and equipment for the field. Nothing of note transpired until the 19th of May, when I was taken sick with symptoms of small-pox; then I was sent to the Rest Hospital at Alexandria. Here I was treated kindly, getting the same treatment as white officers and soldiers, and every thing was kept in the neatest possible manner.

On the 30th of May our regiment was ordered to take transportation from Alexandria for White House Landing, Va., where, on the application of my Captain, I was allowed to rejoin my regiment. The Surgeon in charge of the hospital gave me a new suit of clothing before I started. I then rejoined my regiment, and accompanied it into the field, landing at White House Landing. After disembarking from the boat, we went into camp. For several days, during our stay there, our men were engaged in throwing up redoubts and rifle pits. Then about the 7th of [June], we were ordered to escort a large train of supplies to the front. This was our first march, and a sorry one it was. It was a forced march, and many of the men had to throw away nearly all of their baggage, so as to keep up. We expected to get a rest here for a day or two, but were disappointed. We had to start almost immediately en route for Petersburg. Here, at Old Church Tavern, we joined our corps, and were assigned to the 4th Division, 2d Brigade, 9th Army Corps. Our brigade being the rear guard of the corps, we had a great deal of hard marching; and being in a very important position, we all felt the responsibility that was resting on us as rear guards. We proceeded along finely till we arrived at Dawson Bridge, near the Chickahominy [River], where we rested one day, and a Godsend it was to us. So, the next evening we started, but went only a short distance, and stopped till morning, crossing the Chickahominy. We expected to be attacked. The crossing was accomplished without any difficulty – our regiment being the last to cross the river. We learned since that a brigade of rebels were watching us at the time we crossed, but they did not molest us. We continued on our march until we came to Charles City Point, on the James River, which being a fortified place, we stopped over night; but next day, learning that a large force of rebels intended to attack us, we crossed the river on a pontoon bridge.

No sooner had the crossing been accomplished, than the rebels came in sight and began shelling us; but, luckily for us, a gunboat was lying in the river protecting the bridge, and soon drove them away. After crossing, we rested here one day, when our brigade was ordered to the front immediately, so as to assist in storming the rebel works that night. So on we went, expecting to have battle very soon.

Although the men were very tired, they were anxious to give fight to their enemies; but on arriving at the front, the programme being changed, we were ordered to rest until further orders, which was a godsend to us. We had two days' rest, and then were ordered to the front, to take a position in the rifle pits, which we consider healthier than going into the fight; but, when ordered, we are ready and willing to fight.

Our regiment is not in good fighting trim at present, on account of an insufficiency of officers. In other respects they are all right. We are expecting every day; to be sent to the front; but it is ordered otherwise, probably for the best. Our regiment has built two forts and about three miles of breastworks, which shows that we are not idle, and that we are learning to make fortifications, whether we learn to fight or not.

We are now lying in camp, about a mile and a half from the city, resting a day or two. It is quite a treat for the boys to get a rest after working day and night, four hours on and four hours off. We have worked in that way for eight or ten days, without stopping. But my opinion now is, that the laboring work is nearly over, so that we will have nothing to do but watch the rebels.

There is heavy firing of artillery and small arms every night from both sides, which sounds most beautiful to us. . . .

(Garland H. White, Chaplain, 28th USCI, near Petersburg, Virginia, August 8, 1864; *CR*, August 20, 1864) The "Battle of the Crater" took place near Petersburg on July 30, 1864. Garland H. White, an escaped slave who later became a Methodist minister and chaplain of a black regiment from Indiana, describes the tragic battle as seen by the men themselves. He angrily criticizes newspaper reports that blamed the African Americans for the defeat; the real problem was the generals.

I should remain perfectly silent, so far as the action of the 30th ult. is concerned, but for one reason, which, when presented, I hope the public will accept as being philosophic as well as patriotic.

It is said by a large number of cowards at home that the colored troops under General [Ambrose] Burnside, who participated in the recent attack on Petersburg acted cowardly. This slanderous language I first saw in the *New York Herald* of the 6th inst., it being a paper familiar with political corruption. It did not astonish me to find such calumny heaped upon an innocent and brave people, laboring under disadvantages unparalleled in the history of civilized warfare. These colored troops, who were from New York, Ohio, Indiana, Illinois, and several of the slave States, were led by as brave white men as the country affords. Our friends at home need not think that the failure to accomplish the design of that memorable event or day grew out of any neglect or incompetency upon the part of our regimental or company commanders, nor even the men themselves; for, as an eye-witness to the whole affair, I am compelled, from every consideration of justice to my profession, my God, my country, and my regiment to make some statement respecting the true nature of the case.

At a given hour all the officers of the colored troops were notified to have their men in readiness and at a certain place. This order was carried out to the crossing of a T. Afterward a charge was made, every officer heading his men; and the troops seemed as though they were going to a camp meeting or to a 1st of August dinner.[15] I was with the boys and intended to follow them to the last. Just at this juncture the earth began to shake, as though the hand of God intended a reversal of the laws of nature. This grand convulsion sent both soil and souls to inhabit the air for a while, and then return to be commingled forever with each other, as the word of God commands, "From dust thou art, and unto dust thou shalt return." By this time the colored troops had seen sufficient to convince them of the mighty struggle which would soon follow, and many began to make preparation accordingly, some by saying to me: "I want you, brother White, to write to my father and mother," in New York, Philadelphia, Chicago, Boston, Cincinnati, Cleveland, and other places, "that George (Thomas, John, or Peter, as we call each other out here) died like a man; and when pay-day comes, if it ever does come, send what money is due to my wife, and tell her to raise Sally and Mary in the fear of the Lord."

The Colonel gave the order: "Fix bayonets; charge bayonets!" The last words to me were, "Brother White, good-bye. Take care of yourself – for today someone must die, and, if it be me, I hope our people will get the benefit of it."

---

15. African Americans celebrated August 1 to commemorate the day in 1833 when Great Britain freed slaves throughout its empire.

I must be plain in my remarks, though it should offend some-body. The First Division of Colored Troops, who led the charge, were those who were principally raised in the Slave States. They did not stand up to the work like those from the Free States; for, when the Second Division of Colored Troops went into the action, they charged over the first and carried two lines of rifle pits. They made no stop there; for our gallant Colonel (Charles S. Russell, of Indiana) who led the gallant Twenty-Eighth, told the boys that he intended leading them to Petersburg that day. Colonel [John A.] Bross, who led the Twenty-Ninth, or the Illinois Colored Regi-ment, told his boys the same thing.

Now, I would have the people at home, both white and colored, to understand that the victory of that day was as certainly ours as anything could be. I call upon all candid-hearted men, who stood and saw the affair from beginning to end, to corroborate what I say in making this statement. When I saw our colors waving over the enemy's works, I, with a number of others, said: "Boys, the day is ours, and Petersburg is sure."

For several rods the dead lay thick, both white and colored, Union and rebel. It was a sad sight. Recollect, the colored troops went as far as they were ordered to go, and did just what they were told to do, both in going in and remaining there; and, in coming out the brave officers who led them in, when they saw that bad management had taken place somewhere, and thinking that re-maining longer would endanger that portion of the army, through wisdom and good policy, ordered the retreat.

This statement is the truth, to which I am willing to take my solemn oath. Leave no ground for a set of cowards at home, like Bennett[16] and other foul-hearted buzzards, to attribute the loss that day to the arms of the colored troops. None of the troops, white or colored, are responsible for the actions of the Generals. Let every man answer before the tribunals of his country for him-

16. James Gordon Bennett, publisher of the *New York Herald*, criticized the efforts of black soldiers.

self – Generals as well as privates – for he has grown too [*missing*] to be responsible for his conduct in common with all men.

I hold that there can be no higher sin in all the world than to blame innocent people for consequences for which they are not responsible. I care not who it is, whether king or subject, General or private, it makes no difference with me in a point of exposition of truth. What was lost by the First Division was amply recovered by the Second. . . .

LETTER 44

(James H. Payne, Quartermaster Sergeant, 27th USCI, near Petersburg, Virginia, August 12, 1864; *CR*, August 20, 1864) The Reverend James H. Payne left his home in Kentucky to join an Ohio regiment that was headed for Petersburg. His view of the "Battle of the Crater" provides vivid details of that disaster.

. . . I will now give you a brief and concise account of the battle of the 30th of July, in which I called the members of our regiment together, and delivered an exhortation and held a prayer meeting. Indeed, it was a solemn and interesting time among us. Many professors [of religion] appeared to be greatly stirred up; while sinners seemed to be deeply touched and aroused to a sense of their danger and duty. Our prayer meeting was short but not without good and lasting impressions being made upon the hearts and minds of many. About 12 o'clock that same night, orders came to march. Our brave boys, as on all such occasions, were soon ready to move off. The direction soon proved to them that they were going to contest the strength of the enemy; it was the first time, too. Did they flinch or hang back? No; they went forward with undaunted bravery! About 4 o'clock, on Saturday morning the 30th, one of the enemy's forts in which the garrison were reposing in pleasant slumber, dreaming of no danger, nor apprehending any, was blown up destroying nearly all who were in it at the time. At this moment, the Union line for a mile opened upon the enemy with their batteries, and the most terrific cannonading continued until 10 o'clock A.M. But about 9 o'clock our brave boys, the colored troops belonging to the Fourth Division, Ninth Army Corps, made one of the most daring charges ever made since the commencement of the rebellion. The First Brigade, consisting of four regiments, namely, the Forty-third [USCI] Pennsylvania, Twenty-seventh [USCI] Ohio, and Thirtieth and Thirty-ninth [USCI] Maryland, led in the charge. The first two named regiments drove the enemy from their breastworks, and took possession of the blown up fort; but while they did, all the white soldiers lay in their pits and did nothing to support our men in the struggle; they lay as if there was nothing for them to do for one hour after the explosion took place. The rebels deserted all their forts fearing that some more of their works were about to be blown up.

How easily Petersburg could have been taken on the 30th of July, had the white soldiers and their commanders done their duty! But prejudice against colored troops prevented them. Instead of a general effort being made, as was contemplated, only a few men were taken in to be slaughtered and taken prisoner, which is the equivalent to death, for no mercy is shown to them when captured, although some still plead that the rebels are treating the colored prisoners very well; but before I can be convinced that this is so, I wish to hear one of the prisoners tell the story.

After our men had driven the enemy and taken possession of a portion of their works, I cannot conceive of a plausible reason why it was that reinforcements were not sent to them. This neglect was the cause of their being repulsed with such heavy loss. I can only conclude that our men fell unnecessarily in the battle of the 30th. In their retreat, they received the cross-fire of the enemy, and no small number were killed by our own artillery.

Such was the terrible fate of the day. Time will tell who was in the fault, and who made the great blunder in the battle of the 30th of July.

Among the captured was my brother-in-law, William Johnson of Upper Sandusky, Ohio, where my family now reside; but I can only give him up into the hand of God, who knows just how to deal with his case. If he is murdered by the rebels all is right, his blood will speak for the cause in which he fell. . . .

LETTER 45

(Alexander H. Newton, Sergeant, Co. E, 29th Connecticut Infantry, near Petersburg, Virginia, September 13, 1864; *WAA*, October 1, 1864) The siege of Petersburg lasted from June 15, 1864, to April 2, 1865. During that time the armies fought many battles – some large, some small. Sergeant Alexander H. Newton of New Haven, Connecticut, writes in this letter about two busy weeks of fighting.

Our brigade still holds the line of intrenchments on the right in front of Petersburg to City Point. On the 29th [of August], the rebs opened a heavy firing upon our battery, which proved a costly demonstration to them. Our regiment then held a position of the left of the line of intrenchments, and was pretty well exposed to the enemy's fire. James F. Fowler was killed from the bursting of a shell which fell inside of the intrenchments. Corp'l Cleaveland, private Jacob Robinson and a few in some of the other companies whose names I could not learn were slightly wounded. About 8 o'clock at night we were relieved by the 37th N.J. (white) and moved the length of our regiment to the right. There was a continual firing kept up during our moving. Shortly we arrived at our stopping place and made ourselves as comfortable as we possibly could under the fire, during the night.

On the 30th there was heavy cannonading during the forenoon, but ceased in the afternoon. At night we again moved the length of the regiment, for it was a matter of impossibility to move at any other time; for when we did move we were obliged to go on our hands and knees, and then a ball would whiz by our heads, but fortunately none of us got hurt this day. After moving to our proposed stopping place, one third of us were allowed to rest ourselves the best way we could, whilst the remainder kept awake to watch the movements of the enemy. About 3 o'clock on the morning of the 31st, the entire line was aroused and ordered to prepare for an attack, as there was a continual firing of musketry at our advanced picket line. But the Johns did not succeed in breaking through our lines. At night we moved about a half mile, formed into companies, and lay on our arms all night. There had been no firing during the night, which was something unusual. Early on the morning of Sept. 1st, supposing that we would camp here for a while, we went to work building bomb-proofs. About 8 o'clock p.m. the enemy spied us, and immediately commenced to throw shot, shell, grape, and canister among us, wounding several and killing one private in Co. K, by the name of Burton. We remained here for about two hours, when we came to the conclusion that these pills were too many to take at one dose, and fell back a few rods, and closely stored ourselves behind a long line of breastworks. Our batteries then opened fire upon them and succeeded in silencing them very shortly.

On the 2d we were busily engaged building bombproofs all day. There was no firing today. On the 3d we lay still all day in order to rest a little. There was nothing going on today more than the duel fighting between the pickets. At night they moved us over to the right of the advance line of intrenchments, where we lay for forty-eight hours. Nothing of importance occurred during our stay at this point more than the annoyance of sharpshooters' balls passing swiftly by our heads once in a while. Everything remained quiet for two or three days. We have a 24 pound Parrot gun stationed on the railroad leading from Petersburg to City Point. On the morning of the 10th she sent a dispatch over into Petersburg for Jeff. Davis's special benefit. She is called the "Petersburg Express." Shortly after this the ball commenced. One of the 8th U.S. Colored

Troops was killed. Some of our boys got wounded. Joseph De-
meroy of Co. E, had a ball to pass through his throat, just under the
chin. One man in Co. D was wounded. I did not learn his name. A
man named Mingo in Co. H, was killed. Geo. W. Odell shot
himself through the foot while in the act of cleaning his gun.

The general health of the regiment is pretty good. We anxiously
await the approach of the paymaster. We are now in the 1st Brigade, 3d Division, 10th Army Corps.

LETTER 46

(John C. Brock, Commissary Sergeant, 43d USCI, near Petersburg, Virginia, October 30, 1864; *CR*, November 12, 1864)
Daily life for the men in the trenches around Petersburg and Richmond was full of uncertainty. Sergeant Brock describes in this
letter the highs and lows of emotion faced by the soldiers in the
Battle of Burgess's Mills.

Since the last letter that I wrote to you, we have been engaged with
the enemy. On last Tuesday we were ordered to take six days'
rations, three in our knapsacks and three in our haversacks. On the
same afternoon I saw that each man had the provisions ordered.
Every one thought that a move would be made immediately. All
night, Tuesday, every ear was on the *qui viva* to hear the order to
move, but no order came. All day Wednesday the camp was as
quiet as usual. I don't believe we are going to move at all, says a
youngster. You will sing a different tune from that, replied an older
soldier, before twenty-four hours. On Wednesday evening we went
to bed as usual. At two o'clock on Thursday morning a single
horseman rode into camp, with a dispatch to our commander.
Every man was ordered to strike his tent and get ready to march
immediately. Soon afterwards long columns of troops commenced
to march out past our camp. In about ten minutes every man was

ready to march. But the order to move had not yet arrived; we lay there till broad daylight before we moved. Meanwhile the 2nd and 5th Corps continued to pass us in one continuous column. Many a man lay there with an anxious heart. They shook hands with each other, bidding each other farewell in case they should not meet again. One corporal from the State of Maine handed me a letter, together with his money and watch. "Write my wife," said he, "in case that anything should happen to me." He was only one out of the many that told me the same thing.

What a time for reflection! How many who are now well and hearty going out into the fray will never return again, and how many will returned bruised and mangled! Alas! alas! the desolations of war.

At last, after many hours of delay, the order was given to move forward. The whole division was soon in motion, the first brigade leading. We proceeded along slowly and cautiously about a mile before we met any signs of the enemy. "The Johnnies are all gone," says a new recruit. "You will hear them soon enough," replied an older and wiser soldier. "Hark! What was that?" cried one, as the report of musketry was heard in distance. His companion told him that our skirmishers were chasing in the enemy's pickets. Our brigade advanced in gallant style, driving the rebels before them all day. Towards night the enemy fell back to his works, where he was found to be strongly fortified. Our [men] built breastworks while our skirmishers were busily engaged in watching the enemy.

On Thursday night it commenced to rain, and the boys had to make it rough and ready without tents all night. [By] morning many of them were dripping wet. Soon after dark on Thursday night, the rebels attempted to surprise us, but we were not caught napping. They found the boys ready and waiting to welcome them. . . . On Friday morning everyone thought that the order of the day would be an attempt to make still further advances, but contrary to everyone's expectations, we were ordered to fall back. The Second Corps fell back from their position early in the morning, we following soon afterwards.

Now we are in our old camp where we started from. What good

was accomplished, we have yet to learn. The loss in our brigade was "hot and heavy." In our regiment (the 43rd) we had one officer and several men killed, and some 12 or 14 wounded. Fortunate it was that we lost no more [because] our regiment was flanked several times. The most of the men that were lost belonged to Company B, – as they were the first thrown out as skirmishers, and consequently were most exposed to the enemy's fire. . . .

LETTER 47

(A.W., [Sergeant,] 5th Massachusetts Cavalry, Point Lookout, Maryland, November 26, 1864; *WAA*, December 17, 1864) Life in the army was not all grim tension, especially away from the front. Probably written by Sergeant Amos Webber of Worcester, Massachusetts, this letter describes how its author's regiment, then guarding prisoners in Maryland, celebrated Thanksgiving.

Permit me to inform you of the doings on Thanksgiving day in and about the Fifth Massachusetts Cavalry camp. It was the first holiday that we have witnessed during the eleven months in service. Our officers determined to have some sport most congenial to the feelings of their men, and a sumptuous turkey dinner for each Company; wines excepted.

PROGRAMME OF THE DAY
Reveille – Full Band, 10 a.m.
Horse Race, for officers, at 12 o'clock m.
Thanksgiving Dinner
Sack Race, 1-1/2 o'clock
1st prize, 1 turkey; 2d prize, bale of tobacco.
Climbing Greased Poles; 2 o'clock
1st prize, 1 goose; 2d prize, plug of tobacco
Foot Race; 2-1/2 o'clock.
1st prize, pair of gauntlets; 2d prize, pair of spurs.

Wheelbarrow Race; 3 o'clock.
One Prize – a box of Cigars
A Jig Dance-Prize, pair of Mexican spurs.
A greased pig will be let out every half hour.
Music by the band at intervals during the exercises.
Committee: Maj. H[enry] P. Bowditch of the 2d Battalion;
C[harles] C. Parsons, Captain of Co. D;
F[rederick] G. Parker, Assistant Surgeon in Hospital.

The day proved as clear and fine as an autumn day in the North, and all got ready to see the events of the day as it was ushered in bright and clear. According to programme, the exercises commenced at 12 o'clock. The officers entered the course for the race, and after a spirited run, Lieut. [Curtis] Whittemore's horse won the prize.

Dinner – The turkey dinner was served up to each Company in fine style. I noticed Cos. C, D, and E had a large table spread out in the Co.'s street, about 40 feet long, and the men were all seated around the table, eating away for life, on turkeys, oysters, turnips, onions, bread without butter, etc.

Sack Race – The parties entered for the race with their heads just out of the sack. It was a laughable affair to see them jumping along for the prize. Sergt. Wm. Holmes, Co. G, won the 1st prize; David White, Co.E, the 2d.

Greased Poles – There were two greased poles. On the top of one hung the goose; on the other a plug of tobacco. After many attempts, John Miller, Co. M, succeeded in getting the tobacco; others failed and left the goose high and dry.

Foot Race – 1st prize won by William D. Cooper; 2d by Boyd Hyde, both of Co. E.

Wheelbarrow Race – Won by Peter Smith of Co. D.

Turkey Shooting – The following men shot a turkey for their prize: Sergt. Wm Holmes, Co. G; Corp. David Walker, Thos. Bell, Westley Rhoades, all of Co. I; Franklin Jennings of Co. B, and another whose name I could not learn.

Jig Dance – Prize won by Richard Holmes, Bugler of Co. A.

Pig Chase – One caught by Alexander Ware, Co. H; one by Alexander Davis, Co. D, and by others, names unknown.

Second Foot Race – The officers and visitors, being anxious to see the sport of another Foot Race, soon made up a donation for the prizes. 1st prize, Sergt. James Treadwell, Co. M, $25.00; 2d prize, James C. Greenly, Co. G., can of turkey; 3d prize, James Moulton, Co. D, box of collars and $4.75.

Second Jig Dance – Corp. Ray of Co. E received $5.00 and $4.00 2d prize on the first Jig Dance.

Thus the day was well spent in sport and pleasure to their satisfaction. During the time, Capt. [Horace] Welch of Co. C was recipient of a handsome sabre, two scabbards and a silk sash, all neatly finished. It was presented to the Captain by Sergt. John Davis (Orderly Sergeant) in an eloquent speech. The Captain lifted his hat and responded in a brief manner.

The evening was well spent, to the enjoyment of all. The band poured forth volumes of music from their great horns, during the day and evening, for which they received great credit.

The Chief Bugler of the regiment, Sergt. Rueben Huff, was recipient of a handsome cavalry jacket and sabre-belt, presented to him by the buglers of the regiment as a token of respect to their Chief.

LETTER 48

(James H. Harden, Quartermaster Sergeant, 43d USCI, near Richmond and Petersburg, Virginia, December 3, 1864; *CR*, December 17, 1864) Sudden death was a regular event for the men who served in the siege trenches. Sergeant James H. Harden of Philadelphia tells how shells from Confederate guns dropped into his camp.

. . . We are constantly under the fire of the enemy, who shell our camp nearly every day. There has been some few wounded in our regiment since we have been here, but no one killed as far as I can ascertain.

There is one poor fellow soldier, belonging to the 23d regiment, which is in our brigade, struck in the head by a bullet which caused his death.

The next morning, I saw some four or five men of his company digging a grave, and I inquired after him, and was told that he was dead, and that he was to be buried there. After the grave was finished, his body was borne by some of his comrades to its resting place, and laid in the grave. His clothing formed his shroud, and his blanket the coffin.

The chaplain then made some few remarks, and prayed over the grave where the remains were laid, after which he was covered with earth by some of his comrades.

The same day, another man of the same regiment was struck by a shell, which shattered his thigh to pieces. Another man was struck with a shell which cut him in two.

How will their families and friends feel when they receive the sad tidings of their husbands, fathers, brothers, or sons, or whatever relation they may be, who have fallen in behalf of our glorious Union, and their fellow comrades in the South?

I had a very narrow escape myself, the other day. Commissary Sergeant John C. Brock and myself were standing together, and had just finished issuing rations, when a shell came hissing over us and bursted. We started and ran a few yards, and I fell to the ground, and the pieces flew all around us. One piece struck an old log, which was lying on the ground where we were standing, and glanced off and out through the cook's tent, striking a glass bottle, smashing it, and then struck the upright pole that holds the tent up, which stopped its progress.

I thank God that he has spared my life so far, and still hope to see the city of brotherly love once more.

We have a very nice and attentive chaplain in our regiment. He attends to and furnishes nourishment for the sick and wounded. I do not think that there could be a better one found, for he studies our interests, and tries to supply our wants.

I will now close my letter, for there is neither pen, paper, ink, nor pencil that can describe the desolation of war.

LETTER 49

(James H. Payne, Quartermaster Sergeant, 27th USCI, near Richmond, Virginia, December 21, 1864; *CR*, January 7, 1865) Civilians often accompanied army regiments as servants, wagon drivers, sutlers, or cooks. This was true of both the white and black regiments. In this letter Sergeant James H. Payne of Lima, Ohio, tells of "Sister Penny," a nurse who traveled with the 5th USCI.

Permit me the privilege, through your worthy columns, to give your readers a brief historical introduction to our very worthy and eminent sister and mother in the army, Sister Lydia Penny.

Sister Penny was born a slave in Blount County, East Tennessee, in the year of our Lord 1814. At the time of the Indian War, when General [Winfield] Scott and General Wood [John E. Wool?] drove the Indians from their habitations in Tennessee,[17] Sister Penny served two years as a cook. She was, at the time, only a girl; but she informed me that she subsequently became the mother of a family of children whose companionship she had long been deprived of through slavery, and that she was left a widow to suffer the torments of cruel oppression.

She was finally sold to a Dutch butcher in Memphis, Tennessee. By this time she had learned to trust in God, who had promised to deliver the oppressed and to open the prison doors to them that are

---

17. The Cherokee Indians of East Tennessee and the Carolinas were forced by the Federal government in the 1830s to move to Oklahoma.

bound. She said that she had a falling-out with her Dutch mistress about something, and that she gave her master and mistress both to understand distinctly that she intended to run away from them, which threat she carried into effect about one week after it was made, by which time they thought that she had become contented to remain with them.

Sister Penny says that she kept herself concealed among her friends in Memphis until the Union army had extended its lines near the city, when she made her way within its lines, and again engaged herself as cook. Here, she said, being a lonely widow, and having no one in particular to befriend or protect her, prudence dictated the propriety of making selection of a companion, which she did, as soon as she found one who she thought would treat her as a wife and act the part of a faithful husband by her.

While in the army she formed the acquaintance with Mr. Penny, a native of Pennsylvania, who had enlisted as a servant in the three months' service. They finally came to the city of Cincinnati, Ohio, where Thomas Penny, her husband, re-enlisted in the service, and joined the Fifth United States Colored Troops, at Camp Delaware, Ohio. Sister Penny said that she felt it to be her duty to go along with her husband, not merely on account of the love she had for him, but also for the love which she had for her country – that the cause which nerved the soldiers to pour out their life-blood was her cause, and that of her race, and that she felt it to be her Christian duty to do all she could for the liberty of her afflicted and down-trodden race.

This good woman is called by those who are acquainted with her, "the mother of the army." She well deserves the name, for she has been in the service ever since this rebellion broke out, or very nearly as long.

Sister Penny says that she is not tired of the service, nor does she think of leaving the field until the last gun is fired and peace is declared, and every slave is freed from captivity. Many of our officers and men who were wounded at the battle of Deep Bottom [July 27, 1864] will never forget the kind deeds of Sister Lydia

Penny, who went among them and administered to their wants as they lay weltering in their blood on the banks of the James, near Jones' Landing. There she could be seen, the only woman present, like an angel from above, giving words of cheer, and doing all in her power to relieve the suffering of the wounded and dying.

Yes, while others stood aloof, thinking themselves too good even to go near enough to give them a drink of water to quench their burning thirst, Sister Penny was seen, like a ministering angel, or one of those holy women who in primitive days administered to Christ and His apostles. She gave them water to drink and bread to eat, and assisted the surgeons in dressing their wounds.

When the wounded were placed on the boats to be taken to hospitals at Fortress Monroe, she left her tent and all behind and went on board the boats to minister to their comfort. When they were delivered into the hands of careful nurses, Sister Penny returned to her tent, where she ever waits to administer to the wants of the afflicted soldier.

Her husband seems to be much of a gentleman. I hope that all Christians who shall be permitted to read this short statement of Sister Penny's life and character will pray for her; and I can assure them; they will pray for a worthy woman. . . .

LETTER 50

(James W. Anderson, Sergeant-Major, 31st USCI, Point-of-Rocks, Virginia, [December 1864]; *WAA*, January 14, 1865) Part of the army's strategy around Richmond was to keep the Confederates off balance and confused. Raids behind the lines helped do that. Sergeant-Major James W. Anderson of Sullivan, New York, describes such a raid during the Christmas season.

. . . I suppose you have already heard of our raid; if not I will tell you a little about it. On the evening of the 13th we were ordered to be ready to march at any moment, leaving tents and knapsacks behind. We hardly knew what to make of it, but like true soldiers we asked no questions but got ready. About 7 o'clock on the morning of the 14th we took our line of march for the Appomattox River, reaching which, we took boat and away we went. Leaving the Appomattox at City Point we entered the James, stopping at Bermuda Hundreds and Harrison's Landing, where we were joined by a force of about 200 cavalry. Starting once more on our course, we anchored that night off Fortress Monroe. The next morning we changed the steamboat for a large transport, and off we started again, touching at Point Lookout, where we saw and conversed with some of the 5th Mass. Cavalry. Leaving Point Lookout we took our course Southwardly entering the Rappahannock river at Wind Mill Point.

On the 16th we landed at a point of land, the name of which I could not learn. On the morning of the 17th we all left the boats. It was an interesting sight to see them land cavalry horses, pitching them overboard and allowing them to swim ashore. Everything being landed, we were ordered to cook our dinner as quick as possible, after which we fell into line and then commenced the raid. We took our line of march across the most fertile country that there is in Virginia. Talk about Secession being hard up, it is all a mistake. Passing you would observe in the fields and pastures any amount of cattle and sheep, and around their houses any amount of poultry, and on entering you would find their smoke-houses filled with meat and their barns filled with grain to repletion. But the Philistines were upon them. We helped ourselves to anything that we saw and wanted in the shape of poultry, meat, tobacco, corn, horses, or rebs. The boys emptied their haversacks of all government grub, replacing it with turkeys, chickens, ducks, sweet potatoes, etc., etc. The boys were living high, and it was hard work for them to fall back on hard tack and salt horse again.

We crossed the country to a point on the Potomac where the boats were to meet us, capturing a large number of prisoners and horses, and bringing with us any quantity of tobacco and poultry.

Embarking again, we took our course back to camp. Stopping at Fortress Monroe, we delivered our prisoners to the proper authorities, arriving at camp on the evening of the 24th after an absence of ten days. . . .

LETTER 51

(Christian A. Fleetwood, Sergeant-Major, 4th USCI, Fort Fisher, North Carolina, January 31, 1865; to Moses Lake and quoted in "From Baltimore," *WAA*, March 4, 1865) Death was a sad but frequent part of the war. In each case, someone had to notify the family at home. Sergeant-Major Fleetwood of Baltimore, who later would win the Congressional Medal of Honor, wrote of the death of Sergeant Joshua Coution, who died of wounds from fighting near Fort Fisher, North Carolina.

Mr. Moses Lake has just received the mournful intelligence of the death of his nephew, Joshua Coution, Sergeant Co. D, 4th U.S. Colored Troops. Sergt. Major Fleetwood, in writing of the death of this gallant youth, gives the following interesting details:

"Since the fall of Fort Fisher, our regiment has made three reconnaisances toward the rebel works between us and Wilmington, the last of these being made yesterday (Jan. 30th).

"Coution went with us, acting as the 1st Sergeant of his company. The whole of our regiment was thrown forward as skirmishers, and advanced within about two hundred yards of the works, meeting quite a sharp fire from the enemy.

"While gallantly doing his duty on the skirmish line, Coution was wounded very severely. I saw him carried off from the right, but could not leave my post of duty to ascertain the nature of his wound. We fell back about two hours later, and when we regained our camp, I went as soon as possible off to the hospital to see him. Chaplain [William H.] Hunter, with whom Coution was a great favorite, went also to see him. We found him in a very critical condition. The ball went through his right arm, breaking it too high up to admit of amputation, and passed on into his chest, through his lungs, and was cut out of his back.

"The doctors think that there is no possibility of his recovery, though he may linger for two or three days yet.

"There is a universal regret among all who know him in the regiment. His fine soldierly qualities and manly deportment have made him respected and liked by all with whom he came in contact. May God in His infinite mercy receive him into the rest prepared for His people."

In a letter received a day or two later, the Sergeant Major again writes:

"It becomes my painful duty to inform you that the fears expressed in my letter of the 30th ult., relative to the result of the wound received by Coution, have been realized; and he last night breathed his last in the hospital at this point.

"I visited him again yesterday afternoon, and found him sinking rapidly, though he, poor boy, felt better, and thought himself, as he expressed it, on the mend.

"He was so very weak that I could stay with him but a very few minutes, that he might not weary himself by talking. Early this morning I heard of his death, and at once had a detail sent down for his body, and had it brought to camp.

"Be assured that everything that could be done was done to alleviate his sufferings and soothe his last moments. All that could be done was done to show the respect of the living to the remains of the gallant dead. The last rite has been performed. Our Chaplain read the burial service at the grave, and the companions of his labors have fired a last salute in honor of their comrade.

"He sleeps for the Flag, and may its stars shed pleasant dreams upon his loyal soul forever. A martyr for liberty, he honors a soldier's grave."

LETTER 52

(Isaac Wood, Sergeant, Co. E, 41st USCI, Fort Harrison, Virginia, March 1865; *CR*, March 18, 1865) Young boys accompanied the army into the field, serving as drummer boys or personal servants for officers. Some of them were killed or wounded. Sergeant Isaac Wood met a twelve-year-old boy in the hospital and wrote a letter about him.

While passing through one of the hospital wards recently, I caught the eye of a little colored boy, who looked just as if he desired to speak to me. So I went over to him, and said:

"Well, my little fellow, what is the trouble with you?"

"Oh, no trouble, sir; only, I've lost a leg."

"Why, you are a young hero, to shoulder a musket."

"I wasn't a soldier, sir; I was the Captain's waiter."

"Well, how did you come, then, to get in the way of a ball?"

"I didn't, sir, it got in my way. I wanted to let it pass, but it wouldn't; and so it took my leg off."

"What are you going to do when you get well?"

"Going back to the Captain, sir; he will take care of me."

Brave little fellow! Only twelve years old, and yet a hero! Regardless of danger, he had followed his Captain to the field, and fell, where his impulse led him, among the veteran soldiers of Grant's army. He has the material in him of which soldiers are made; and, had he been older and stronger, would have been quick to shoulder his musket in defense of the Union.

LETTER 53

(J. Roberts, Orderly Sergeant, Co. F, 28th USCI, City Point, Virginia, [March 1865]; *CR*, April 1, 1865) Although many black soldiers criticized their white officers for racism, cowardice, or incompetence, there were also many examples of good relations between them. In this letter, Sergeant Roberts tells how he and his men proudly rewarded their captain for his loyalty and bravery.

It was a beautiful evening in the month of February, and that which took place in Co. F, 28th Regiment U.S.C.T., now stationed at City Point, Va., made it more pleasant.

Sergeant Roberts, Orderly of the company, immediately after retreat roll-call, marched his men up before our worthy Captain's quarters, and after delivering a short speech, which had been prepared for the occasion, presented him with a handsome sword, sash, and belt, for which they paid ($150) one hundred and fifty dollars. The men raised the money, bought the article without the knowledge of their commander, and of course, it took him by surprise. The following is the address of Sergt. Roberts:

"Captain, we, the members of Company F, 28th Regt. U.S.C.T., assemble here at this time, for the purpose of paying our respects to you for the interest you have always taken in our welfare, for the kindness you have manifested toward us, and for the undaunted gallantry you have displayed on many different battlefields, several of which your company witnessed. We know, Captain, that you are still ever ready to lead us whenever the hour of trial comes, and your fearless boys stand here now to renew our vows, that we will be with you 'although we are far from home.'

"We know, Captain, that on the ever memorable 30th of July last, you were wounded, lost your sword, and were afterwards taken prisoner, and fell while at the head of your company, manifesting as much nonchalance with your half-smiling, but determined look as though you were drinking a glass of ice-cold water. Many signs were given during your absence from us, and many shouts of joy have been heard on account of your presence; and now, since the good Lord has permitted you to return safely to us, we feel it a duty we owe to you to make you a present.

"I, in the name of Company F, have the honor to ask you to accept this sword, sash, and belt, as a token of our respect. We hope you will wear them wherever you go, and with our prayers we trust that you will be guided and protected safely through the conflict, and when all is over, when peace shall have been restored to our once-happy country, that you will be permitted to return to the loved ones at home, who have, doubtless, mourned often and passed many sleepless hours while you have been undergoing many hardships, and passing through many dangerous scenes that they know not of. May the Lord bless you, Captain, is the wish of the humble men who now stand before you."

During this speech, Captain [John M.] Ridenour stood in the door of his neat little hut, looking perfectly amazed. After a few moments' silence he stepped out, took off his hat, and addressed them as follows. (Allow me to remark here that I have been acquainted with Captain Ridenour for some time: never before that evening did I think he was so handsome, his pale, blushing face, his manly deportment, induced us to look upon him with more pride than ever before.)

"Non-commissioned officers and men of Co. F. With a heart full of thanks, but no tongue to express them, I accept the present you have so kindly offered. Owing to the surprise this evening, which has caused me to be somewhat embarrassed, you will excuse me for not saying more. You ask me to wear the sword: I will do as you request, as I have confidence that you will protect me from all harm, as far as lies in your power. I hope that this most execrable rebellion will soon be crushed, that every traitor will soon have found the 'last ditch,' or [be] totally destroyed from the face of the earth.

"Asking many pardons for the short remarks I have made, and hoping that when the time comes again, I will have the honor to go with you into action."

After this the company gave three hearty cheers, and returned to their quarters.

Capt. Ridenour was complimented for his speech and present by many of his brother officers.

LETTER 54

("Clerk," Headquarters, 25th Corps, in the field, Virginia, March 14, 1865; *WAA*, March 25, 1865) As the war drew toward its end in April 1865, African-American soldiers still resented the fact that they could not have black officers. Government policy was changing, however, and "Clerk" thinks blacks can command as well as whites.

. . . This afternoon, could you have but witnessed the grand sight of a review (by our tried and equal rights friend, Gen. Wm. Birney) you would have been highly pleased. It was rather a grand affair, consisting of the 1st Brigade, in which is the noble 7th U.S. Colored Troops (the drum corps of these looking splendid in their dress of scarlet pants, with a dark gimp cord, fitting in the neatest possible manner, the round about of dark cloth, and their caps, dark-blue cloth, trimmed with gold lace); the 2d Brigade, looking in fine order, as did the 3d brigade; the drum corps belonging to the 116th U.S. Colored Troops, with these looking in an excellent manner. The music (brass bands) was furnished from the heroes of Olustee, the 8th U.S. Colored Troops, Orange C. Thompson, leader, and a brass band belonging to the 109th U.S. Colored Troops.

Our zealous friend, Gen. Birney, has just returned from a twenty days leave of absence, on a visit to his family. On his return, he found his command ready to greet him, and they hailed him with thankfulness, as some had been informed that he had been assigned to another field of military labor. I presume if it had turned out so, some of the head officers of this corps would have felt elated; and why? because he strongly favors the promotion of colored men as line officers. It was a death blow to them to hear that Martin R. Delany was made a Major, and I expect to see many resignations come in from that one instance; but the sooner they are rid of the better the service will fare. The General has at his back hosts of military admirers, and he can spare the Copperhead fraternity, I think, and fill their places with men who are loyal (black men); for the material is here, ready [and] waiting to show the world that the Anglo-Africans can do duty as officers.

I saw an Orderly Sergeant commanding his company today on the general review, and they were commanded every whit as good as the rest, while as regards to dressing on the Guide and marching in company front, none looked better. I do not think that, in speaking of this instance, I am aspiring to be a military critic; but I merely do so to show that colored soldiers will conform to military discipline under colored officers as well as white, because it is said that ere long we will be able to record the names of some colored officers in the Army of the James. . . .

LETTER 55

(Garland H. White, Chaplain, 28th USCI, City Point, Virginia, April 20, 1865; *CR*, May 6, 1865) Like other soldiers, some of the black troops ran afoul of military law. Samuel Mapps was convicted of trying to murder his captain. It was the sad duty of Chaplain Garland White to tell Mapps about his fate and to prepare him for his execution.

On the 19th inst., about 10 o'clock, P.M., the Orderly from Brevet Brig. Gen. Charles S. Russell came to my tent, woke me up, and handed me an order reading thus:

Rev. Garland H. White, Chaplain of the 28th U.S. Colored
Troops:

Sir: – You are requested to call upon Samuel Mapps, private in
Co. D, 10th U.S.C.T., now under sentence of death, and now
confined in the Bull-pen, to prepare him to meet his Savior.

By official orders,

Gen. C.S. Russell

T. Latchford, Assist. Adj. Gen.

Reply

Gen. C.S. Russell, Commanding this Post:

Sir: – I have the honor to acknowledge receipt of your order
respecting my visiting private Samuel Mapps, Co.D, 10th
U.S.C.T. In reply, I would say I will comply promptly, and do all in
my power to point him to the Lamb of God that taketh away the
sins of the world.

Yours,

G.H. White

Chaplain

At the prison

"Well, my friend, how stands your case?"

He began to plead innocence, and commenced to enter into a
lengthy discussion of all that was connected with his trial.

To this I said in reply, "I came to see you, not to discuss a point
of law as to the nature of your trial and decision, for that is all
useless, and, my friend, I must tell you that to-day, at 12 o'clock
you will be executed – yes, you will be shot. Now, let you and
myself kneel down and address a throne of grace where you may
obtain mercy and help in time of need." He complied and prayed
fervently, after which I read several passages of Scripture, and sang
a hymn – "Jesus, Lover of My Soul," &c, at the conclusion of
which we bowed again in prayer to God.

I then spent some time in reasoning upon what he thought about
religion.

He replied, "It is very good, and I wish I had it."

I then cited in plain terms the case of the dying thief: – that seemed to give him hope. We prayed again and he appeared some-what relieved; but at this moment the wagon with a squad of guards appeared at the door. He did not see them; I did. He continued to pray fervently, and an officer came in and announced that the time to repair to the place of execution had come. I told him to stand up and walk with me. I took his arm, and went out to the gate where thousands of persons had assembled to see him. He entered the wagon, and sat on his coffin. I then got in with him, took a seat by his side, and commenced talking and praying all the way to a large open field, about a mile out of the village, where it appeared to me, all the people in the place had congregated.

At the grave

The officer went through all the necessary arrangements, and then made a sign for me to proceed to pray for the last time, with the poor man who would soon be in eternity.

I asked him for the last time, "Do you feel that Jesus will be with you?"

"Yes," he replied.

"Do you put all your trust in him?"

"I do," was the answer.

"Do you believe that you will be saved?"

"I do; for though they may destroy the body, they cannot hurt the soul."

"Let us pray," I replied. "Eternal God, the Master of all the living and Judge of all the dead, we commit this our dying comrade into thy hands from whence he came. Now, O my Lord and my God, for thy Son's sake, receive his soul unto thyself in glory. Forgive him – forgive, O thou Blessed Jesus, for thou didst die for all mankind, and bid them to come unto thee, and partake of ever-lasting life. Save him, Lord – save him, for none can save but thee, and thee alone. Amen. Good-by, my brother, good-by."

The order was now given: ready! aim! fire! About as long as it would take me to speak the word was the interval. I approached the corpse and found that all of life was gone. Five or six bullets had pierced his heart. It was the saddest spectacle I ever witnessed, and

I hope never to witness another the longest day I live. He was the first colored man shot in this army, to my knowledge, during the war, and [I] hope it may be a warning to others.

He was charged with having attempted to kill his captain and insubordination. He was a Virginian and had never lived North. His regiment was raised in Virginia, and has a white chaplain, who is not here at present.

4

The Gulf States

ON MAY 27, 1863, Captain André Cailloux led his company of African-American soldiers in a hopeless charge against the Confederate forts at Port Hudson, Louisiana. As a free man in New Orleans, he had gained wealth and respect among both whites and blacks. He had been educated in Paris, and in the black community of Louisiana he was a natural leader; Cailloux was proud to be the "blackest man in America." When Federal forces took New Orleans in April 1862, he volunteered for the Union Army and personally recruited a company of men for the 1st Louisiana Native Guards, one of three regiments that had black officers.

The 1st Louisiana got its baptism of fire at Port Hudson, which controlled the Mississippi River between New Orleans and Vicksburg. Port Hudson stopped Union shipping and was strongly defended by rebel soldiers. The Federal army surrounded the town in May 1863. Black troops had not yet been tried in battle, but they were put on the right wing of the Union force and ordered to attack across a half mile of swamps and fallen trees to get at a rebel fort. Captain Cailloux lined up his men for the charge and, as they worked their way through the swamp, went up and down the line urging his men forward against heavy fire from Confederate sharpshooters and artillery. He shouted his orders in both English and French so he could be understood by his black Creole troops. The enemy fire was brutal for three hours, and the black troops stopped, regrouped, and charged again and again. Men fell all around him, but Cailloux led them onward. A bullet smashed into his left arm, but he continued at the front of his company, advancing to within fifty yards of the enemy trenches. Finally, early in the afternoon, a rebel shell killed him. After three charges against rebel lines, the black troops had to fall back because of their heavy casualties. But General Nathaniel P. Banks, who commanded the Department of the Gulf, reported to the War Department: "The history of this day proves conclusively that the Government will find in this class of troops effective supporters and defenders."

Although the two armies arranged a truce to remove the dead and wounded, the rebels refused to let the Union troops retrieve the bodies of black soldiers. Captain Cailloux's body was finally recovered on July 8, when Port Hudson fell. His magnificent funeral in New Orleans was attended by blacks and whites alike; he had lived as a leader and died as a hero. Cailloux had indeed showed that black officers could organize and lead soldiers in battle; he was one of only three black officers who died in combat during the Civil War.[1]

African-American soldiers proved themselves in other battles in the Gulf states, including Milliken's Bend, Pascagoula, and Mobile. As a result, Union officials recruited thousands of newly

---

1. Williams, *A History of the Negro Troops in the War of the Rebellion, 1861–1865*, 214–221. Dudley Cornish, *The Sable Arm* (New York, Norton, 1966) 142–145. Joseph T. Glatthaar, *Forged in Battle* (New York, Free Press, 1990) 123–130. Wilson, *The Black Phalanx*, 212–219. Quarles, *The Negro in the Civil War*, 214–220.

freed slaves in the Gulf region. These black soldiers served as garrison troops, building fortifications and defending towns and rail lines against rebel raiders. Racial prejudice in the army quickly forced the black officers to resign, and soon all these troops were commanded by white officers. Most of the soldiers themselves were illiterate, so relatively few letters from the Gulf appeared in the newspapers. The educated men in the Louisiana regiments wrote few letters to the press. Most of the letters from that region came from three regiments of free blacks from the North.

Those regiments primarily defended fortifications in Louisiana and West Florida and took part in raids in Mississippi and Alabama. In Louisiana, African Americans manned fortifications along the Mississippi River around New Orleans. The 14th Rhode Island Colored Heavy Artillery (renamed the 11th U. S. Colored Heavy Artillery) had detachments at several places where large Union cannon guarded the river. The 20th U.S. Colored Infantry served in the same area, giving protection to the landward side of those forts, guarding against rebel guerrilla attacks, and occasionally raiding rebel-held country.

In West Florida, Fort Pickens was the main Union base. Located on an island in Pensacola harbor, it had stayed in Federal hands since the beginning of the war. It kept Pensacola from being used by blockade runners, and it made a good base for the blockading ships of the Union. The 25th USCI, a Pennsylvania regiment, helped man Fort Pickens and its outposts on the mainland. From there, the black troops launched raids into nearby Florida and Alabama.

Mobile, Alabama, between New Orleans and Pensacola, had an excellent harbor and rail lines that led to the rest of the Confederate states. It was, therefore, a major blockade-running port, and the Union wanted to close it down. In August 1864, navy ships steamed into the harbor and seized the forts at its mouth, thus closing the port of Mobile. But the city itself stayed in rebel hands until April 1865. Black soldiers, who had marched from bases in Louisiana, helped capture the city as the war ended.

The letters in this chapter tell of daily life in the Union forts, the raids into enemy territory, the efforts of the soldiers to help the slaves, and the problems the men faced in the racial climate of the Deep South. Pride in themselves and in their race, as well as a strong desire for civil rights, shows through each letter.

LETTER 56

(Robert H. Isabelle, Lieutenant, 2nd Louisiana Native Guards [74th USCI], New Orleans, Louisiana, February 27, 1863; *WAA*, March 14, 1863) Lieutenant Isabelle, one of the early black commissioned officers in Louisiana, helped recruit men for new regiments. Certainly most of the black soldiers there were Creoles, American-born. But in this letter, Lieutenant Isabelle describes two eager volunteers from Africa.

In Co. A, 2nd Regt, La. Vols., Native Guards, there are two privates, Wimba Congo and August Congo, who are natives of Africa. They were brought here some three years ago, on board of the celebrated yacht Wanderer,[2] and sold as slaves to a slaveholder on the opposite side of the river, and were compelled to work until the city was captured by the United States troops. As soon as Gen. [Benjamin] Butler issued his order calling on the colored people of Louisiana to take up arms to defend their homes, these two patriotic sons of Africa threw down their hoes in the field and marched boldly to the Touro Building, and in broken language declared that they wanted to fight for the United States. Capt. [P. B. S.] Pinchback[3] at first declined to enlist them because they could not speak the English language plain enough to be soldiers, but Lieut.

2. The *Wanderer* illegally brought a cargo of slaves to the United States in 1858.
3. P. B. S. Pinchback, an African American, became lieutenant governor of Louisiana during Reconstruction.

[Wm. F.] Keeling insisted on taking them, which was done, and they have proved as good soldiers as we can find in the whole three colored regiments. They are from the Congo river. They gave wonderful accounts of Africa, and tell how they were stolen from there and brought to America. They speak high of their King Lewis, but they are from King George's country. We want ten thousand more brave sons of Africa like these, so if the Wanderer and her officers would like to go into the recruiting business, we will pay two dollars for each able-bodied man they may steal from Africa and bring to the United States army. . . .

LETTER 57

(James F. Jones, Hospital Wardmaster, 3rd Battalion, 14th Rhode Island Heavy Artillery, [11th USCHA,] Camp Parapet, New Orleans, Louisiana, May 8, 1864; *CR*, May 28, 1864) Although most Northern black regiments served in Virginia or the Department of the South, this Rhode Island regiment, recruited from across the North, was sent to help protect New Orleans with heavy artillery. Wardmaster Jones, who hailed from Richmond, Indiana, told in this letter how his unit moved from its training base in the North to the forts on the Mississippi River.

After a brief silence, I thought that I would scribble a few lines to the Christian Recorder, thereby informing the many readers thereof, that the 3d Battalion of the 14th regiment, R.I. heavy artillery, numbering 600 men, rank and file, had turned up under command of Lt. Col. Nelson Vial. On the 29th of March, in the evening, the steam transport America quietly steamed into Narragansett Bay, and, with but little ado, cast anchor in such close proximity to Camp Bailey, our camp in Rhode Island, that our boys, as many of them expressed it, "began to smell a mice," as we were all anxious to learn why so large a vessel cast anchor in the Narragansett, we were not kept in suspense long; for soon the order came for us to be ready to embark by early dawn next morning. But who can tell what a day may bring forth? The morning came, and with it a terrible storm, so furious and fearful in its demonstrations, that we wisely concluded to wait and let the sea become more calm. For this we waited until the first of April, when we embarked. At 6 o'clock on the morning of the 4th, we hoisted anchors, and were soon out of sight of Dutch Island, a small strip of earth that we will never forget, after experiencing a tedious journey of seven long, and, to us, weary months. We were scarcely well out at sea, before most of the boys began to show symptoms of sea-sickness, a scourge that but few of us escaped; the effects of which none but those who have experienced [it] can properly describe. With fair winds and plenty of steam we were not long in making Cape Hatteras, the Gulf Stream, and coming in sight of a portion of the blockading fleet. Here we were brought to by an ugly-looking customer, firing a blank shot across our bow, which unceremonious action promptly brought our noble craft to. She was soon boarded by the commander of the before mentioned ugly-looking customer, which proved to be one of Uncle Sam's gunboat cruisers, who, having satisfied himself that we were all right, suffered us to proceed on our journey in peace.

At length we passed the quarantine grounds, and were soon made fast to the wharf in New Orleans, the present home and headquarters of Major General [Nathaniel P.] Banks. I omitted saying that as we passed up to the city, from Fort Jackson, we were hailed by the people on each shore (which were visible) with cheers, and every demonstration of joy and gladness. These demonstrations did not arise from the scarcity of Union troops in this section, but from the fact that the "contrabands" and Union people of the South look for more certain help, and a more speedy termination of the war, at the hands of the colored soldiers than from any other source; hence their delight at seeing us.

In the city of New Orleans, we could see signs of smothered hate and prejudice to both our color and present character as Union soldiers. But, for once in his life, your humble correspondent walked fearlessly and boldly through the streets of a southern city! And he did this without being required to take off his cap at every step, or give all the side walks to those lordly princes of the sunny south, the planter's sons! Oh, chivalry! how hast thou lost thy potent power and charms! . . .

We had been here but a short time before the 25th U.S. Colored Troops made their appearance, and we are all encamped here in Camp Parapet. This camp, Esfesti, as it may more properly be called, is nine miles above the city of New Orleans, directly on the Mississippi River. This was one of the strongest defenses of the city at the time General Butler appeared to them in his usual unceremonious manner. Since that time it has been in the hands of the Union forces, and has been greatly improved by them. So much so that the place is considered impregnable to any force that the enemy can bring against it.

I am happy to be able to inform the many readers of the precious Recorder that our battalion has the honor of the post of honor here. Not only is this true, but our Colonel has the honor of holding the prominent position of acting Brigadier General – commanding the rest. The same is true of our Messrs. Adjutant and Surgeon; and our boys occupy the place of guards to headquarters.

There are some white regiments here, some of which thought to deride us and disrespect us as soldiers because we were colored; but our noble Colonel promptly informed them that his command must and should be respected. Just here, let me say that Colonel Vial is the right man in the right place. He has the cause of the country at heart, and he is the strong friend of the colored soldiers, working day and night for their rights and protection.

The health of our battalion is very good, considering the change of climate and weather. At present there are only eighteen in the hospital, most of whom are subjects of chronic diseases.

Today, Company I, 1st Lieutenant [Alfred M.] Taylor commanding, have gone out on a foraging and scouting expedition. We expect them to do wonders, and achieve many a bloodless victory. I hope to be able to give you a good account of Battery I, in my next.

I am more fully convinced of the righteousness of our cause, and the great importance of the work that we have in hand, than ever before. I see daily occurrences, which convince me more fully of this truth, namely, that if our cause were not a just one, if an infinitely wise and just God did not watch over, guide and protect the colored soldier, certainly he could not stand. Betrayed and cheated by conniving recruiting officers, by being unfaithfully and unjustly dealt with by the general Government in regards to our rights and protection guaranteed to soldiers, by being subject to the sneers and abuse of pretending Union men in Uncle Sam's uniform, but merely playing soldiers and enemies to the cause they have from some sinister motives espoused.

This, Mr. Editor, this, and more too, is what the colored soldier has to endure; yet he prospers; yet he becomes thoroughly trained in the mysteries of modern warfare; yea, he makes rapid proficiency in the art, and notwithstanding the unfairness with which he is dealt, the unjustness of the privation he has been called to undergo, he receives them all, and is willing to fight. . . .

LETTER 58

("A," 2nd Battalion, 11th USCHA, Plaquemine, Louisiana, February 15, 1865; *CR*, March 18, 1865) Garrison duty in the Louisiana forts included drill, construction work, more drill, emergency alerts, drill again, going to church, and payday, followed by more drill. Whatever the weather, the men managed to keep busy.

I have been promising myself, for a long time, to write a few lines for your valuable columns, to give you some idea of our manner of life in this portion of our country. We still remain in this locality, where we have been for the last ten months, on the Mississippi River, above the city of New Orleans.

The 2d Battalion, 11th U.S.C. Artillery, came to Plaquemine on the 26th of March last, since which time we have performed the garrison duty of the post.

We have a fort, not yet completed, which mounts ten guns, nine thirty-two pounders, and a thirty-pound Parrot gun, which throws a shot at a distance of four miles.

Our routine of duty consists mostly of guard and picket duty, of which we enjoy a liberal supply.

We are quite proficient in heavy artillery and infantry drill, but have never yet had a chance to exercise our knowledge of the use of arms with the enemies of our country and race.

Major R[ichard] G. Shaw, commandant of the battalion, commands the post. There are two companies of the 3d R.I. Cavalry at the post besides the battalion.

The country here is beautiful, and we enjoy it very much. The health of the battalion is very good, owing the exertions of our beloved surgeon, Dr. Horace McCorney, attended by the blessing of God.

We have lost by death, I think, during the past year, about forty men; not a very large mortality for this climate. We are comfortably housed, and bid defiance to the blasts of old winter, of which we have felt not a little even in this sunny country.

Rainy weather seems to be the order of the day, at the present time. Storms are frequent, and often very severe.

We were forcibly reminded of the flood the other day, in the midst of one of these storms. It had rained violently at intervals for seven days, and was preparing to continue its course on the eighth, when old Sol broke through the clouds, and brought sunshine and the remembrance of God's promise to light.

We are just now enjoying fine weather, and every thing seems to praise God for his goodness to us.

The usual excitement incident to camp life prevails to a great extent in the battalion; the boys enjoying themselves hugely with every thing that turns up, consoling themselves with the remark, "It's all in the three years," and hence is to be borne with as good a grace as possible.

The pay-master visited us on the 6th of last month, and left a good stock of "green-backs" behind, though I consider it somewhat doubtful whether a large stock can be found at the present time. The usual results followed the pay-master's visit, but everything has assumed its usual quiet at the present time.

Occasionally, at the dark hour of midnight, we are turned from our beds by the beating of the "long roll," when we await, with breathless suspense, the appearance of the foe. But no foe appears, and we seek our couches again for the rest from which we have been summarily torn by a false and needless alarm.

Military matters in this department are somewhat active. Troops are constantly going down the river, and it is very evident that earnest, decisive work is anticipated in the approaching campaign. What our part is to be remains to be seen. As soldiers, it is our first duty to obey orders, so we must be content with whatever purports to be our lot. . . .

We have the use of the old Methodist Church in town, where the boys hold services two or three times a week. We have an excellent Sabbath School headed by one of our members, and every thing looks bright for the cause of Christ. Our doors are thrown open to all, and large numbers of our race in this locality take advantage of these opportunities to increase their sphere of knowledge, and make them wise and more useful among their brethren at home. God is blessing us by these means of grace, and we earnestly pray that much good may be done in the name of the Lord Jesus.

The cause of the nation is everywhere brightening, and soon I believe the rebellion will succumb. The victorious armies of freedom will continue their triumphant march through the South until victory shall perch upon all our banners, and the Prince of Peace, clad in the beautiful garments of liberty and righteousness, will reign in all our borders, North, South, East, and West. Then will Christ acknowledge us, and make us, indeed, that people whose God shall be the Lord.

LETTER 59

(James C. Taylor, Orderly Sergeant, Co. A, 93d USCI, Bashear City, Louisiana, April 14, 1865; *CR*, May 6, 1865) Sergeant Taylor, born free and raised in Statesville, Pennsylvania, served in a Louisiana regiment made up of French-speaking ex-slaves. They told him about the horrors of slavery; he told them about the better life of freedom.

Through the kindness of my sister, Mrs. E. J. Sterrett, one of your subscribers, I received a copy of your valuable paper last evening. I read it over and over again to the members of my company, which afforded a great deal of pleasure. Being all creoles of this state, and born in slavery, they had not the chance of learning to read. Among ourselves the conversations are carried on in French; in fact, some of us can speak very little English.

There is an old man in my Company, that showed me the scars on his back where his master had whipped him until the blood stood in puddles at his feet. And what for? For praying to the Almighty God. Nor is this the only case of fiendish cruelty that has been done for the same offense, that is, if it is an offense to bow ourselves down and worship Him who gave up his only begotten Son to die on the cross, that sinful man might be saved through repentance.

But God, in his divine wisdom, through the instrumentality of our noble President Abraham Lincoln, saw fit to remove the only dark spot (slavery) from one of the most glorious flags the sun ever shone upon.

And to show our gratitude we are now fighting, and ask no more glorious death than to die for it. But for our race to go back into bondage again, to be hunted by dogs through the swamps and cane-brakes, to be set up on the block and sold for gold and silver, and what is yet meaner (Confederate money) no never; gladly would we die first.

We now, and have been for the last eight months doing garrison duty at one of the southwest outposts of the defenses of New Orleans: the rebel pickets are three miles distant in our front. There are scouting parties sent from our Regiment about once a week. Every time we go, we generally have a smart brush with them, which is sometimes right smart for a small party, but generally results in our favor.

(A. J. Bedford, Sergeant, 25th USCI, Fort Pickens, Florida, November 7, 1864; *CR*, March 4, 1865) Fort Pickens, at Pensacola, Florida, served not only for defense against blockade runners but also as a Union base in the Deep South, surrounded by hostile Confederates. Sergeant Alexander Bedford of Philadelphia tells in this letter of raids by rebel troops and of a counterraid by his regiment of African-American soldiers.

. . . With a fort as formidable as Fort Pickens, through whose embrasures between two and three hundred angry-looking howitzers and rifled cannon seem to be angrily looking for a reb, besides there are some sixty-four-gun men-of-war, and some eighteen or twenty smaller ones lying out upon the deep blue sea in front of us, ready at a moment's notice to belch forth their vengeance in to the planks of the vessels of any invading foe, by sea or land, that may approach.

I will tell you of a circumstance that occurred the other night. Our officers of the 25th used to go the grand round every night, and try to fool the pickets. They did it so often that the boys got used to it. But, mind you, the rebels were watching all their movements, so they thought they would take the advantage of our pickets some dark night, and so they did. One rebel officer approached one of the cavalry pickets, same as our own officers, and got so close he just out with his pistol and let our picket down. So then there were some forty rebel pickets came over, and there was a general skirmish among our pickets and the rebel pickets, and out of forty or more that crossed into our lines, there were none that went back. The whole of them were captured and marched off to the guard-house under a heavy escort of guards, and all the casualties that happened to our men was one shot severely, and one run overboard by three rebs and not much hurt, and four or five slightly wounded. The next day the forts opened fire with bomb-shells in and up and down the wood for five or six miles. Fort Pickens, Fort Barrancas, and Fort Reed belched forth fire, ball, and destruction to everything that happened to meet their rage, and we have heard of no rebels since in that quarter.

A few days since, two companies of the 25th, two of the 82d, two of the Louisiana cavalry, and two of the white cavalry, who had been captured rebs and enlisted in the cavalry troops, went out on a scout, a hundred or two miles up the island, to a small town called Mariana, in West Florida, where there was supposed to be some eight hundred or a thousand inhabitants. The general sent the white cavalry into the town to capture all inside from the biggest white reb to the darkest contraband, while two more companies went to the west end of the town to meet them as the cavalry drove them out, but they did not come, for they went in on a trot, but they galloped out, and the general told them to go in again, but they refused, and the general took their battle flag from them, and then he told the Louisiana cavalry to perform that duty, at which they jumped. They had not been in the town many minutes before there was a smoke seen, and rebs skedaddling in all directions, but the infantry stopped them when they came outside of the town, for it was too hot for them to stay in it, as the colored cavalry had the town half burnt down before the general stopped them. It was the women that did all the fighting, for they fired out of the windows and every by-place they met us. One woman walked right into the street with a pistol, and aimed at the general. She fired and shot him in the left arm, breaking it between the shoulder and elbow. Another came out from another place and shot Captain Young, of the 7th Vermont, through the heart, killing him instantly. Then the boys rushed on the women, and they had to bayonet several of them before they could get them out of the way. So we captured one hundred and sixty-seven rebs, including one general and several of the other officers, and two companies of the regiment brought them down the island safe to Fort Pickens, and next came two more companies with two hundred head of cattle – plenty of fresh beef. Now, then came the general, and the Fort Pickens boys with four hundred and fifty contrabands, men, women, and children of all kinds and sizes. As soon as they came to the Fort, we, the 25th boys, gave them our tents, and they put them up in our old camping place, and at night all the companies, B, H, E, and C, made them three kettles of coffee apiece, twelve in all, by the authority of our noble Major [I. W. H.] Reisinger, of the Fort. Then came the cowardly cavalry, with the colored Louisiana cavalry behind them, bringing up the rear with about one hundred and forty horses and mules; so this ends our capture at this time. But if the general had known there were one thousand contrabands just three miles distant on a small plantation, before he got so far away, he would have had all of them. They are going again next week.

LETTER 61

(Milton Harris, Orderly Sergeant, Co. F, 25th USCI, Fort Redoubt, Florida, November 21, 1864; *CR*, December 17, 1864) Daily life at Fort Pickens and its outposts was usually quiet. That left time for the men to think about their living quarters, their health, their officers, and, for many, their education. Sergeant Milton Harris of Lancaster County, Pennsylvania, tells in this letter about his officers, "as good as [those of] any colored regiment that has come from the North."

... The 25th is doing garrison duty now. Our regiment has three forts in charge – Redoubt, Barrancas, and Pekins [Pickens]. Pekins is the principal; Barrancas is the second in size, and Redoubt is the smallest. My company (F) and Company G hold Redoubt, and have nice and comfortable quarters, and we can keep ourselves clean and dry much better than in camp, where we have nothing but shelter tents.

We have had no picket duty to do, as yet, though there is some talk of our regiment being assigned to that important duty. The health of our regiment is getting quite good now. At one time nearly all of our men were sick. My company could not muster but seventeen men fit for duty, and some of the other companies could not muster as many.

We have not yet been in any engagement, with the exception of a part of our regiment, which was sent out on a scouting expedition, and who all returned safely. When the Johnny Rebs saw our boys, they skedaddled away so fast that they could not do much with them. They captured a few of the rebel cavalry. Everything is now quiet with us.

Our chaplain has done a great deal for us in many circumstances. When so many of our men were sick with the scurvy, he went to New Orleans, and got vegetables for us. Our men soon began to mend.

I must say that the 25th Regiment has been blessed with good officers – as good as any colored regiment that has come from the North. They take a deep interest in the boys of the 25th, and endeavor to make everything as pleasant and comfortable as possible. They are going to have a school for us in the fort. Capt. Wm. A. Prickett, of Co. G, has lately returned from New Orleans, with a considerable number of books, for the benefit of our men, in the way of educating them. He has been furnishing them with books, so that a great many of them could learn to read and write. Some of them have improved a great deal by the teaching of the orderly sergeant of that company, Lewis Willis.

Captain Chester A. Greenleaf, of Co. F, is one who takes a deep interest in getting books for our men. He has already furnished quite a number.

Our regular school has not yet commenced. We expect to begin this week. I will tell you about it the next time I write.

LETTER 62

("A Colored Soldier," 25th USCI, Fort Pickens, Florida, December 19, 1864, and January 21, 1865; *Philadelphia Press*, February 15, 1865) Among the thousands of African Americans who served in the Union Army there must have been hundreds of remarkable stories of individual soldiers who fought against their former masters. One of them who joined a Pennsylvania regiment tells a white friend what happened when the Confederate Army tried to use black troops.

"For whom will the colored soldiers fight?"

In answer to this question we give below a significant fact, copied from letters received by a gentleman of this city from a fugitive slave, who was employed by the former on his farm in New Jersey, the once-slave now being a freeman and belonging to the 25th United States Colored Regiment, garrisoning Fort Pickens, Florida. This young colored man, though unable to tell one letter of the alphabet from another at the time of his escape from his master, at the battle of Gettysburg, was nevertheless quite intelligent and appears now to be able to write his own letters. He was the body servant of Captain Gilbert, of South Carolina, who lost a leg at the above-named battle. After conveying his master from the field to one of the hospitals in the vicinity, he fled to the land of liberty, and is now fighting on the side of our common country. Here are the extracts:

"Fort Pickens, Florida
"Dec 19 1864 and Jan 21 1865

"Dear Friend: When our regiment arrived at Fort Pickens, after leaving Philadelphia, I cannot tell the joy I felt at seeing my brother there, who had escaped from slavery in South Carolina like myself. I knew him at once, but he did not know me, as we had not seen each other for seven years. We had both become men in that time, and both are now serving our country against the rebels, who held us wrongfully in slavery. Our mother was not born a slave, but our father was, and so they held all of us as slaves. . . .[4]

I have not as yet been in any regular battle, but have been on scouting parties a number of times. The last scout we were on we met the rebs, who had six companies of colored soldiers with them, all armed with guns.[5] As soon as the colored soldiers among the rebs saw our colored troops they threw down their arms and ran over to us, crying out '*we are free, we are free!*' This comes of putting arms in the hands of slaves to secure their own bondage. It will always be so, for they all know who are their friends! What will the proposed 200,000 do when armed by their masters? We shall speedily know."

LETTER 63

(William H. Watson, [Sergeant,] Co. K, 25th USCI, Barrancas, Florida, February 14, 1865; *CR*, March 18, 1865) Black soldiers

---

4. Legally black children had the same status as their mothers, but in slave states it was difficult for them to protest if white considered them slaves.
5. There is no reliable evidence that the Confederate Army used black troops in the Gulf states.

from Pennsylvania saw slavery at first hand around Pensacola and
Fort Pickens. Sergeant William Watson of Carlisle, Pennsylvania,
reacts with strong emotions to what he saw of slavery.

. . . Our company is divided into two parts, viz, the first and second platoon. The Captain is with the first platoon, stationed at
Ball's Battery, along the Pensacola Bay, and the second is stationed
at Bragg's Ridge, under Lieutenant [James M.] Adams.

We lived in tents all summer, until about five weeks ago, when
we got lumber from the rebels' side, and built barracks. We live
better now. Our Company is doing picket duty, and Co I has been
relieved from Gunboat Point, and Co. G takes their place. Company I has gone into Fort Redoubt. There has been no snow here,
but we have plenty of rain. No mud, but plenty of sand to walk
through. We have got a fine chaplain to our regiment. He came
down to see our little band, and preached to us. I intend to take
your paper as long as I live. If I ever get out the war, I can sit down
at my mother's house and read to her. I enlisted on the 11th of
February, 1864. I am more than one year in the army, and do not
wish to go home till every slave in the South is set free. I often sit
down and hear the old mothers down here tell how they have been
treated. It would make your heart ache. But never mind; there is a
day coming when there will be no such thing known as lashing the
colored man till the blood runs down his back in streams. They
have frequently shown me the deep marks of the cruel whip upon
their backs.

Oh! is not this picture enough to curdle the blood in the veins
and make the heart stand still in horror? In a Christian land – in
the 19th century – a human being pinioned to a stake so tightly that
the veins of this forehead and brawny arms start out and burst in
his agony – lashed right unto death, and then dragged into the old
cotton-shed to linger and to die! Oh, if there be a God of mercy
and justice, how fearful is the crime of those who uphold slavery!

Come with me, ye victims of prejudice, where the grave of the white and the black soldier lie side by side, and tell me which is the colored man and which is the white, and which of the two you would rather be? Would you base your answer upon color?

The rebels that come in here look hard, being but half-clothed. And to see the poor colored people brought in by our soldiers when they go out on raids! It is shameful. We have rumors of peace going to be made before a great while. . . .

LETTER 64

(Theodore A. Anthony, Sergeant, 20th USCI, Pascagoula, Mississippi, [March 1865]; *WAA*, March 25, 1865) Mobile, Alabama, was still in Confederate hands late in the war. The Union Army marched overland in the spring of 1865 to attack the city. Sergeant Anthony of Jamaica, New York, describes in this letter his adventures along the way from New Orleans.

. . . We had orders to pack up and get ready to march. We were in marching order at 12 o'clock. We took our rubber and woolen blankets and three days rations. We marched from our camp to Lake Point, which is 17 miles from New Orleans. We arrived at the dock at 8 o'clock and found the transport waiting for us. We were sent to reinforce Gen. Ranger[?] at West Pascagoula; but he had defeated the rebs and caused them to retreat 14 miles on the road toward Mobile.

We landed at 6 o'clock this morning; and it was well we did, for our rations had given out. We had no trouble, however, in getting what we wanted, for the rebs had left cows, hogs, chickens, sheep and sweet potatoes. When we got there the colonel told us to slay and eat. In ten minutes there were fires through all the camp and each man cooking for himself. It was fun to see the boys chasing the cows and sheep over the fields and through the woods, and see them come with half a sheep on their backs and poke a stick through it, and roast it over the fire. Well, after we got a full supply of food we set to work to build our tents which we made of pine boughs. When we had finished that, there was still something wanting; such as chairs and tables. We soon found some in the houses of the rebs, and of a quality that not only soldiers but citizens might be glad to own. We only laid on beadsteads and sat on chairs one night, for Gen Ranger heard of it and ordered us to take them back, for, he said, we were getting too grand; he wanted us to understand that we did not come there on a pic-nic. I did not blame him, for I thought we were laying the thing on a little too thick. Our fun did not last long, for we were there but five days when we had orders to move from there, and go 15 miles further towards Mobile, to East Pascagoula, where I expect we will stay until the attack on Mobile, in which fight I suppose our regiment will join. We are looking for an attack in the rear. We have a large land force and are lying under cover of the gunboats.

LETTER 65

(Cassius M. Clay Alexander, 1st Sergeant, Co. C, 50th USCI, Mobile, Alabama [October 1865]; *WAA*, November 18, 1865) Mobile, Alabama, fell to Union troops on April 9, 1865. Its main defense was Fort Blakely, built with the aid of black Union soldiers who had been captured elsewhere in the South. There was some justice, therefore, in that black regiments played a major role in capturing the fort. Sergeant Alexander of Lexington, Kentucky, recalls in this letter some of the fighting at Mobile.

I have never before attempted to pen a line for your columns, but in this case I am compelled to, because I have been waiting patiently to see if I could see anything in regard to our noble Regiment, and have seen nothing. We have fought and captured

Blakesly's Fort. We were only ten days on the siege, and had nothing to eat but Parched Corn. But as luck would have it, I crept out
of my hole at night and scared one of the Jonnys so bad that he left
his rifle pit, gun and accouterments, also one corn dodger and
about one pint of buttermilk, all of which I devoured with a will,
and returned to my hole safe and sound. After sleeping the remainder of the night, about day I was awakened by our turtle-
backs[6] that were playing with the enemy's works. At that time I
forgot myself and poked my head out of my hole, and came very
near getting one of Jonny's cough pills. We had to keep our heads
down all the time or else run the risk of getting shot. So me and my
friend of whom I was speaking had it all that day, shooting at each
other. Finally, he got hungry and cried out to me, "Say, Blacky, let's
stop and eat some Dinner." I told him, "All right." By the time I
thought he was done eating, I cried, "Hello, Reb." He answered,
"What do you want?" I said, "Are you ready?" "No, not yet," he
said. Then I waited for a while. I finally got tired and cried for a
chew of tobacco. He then shot at me and said, "Chew that!" I
thanked him kindly and commenced exchanging shots with him.

I must not take too much time in relating all the incidents, for
Parched Corn takes the day also. We have accomplished all under-
takings, and excel in the drill. We ask nothing now but to be
mustered out.

6. A nickname for the ironclad "monitors."

5

Occupation Duty

ON JANUARY 30, 1865, Chaplain Henry M. Turner crossed the Cape Fear River from Fort Fisher to Smithville, North Carolina. His regiment, the 1st U.S. Colored Infantry, occupied Smithville after Confederate troops fled; they were the first black soldiers the local people had ever seen, and Turner was certainly the first black officer.

Turner's primary job was to recruit freed slaves for the Union Army. He made speeches, cared for the sick, and visited the homes of all he could reach. "Recruiting in this department goes on finely," he wrote. "We have enlisted several hale, stalwart-looking fellows, whom we think will fill their places nicely. One man wants his gun now, so he can get to killing right off."

Slaves from adjacent counties fled to Smithville, and Turner observed them closely. "They are coming in by droves, sometimes fifteen or twenty in a gang, some of whom are pitiful-looking creatures. Oh," he wrote, "how the foul curse of slavery has blighted the natural greatness of my race!" As a Methodist minister, Turner did not like the morality of the slaves; they had been encouraged to breed and produce new slaves for their owners. But he found them eager not only to join the army but also to enter school, start new churches, and work as free people. There was much to be done among them, and he urged his Northern readers to come to the South to serve the freedmen.

Southern whites also attracted Turner's attention. "White people," he wrote, "nearly without exception, showed a bitter and chagrined countenance" in Smithville. "Small squads of rebels could be seen standing on the corners, conversing, I presumed, over the dubious records of blighted prospects." A black woman had argued with two white women about ownership of some firewood; Turner had defended the black and threatened to arrest the whites. Next day, he met two of them: "Two of the same party met me on the street, and when they saw I was going to take the inside of the pavement, they gazed at me with unrestricted frowns, and rubbed the very palings to compel me to go into the street and give them the entire side-walk; but I returned the gazing compliment and kept on until we had effected a collision."

The change from slavery to freedom in Smithville created problems. Not only did it make race relations more difficult; it also left the ex-slaves without work. According to Chaplain Turner, some landowners offered their former servants contracts to work for the year; the farmers were "offering them the use of their present homes (slave huts) and the use of their horses, wagons, lands, and other farming utensils." In return, the former slave was to pay the owner one-third of the proceeds from the farm. Turner suspected that this was a plan to keep the blacks in bondage: "This ingenious trickery is designed to keep the old master fat doing nothing, making the Yankees believe 'dis old nigga no wants to leave massa,' and for the purpose of fizzling them out of all their claims upon the real estate."[1]

1. H. M. Turner to Editor, *CR*, February 25, March 4, 18, and 25, 1865.

Chaplain Turner's experiences in Smithville were a preview of what other Northern African Americans would see while occupying the defeated Confederacy. In the spring and summer of 1865 the army became the only official government in the ex-Confederate states. Once the fighting stopped in a particular place, the Union Army left units behind to keep order, guard against guerrilla attack, and protect the helpless. Many of those units were black.

Black soldiers were particularly hard for Southern whites to accept. Even though slavery was gone, racial tensions still thrived. Many of the Union soldiers had recently been slaves, and their presence constantly reminded whites that they had lost the war, lost their independence, lost their wealth, and lost their status. Their first reaction was sullen bitterness, usually quiet but sometimes violent. As the summer went on, and as President Andrew Johnson let the Southern states have more and more self-government, whites became more openly hostile to occupying black soldiers. The soldiers, in response, wrote that the only real protection from racism was the right to vote.

Although most of the white officers of the black troops were loyal to their men, many others shared the race prejudice of the white Southerners. Such officers often sided with the ex-rebels against the soldiers. With the dangers of war ended, these white officers were free to be unfair, harsh, even brutal to their black men. The men, especially those from the Northern states, complained bitterly about their treatment.

Most of those Northern African Americans were seeing slaves and the slave system for the first time. They believed that their own destiny was closely tied to that of the slaves, so they observed the freedmen closely. The downfall of the slave system made problems for the ex-slaves: How could they make a living without land to farm? How could they find their relatives? How could they compete without money or education? How could they get free of racism? But it also made opportunities. They were no longer bound to an owner. They could have their own churches and schools. They could marry and live as families. When Northern black soldiers had opportunities to watch the freedmen closely, they could see not only the problems left by slavery but also the newly opened doors. The troops wrote about the joy of the slaves when freedom came, and they told how they were welcomed by the black population as they marched into Southern cities and towns. They told how the freedmen, with the help of black soldiers from the North, started new schools. Black chaplains helped start new churches where the people could hear sermons on something other than how to be good slaves.

Most African-American soldiers had enlisted for three years; hence they were expected to stay in the army at least through 1865. Most white soldiers had enlisted earlier, and when the fighting stopped they were discharged earlier. This made many black troops unhappy: They were as eager as the whites to get home to their families. But most of them were disappointed. Some were mustered out as early as August 1865; most of the men from the Northern states were out by Christmas, but many regiments raised in the slave states had to serve out their full three-year enlistments. Once the war ended, they wrote of their longing to be home.

Soldiers from the Northern states wrote home about their occupation duties. The first letters came from North Carolina, where several regiments of African Americans had helped liberate Fort Fisher and Wilmington. Those regiments had then joined General William T. Sherman's march through the Carolinas and occupied other towns and Roanoke Island. When the Confederate government and army abandoned Richmond, Virginia, on April 2, 1865, black soldiers were among the very first troops to occupy the city; but they were quickly moved away to other places. Several black regiments stayed in and near Jacksonville, Florida, during 1864 and 1865. When the fighting ended, some were sent to other towns, such as Tallahassee, Lake City, and Gainesville, to establish law and order. Kentucky, of course, had not seceded from the Union; nevertheless, it was a slave state, and black soldiers based there helped officials emancipate the slaves when the war ended. In

Louisiana, Northern black troops had served since 1863, but once the fighting stopped, they found themselves victims of the prejudice and hatred of their racist officers and defeated enemies.

Texas was a special case of occupation duty. As soon as Federal authority was established in and around Richmond, Virginia, African-American soldiers were transferred from there to Texas. General Henry W. Halleck, military governor of Virginia, thought the black troops not well disciplined enough for occupation duty there. So he ordered them to help set up Federal control in southern Texas, from Corpus Christi to the Rio Grande. This occupation was aimed not only at the former rebels in Texas but also at the new government in Mexico, which had been taken over by the French. Most of the black troops were unhappy about being sent so far away from their families. They suffered from boredom, fever, racism, and homesickness. Although most of the regiments in Texas went home to civilian life by December 1865, some stayed on until 1867.[2]

The letters in this chapter are arranged first by place and then by date of writing.

NORTH CAROLINA

LETTER 66

(J. H. Payne, Sergeant, 27th USCI, Wilmington, North Carolina, February 28, 1865; *CR*, March 18, 1865) Quartermaster Sergeant James H. Payne had been a minister in the African Methodist Episcopal Church in Lima, Ohio, before he had enlisted in the army. When his regiment got to Wilmington, he saw the release of

2. Glatthaar, *Forged in Battle*, 207–230. Berlin, Reidy, and Rowland, *The Black Military Experience*, 733–764.

some prisoners of war by the Confederates. Rumors about their mistreatment abounded, but the reality was just as bad.

I take this opportunity of writing you and the numerous readers of your highly esteemed and interesting paper, a brief letter, in order that you may know we are safe in the town of Wilmington, North Carolina. Our arrival in this city was quite unexpected to us, as we expected to meet the land forces at Fort Fisher; but, to our great and happy disappointment, when our transport, the "Daniel Webster," arrived in the harbor at Fort Fisher, we were informed that our troops had passed Wilmington, and were ten miles north of the town. Hence, the boat landed us on the wharf at this noble-looking little town, which has been so long disgraced by the cause of slavery. But now, thank God, the foul curse is swept away, and at present, the atmosphere seems in a little healthier state.

Last Sabbath was our people's great day of Jubilee. It was their first free Sabbath. Oh! could you have been here to witness their expressions and tokens of joy on that occasion, even in their religious exercises, you could not otherwise than [have] been animated and delighted to hear and see them.

Our men here are enlisting very fast. We have recruiting offices open, and they are generally delighted with the opportunity which presents itself for their enlistment.

Chaplain W. H. Hunter addressed the citizens of color in this place yesterday, by way of encouraging the young men to enlist. I am sorry I was not apprised of the fact until too late to attend the meeting.

While I am writing this letter, I am surrounded by nearly a thousand of our Union prisoners who have been brought in under a flag of truce. Of all the wretchedness ever my eyes beheld, I never saw any thing equal to the appearance of these suffering, famished, and half-starved men. Some of them were without shoes to cover their torn and bleeding feet, while others were without even a hat. Most of them wore the old clothes the rebels had thrown away. They truly presented a picture of distress and despair, which would cause the hardest heart to ache and feel for them.

But the worst of all which has disgraced the Southern Confederacy, and will continue to be a stain on their character forever – is their barbarism. The rebels, just before our men entered the town, tied the sick prisoners up by their heels in the barracks, set fire to the barracks, and *burnt them alive.* This, I am assured by good authority, is a positive fact. I recollect of but one case which surpasses this in wickedness, which we have in Josephus. He informs us of a woman who was in such a pitiable condition from starvation, in the time of the destruction of Jerusalem, that she slew and ate her own child.

There is another wicked act of the rebels here which they practice toward the Union prisoners, especially the colored ones. They give them nothing but corn-meal and rice, and allow them no tobacco. When any of the citizens would bring them something to eat, the guards would take it from them, and trample it under foot. I am almost ready to believe that any punishment that may be inflicted hereafter upon such base men is hardly sufficient for their wicked crimes. But yet I should content myself to know by the authority of God's word that every man will be punished according to his crimes. Though the wicked may go on hand in hand for a while, yet they shall not escape punishment.

LETTER 67

("Arnold," Wilmington, North Carolina, March 29, 1865; *CR,* April 15, 1865) After getting free of slavery, one of the first things blacks in the South wanted to do was to get their own churches. "Arnold," probably a soldier in the 4th USCI, tells in this letter

how the black Methodists of Wilmington got their church with the
help of the army.

February 20th – We had something of a skirmish with one of
General [Braxton] Bragg's "bad men," General [Robert] Hoke,
and as usual he fell back. On the 21st, we built a line, and bivouacked for the night; being only four miles from the largest and
oldest city in the State. We asked ourselves as well as others, "How
would you like to march through Wilmington tomorrow, February
22d, the anniversary of the birthday of Washington?" The answer
was, "It would be the proudest moment of my life!" But little does
a soldier know when, or at what time, he may be ordered to "fall
in." We slept behind our works that night. The 22d came, and a
more lovely day I never saw. By half pat six o'clock we were on the
move, as General Hoke had evacuated during the night, and one
hour's march brought us on the corporation line of Wilmington,
when large volumes of smoke were seen rising in the eastern part
of the city. For a time, we thought Hoke had set fire to the city as he
went through. But not so. It was the burning of cotton and turpen-
tine at and near the Wilmington and Weldon Railroad. The column halted for a few moments, when the mayor met General
[Alfred] Terry, and begged for protection. We finally moved, and
entered the blockaded city of the Confederacy – the place where
all the southern and some of the northern men have made their
piles of money – the once [rising] city of the Confederacy; the
place noted for its slave market! But now, alas! we march through
these fine thoroughfares, where once the slave was forbid[den]
being out after nine P.M., or to puff a "regalia," or to walk with a
cane, or to ride in a carriage! Negro soldiers! with banners floating!
with their splendid brass bands and drum corps, discoursing the
National airs and marches! – the colored division of the 25th army
corps, commanded by General Charles J. Payne. It would be a
mere attempt for one such as myself to describe the manner in

which the colored people of Wilmington welcomed the Union troops – cheer after cheer they gave us – they had prayed long for their deliverance, and the 22d day of February, 1865, realized their earnest hopes. Were they not happy that day? Free, for evermore! The streets were crowded with them, old and young; they shook hands with the troops, and some exclaimed, "The chain is broken!" "Joy! Freedom today!" "Hurrah for Uncle Abe!"

"There goes my son!" said a lady. "Which one?" asked a corporal. "That one, just gone ahead!" And, sure enough, it was her son. She overtook him and embraced him; and how proudly she felt, none but those similarly situated can ever feel. The man knew that his mother was living when he entered the service, for some friend had so informed him. He had left his home a slave, but had returned in the garb of a Union soldier, free, a man. Similar incidents have happened in other colored regiments. At one corner, near the market, the colored people had boxes of tobacco which they distributed to the troops as they passed. At almost every door was a bucket of water; and, in many places, ladies gave bread and meat to the boys, saying, "'Tis the best we have." The farther we advanced, the more numerous the people. At one corner, my attention was attracted to a crowd who were "jumping for joy!" One old man among them said he was nearly ninety-three years old, and had not been in the street since last July; but hearing the music of the Union troops, it had revived him, and he felt so happy that he came out; and there he stood, with his long white locks and his wrinkled cheeks, saying, "Welcome, welcome!"

We passed out of the town, and were soon on Hoke's track. We came up with him at North East Bridge, or Station, nine miles from town – the 4th, 6th, and 30th U.S.C.T. Gen. [Samuel] Duncan's Brigade, gave him battle at this place, and during the night – as usual – Gen. Hoke retired.

Back to Wilmington

On the 25th, details from the different regiments were made for the purpose of recruiting. War meetings were announced, and the work went bravely on. Gen. Payne's Division obtained near one thousand men in a few days.

What I saw while in town

One of the first things I did while in the city was to take a view of the A.M.E. Church that I have heard so much of. Having the good fortune to be introduced to Mr. Edward Avis, he kindly volunteered to accompany me. The church is built in the latest style, and is very commodious, seats sixteen hundred persons, has a large and convenient gallery, and splendid basement. It is situated on "Zion's Hill," so named by the Rev. Wm. Meredith, the founder of the church. On each side of the steps are two marble slabs, one dedicated to the Rev. Mr. Meredith, the other to a South Carolina Bishop. The former is on the left side, and reads:

"This marble is erected in Memory of the late William Meredith, who died in 1799, by those for whom in life he labored." The ground on which this church stands was willed by this man to the colored people of Wilmington, N.C. Shortly after his death a church was built; some years after it was burned, another was built; this was burned. When the colored people began another the whites interfered, and informed them that unless they had white people to act with them, no church could be erected. Thus was their plan to build a place for worshiping God severed. Finding them otherwise as the whites desired impossible, they of course had to yield. The church was finished; the colored people, who paid the largest portion of the money, and who owned the ground, were not allowed to assemble in it unless a white man was present. Marriage ceremonies among the colored people must be in the basement. "Your seat is in the Gallery." Thus it was until February 22d, 1865, when things generally in Wilmington took a sudden change. The first sermon ever delivered in Wilmington, N.C., by a colored man was by Rev. [William] H. Hunter, Chaplain of the 4th U.S.C.T, who will be known as the second Meredith. The present, or at least the late pastor, Mr. Burkhead, strongly objected; but the colored leaders insisted, and on Sunday, March 5th, 1865, at 8 o'clock P.M., "Old Bethel" was crowded. Among the distinguished persons I recognized General Harley [Joseph R. Hawley] and staff, General [Henry] Abbot, and many of Generals [John] Schofield and [Alfred] Terry's staffs, and a number of officers of the navy, and a host of persona from all parts of the world. The audience as it was, could not be excelled in regard to decorum or interest to the sermon.

Immediately over the pulpit reads: "For my house shall be called a house of prayer for all people." Thirteen leaders were represented, and they are worthy of their titles, not only as of this church, but of the very best society and morality that can be found. Accompanied by the Rev. Jeremiah Asher, Chaplain, 6th U.S.C.T., Mr. Hunter entered. Robed in his army uniform, that manly form failed, I am sure, to please the eye of one or two Secesh Gents, who came, not to hear him preach, but to see what was going to be done by the Negroes, and how the Negroes were going to act.

The hymn chosen was "Sing unto the Lord a new song." I thought, as did others, that it was the best singing we ever heard. The text was from Psalms: "Sing unto the lord a new song, for he hath done marvelous things; with his right arm he hath gotten him the victory." Eloquence never flowed so freely as on that day: few in the church could say their eyes were dry. Mr. Hunter himself was born a slave on this very soil; sixteen years previously he left the state a slave. But now he come to the land of his birth an officer in the United States Army. Was not that congregation of citizens proud of him? Yes! they are; they will never cease to remember him. How can they? He worked day and night for them.

He had interviews with General Schofield and with General Terry, when finally he showed the letter he received from the former, informing the colored people that they should be protected while worshiping God according to the dictates of their own conscience and loyalty to the Government of the United States, and, that they might choose whom they desired to preach to them the Gospel. Mr. Hunter has thus turned over to the A.M.E. Church of the United States the largest Methodist congregation of any city that has been in the Confederacy. Every leader voted for being transferred to the A.M.E. Church of the U.S., and each voted for the bill which dispensed with the services of the white pastor, Mr. Burkhead, of the M.E. Church South, and who still thought his church in authority.

"Freedmen's schools"

Nearly or quite seven hundred children were in the basement of the church on March 11th, it having been announced that schools were about to be organized. Speeches were made by Mr. Asher, Mr. Hunter, Mr. Conn, and Mr. [Mansfield] French, A[merican] M[issionary] A[ssociation], and others. At 10:30 Brig. General [Joseph] Hawley entered and spoke for half an hour. He, as all others, was pleased with the children, and I heard several say that a more intelligent body of little ones they never saw, and it was just so. One little boy, Master Horte (slave), made a neat speech to that vast audience of people from all parts, and strangers to him. Some little Misses made little speeches, and did it as though it was common to them, and they sang splendidly.

The above named gentlemen, assisted by Misses Day, Sampson, and Cowan, organized the school, and it is now in splendid running order. The "underground" schools have been taught in this city for a number of years by the young ladies and others. . . . The people are generally refined and well informed. Union to the bone, liberal and modest. Almost, or I may say, all of the colored people have been engaged in the business of hiding Yankee prisoners. Almost every house in the city occupied by colored people has done this favor for our prisoners. . . .

LETTER 68

(J. H. Payne, [Sergeant,] 27th USCI, Wilmington, North Carolina, August 12, 1865; *CR*, August 19, 1865) North Carolina was quick to reorganize its government under the guidance of President Andrew Johnson. That meant that the prewar white leadership gained control and started passing laws that kept blacks from voting or using other freedoms. Sergeant Payne describes this state of affairs for readers in the North.

As to the conditions of things as they are, and appear to exist here in the city of Wilmington, and I may say throughout North Carolina. So far as I can learn, trouble and destitution, as well as hatred and revenge, await our poor people in these Southern States, and it is to be regretted that the President has left so much to be decided by the choice of the prejudiced loyal white men of the South in the reconstruction of the States. Here the black man, though having fought to bring peace to the distracted country, after the victory is obtained, can have no voice in making the laws which are to govern his future destiny in this country. No, but he must sit in a state of perfect dormancy, as though he were under slavery's cruel power still.

I wonder, as the Southern black man has got sense enough to fight for this country, if he ain't got sense enough to vote, whether he is educated or not. It seems to me, if he knew where to strike with his steel and firearms, he will also know where to strike with his vote. The opinion of most white men in reference to the colored man is something like the opinion of some people about the turtle: they say the turtle has all kinds of meats in him. So the white men of this nation, or at least a majority of them, think the same of the colored man; they think he has all kinds of material in him, and seem to be under doubts as to which of these principles will prevail in the colored man, whether this or that. But one principle they seem to be determined shall not prevail, and that is the pure principle of his manhood; for they say, "We will not give him the privilege of developing that principle."

But the President has left the matter of reconstruction with the loyal whites of the South, and now the argument attempted to be deduced is this: that no colored man should be allowed to vote, unless he can read and write. Now, if this is to be the motto, let it be applied to all men, for one unlearned man is just as unqualified to vote as another.

But this would cripple the President's decision, for it would cut off a large portion of the votes of the loyal white men of the South, who must, by their votes, assist in the reconstruction of our State laws. Then, in order to justify themselves in this matter, they plead the colored man's inferiority to the white race. But they forget that we have proved ourselves their superiors in every privilege we have been permitted to enjoy. . . .

There is a great deal to be done yet before the full attainment of our liberty in this country, and none can accomplish so great a work but God, and He alone. Then let every minister among us teach his congregation the importance of asking God in every petition to turn the strong current of prejudice away from us. May our God work marvelous things for us now and forever. Amen.

LETTER 69

(N. B. Sterrett, [Commissary Sergeant,] 39th USCI, Kinston, North Carolina, July 2, 1865; *CR*, July 8, 1865) Sergeant Norman B. Sterrett of Baltimore describes race relations in the small town of Kinston. Citizens of the town reacted strongly to the presence of the "smoked Yankees" in their midst, and one soldier was killed by a local rebel.

. . . Kinston would be a very fine little town, if the inhabitants did not consist of inveterate secessionists. The town is inhabited principally by them, and no place is pretty or nice that has a rebel in it. The introduction of a colored regiment here was perfectly exasperating to the citizens. I heard them calling in all manner of names that were never applied to the Deity, to deliver them from the hands of the *smoked Yankees*. But their prayers in this case were like all others offered by rebel hearts; and the next thing they saw was the *smoked Yankees* marching some of their fellow citizens to jail at the point of a bayonet.

There are a great many colored people here, but civilization is very much needed among them.

Rev. Mr. [James] Hood came here the first sabbath after we arrived, and organized a church.[3] I was very much surprised to find that he had not organized one before, as he has so often passed this place.

Our camp ground is a few hundred yards from the city, upon the plantation of Sir John G. Washington. His house is occupied as head quarter. It is a large brick building. This gentleman was the owner of some 400 or 500 slaves, and when the Union forces entered this State, he scattered them for hundreds of miles around. Master John comes out occasionally to see his old house. But instead of seeing the negroes busy at work, he finds a number of gigantic soldiers (colored) going through the manual of arms second to none. I imagine that I can hear his heart praying for days of slavery to roll back. But it is no use, Mr. Washington, for thou in thy life-time hast received many good things and thy slaves likewise evil. But now they are comforted and thou art tormented. . . . The citizens of Goldsboro, I learn, have sent to the head authorities to have a colored regiment sent back there. I think their attempts will prove fruitless. We are needed in other places of more importance.

Since writing the above, David C. Bracker, of Co. F, has been brought into camp a corpse. He was shot by a notorious rebel by the name of John Henry Jackson. Col. [Ozora] Stearns has ordered out squads of men to scour the country, until he is caught and brought to camp, there to receive his merited punishment.

LETTER 70

(William H. Brown, [Private,] Co. C, 1st USCI, Roanoke Island, North Carolina, July 6, 1865; *CR*, July 22, 1865) Roanoke Island

3. Hood was a missionary of the African Methodist Episcopal Zion Church.

had been taken by Union troops early in 1862. It soon became a temporary home for thousands of contrabands, slaves who had escaped to Federal lines. When the war ended, the island was garrisoned by a black regiment. Private William H. Brown of Washington, D.C., tells in this letter how the people on Roanoke Island celebrated Independence Day, 1865.

It may be that some of your readers would be pleased to know how we spent the Fourth of July on Roanoke Island. I am a very poor writer, but I hope you will excuse all defects.

About sunrise there were 36 cannons fired, which sounded very much like war times, and appeared to arouse the very fish in the waters. The band then played several airs, and every body seemed to be alive. About 9 o'clock our Regiment turned out, the soldiers marching to the music of the drum corps, and then halting in front of head quarters, where the old flag was flung to the breeze amid the cheers of the assembled multitudes.

By this time about 3500 persons had collected. The regiment then stacked arms, and our most worthy and industrious chaplain, H[enry] M. Turner, came along with his little wife by his side, who, by the way, appears to be a noble woman. Taking his position in front under a shade tree, he delivered one of the finest orations, I can safely say, that was ever heard on this island. Mr. Turner has always been the idol of our men, he goes with us every where in cold or heat, battle or sickness, he is always there, and every time he has something new to say. I could not realize that I had ever heard him before.

In his address to the Fourth, he reviewed the history of the country from the discovery by Columbus, and spoke on slavery from its inaugurating until it was destroyed by the proclamation of our lamented President. He concluded by paying the nation's flag a glorious tribute; he said the extremities of color, white and black in this country, had made it the world's theatre, and that every despotic nation under heaven should yet dance to American music, and that Daniel's stone made it the regulation in 1776, and would make its last when the whole world would be one great republic, and that as soon as God would knock down the wall of prejudice between the whites and blacks, sectional divisions would crumble into dust throughout the entire Globe. He handled his subject in a masterly manner, and the secessionists that heard him looked wild at its conclusion. Every body then returned to their homes, and the rest of the day went off quietly.

VIRGINIA

LETTER 71

(Garland H. White, Chaplain, 28th USCI, Richmond, Virginia, April 12, 1865; *CR*, April 22, 1865) Richmond, the capital of the Confederacy, had been the main target of Union armies since 1861. When General Robert E. Lee abandoned the city on April 2, 1865, black soldiers who had besieged it for months rushed to be the first Union troops to enter. Among them was Chaplain Garland H. White, who had been born and raised nearby as a slave. In this moving letter he tells of his experiences on that first day in Richmond.

I have just returned from the city of Richmond; my regiment was among the first that entered that city. I marched at the head of the column, and soon I found myself called upon by the officers and men of my regiment to make a speech, with which, of course, I readily complied. A vast multitude assembled on Broad Street, and I was aroused amid the shouts of ten thousand voices, and proclaimed for the first time in that city freedom to all mankind. After which the doors of all the slave pens were thrown open, and thousands came out shouting and praising God, and Father, or Master Abe, as they termed him. In this mighty consternation I became so overcome with tears that I could not stand up under the pressure of such fullness of joy in my own heart. I retired to gain strength, so I lost many important topics worthy of note.

Among the densely crowded concourse there were parents looking for children who had been sold south of this state in tribes, and husbands came for the same purpose; here and there one was singled out in the ranks, and an effort was made to approach the gallant and marching soldiers, who were too obedient to orders to break ranks.

We continued our march as far as Camp Lee, at the extreme end of Broad Street, running westwards. In camp the multitude followed, and everybody could participate in shaking the friendly but hard hands of the poor slaves. Among the many broken-hearted mothers looking for their children who had been sold to Georgia and elsewhere, was an aged woman, passing through the vast crowd of colored, inquiring for [one] by the name of Garland H. White, who had been sold from her when a small boy, and was bought by a lawyer named Robert Toombs, who lived in Georgia.[4] Since the war has been going on she has seen Mr. Toombs in Richmond with troops from his state, and upon her asking him where his body-servant Garland was, he replied: "He ran off from me at Washington, and went to Canada. I have since learned that he is living somewhere in the State of Ohio." Some of the boys knowing that I lived in Ohio, soon found me and said, "Chaplain, here is a lady that wishes to see you." I quickly turned, following the soldier until coming to a group of colored ladies. I was questioned as follows:

"What is your name, sir?"

"My name is Garland H. White."

What was your mother's name?"

"Nancy."

4. Toombs was a U.S. senator and a Confederate secretary of state and general.

"Where was you born?"

"In Hanover County, in this State."

"Where was you sold from?"

"From this city."

"What was the name of the man who bought you?"

"Robert Toombs."

"Where did he live?"

"In the State of Georgia."

"Where did you leave him?"

"At Washington."

"Where did you go then?"

"To Canada."

"Where do you live now?"

"In Ohio."

"This is your mother, Garland, whom you are now talking to, who has spent twenty years of grief about her son."

I cannot express the joy I felt at this happy meeting of my mother and other friends. But suffice it to say that God is on the side of the righteous, and will in due time reward them. I have witnessed several such scenes among the other colored regiments.

Late in the afternoon, we were honored with his Excellency, the President of the United States, Lieutenant-General Grant, and other gentlemen of distinction.[5] We made a grand parade through most of the principal streets of the city, beginning at Jeff Davis's mansion, and it appeared to me that all the colored people in the world had collected in that city for that purpose. I never saw so many colored people in all my life, women and children of all sizes running after Father, or Master Abraham, as they called him. To see the colored people, one would think they had all gone crazy. The excitement at this period was unabated, the tumbling of walls, the bursting of shells, could be heard in all directions, dead bodies being found, rebel prisoners being brought in, starving women and children begging for greenbacks and hard tack, constituted the

5. Lincoln visited Richmond on April 4, 1865.

order of the day. The Fifth [Massachusetts] Cavalry, colored, were still dashing through the streets to protect and preserve the peace, and see that no one suffered violence, they having fought so often over the walls of Richmond, driving the enemy at every point.

Among the first to enter Richmond was the 28th U.S.C.T. – better known as the First Indiana Colored Volunteers. . . .

Some people do not seem to believe that the colored troops were the first that entered Richmond. Why, you need not feel at all timid in giving the truthfulness of my assertion to the four winds of the heavens, and let the angels re-echo it back to the earth, that the *colored soldiers of the Army of the James were the first to enter the city of Richmond*. I was with them, and am still with them, and am willing to stay with them until freedom is proclaimed throughout the world. Yes, we will follow this race of men in search of liberty through the whole Island of Cuba. All the boys are well, and send their love to all the kind ones at home.

FLORIDA

LETTER 72

(William B. Johnson, [Private,] Co. A, 3rd USCI, Jacksonville, Florida, June 22, 1865; *CR*, July 8, 1865) When the war ended, a black regiment went from Jacksonville to occupy Tallahassee, the state capital. As Private William B. Johnson of Philadelphia records in this letter, the local whites gave the black troops a hostile reception.

Our regiment was ordered to Tallahassee on the 19th of May. On the evening of the 20th we marched to Baldwin, and on the morning of the 21st took the cars at Baldwin Station, enroute for Tallahassee. Nothing of note occurred until we arrived at Olustee Station, where one year before, we fought the Confederate forces. The cars stopped for wood, when the platforms of the cars were immediately crowded with white and colored persons all eager to catch a glimpse of the "black soldiers." Some deep-dyed citizen made the remark that all the niggers should be in ———— (a place of not very moderate temperature). A moment afterward, twenty guns were pointed at his heart; and one man more angry and revengeful than the rest discharged his piece, the ball grazing the speaker's head; and if it had been a little closer Johnnie would have been nowhere and would in all probability have received a through ticket for the locality which he named.

For a period of about half an hour, the wildest excitement prevailed around the immediate vicinity.

Finally, Brigadier General B[enjamin] C. Tilghman made his appearance upon the scene and demanded the cause of so much disorder and confusion, and in a little while I saw him lead the wounded man aside with but a little lost grace, and bid him depart in peace, lest a worse evil come upon him.

About half past ten o'clock, the same evening, we arrived at the Capital. The place was wrapped in slumber, and a quietness as profound as that which brooded over Goldsmith's Deserted Village reigned around. No sound arose to break the dead silence, save the soft humming of the steam as it escaped through the valves of the reposing engine.

In the morning, however, we had plenty of visitors, and among them the most inhuman and brutal man that ever lived, in the person of the *Hon.* Benjamin Cheers of Tallahassee; and if ever there was a demon in human form, he is one. The day before we came up, he took one of his slaves, a boy of twelve years, and laid upon his naked back *Three Hundred Lashes*. But thank God, today he stands awaiting his trial. . . .

The rebs here seem to die very hard at the idea of having black troops to guard them, but they have been very quiet, and do not have much to say. How true is the saying that we know not what a day may bring forth! Great changes are being wrought.

On Monday last a man calling himself General Myers stabbed a colored man. He was immediately arrested, and is at this time awaiting his trial. . . .

LETTER 73

(William B. Johnson, [Private,] Co. A, 3rd USCI, Jacksonville, Florida, July 27, 1865; *CR*, August 12, 1865) After a few weeks in Tallahassee, the 3rd USCI was sent back to Jacksonville. Despite the hostility of whites there, Private Johnson recalls some good things that happened back in Tallahassee.

. . . I will say now that few of the old soldiers who enlisted in the beginning of the war remain. Sickness has made a fearful havoc in this regiment.

I wrote to you some time ago that we were ordered to Tallahassee, the capital of the State of Florida. While there the men suffered – fevers raged throughout the camp, and out of 800 men, there were not 300 fit for active service. It being so unhealthy, we were ordered back to Jacksonville, and at present are commencing to improve.

Tallahassee is quite an extensive place, being laid out something like Burlington, N.J. The people of color were glad to see us, and cheer after cheer rent the air as we marched through the principal streets, led by the gallant Brevet Brigadier General B[enjamin] G. Tilghman, with colors flying and our band playing (John Brown's marching on.) The would-be rebels looked on in silence, not daring to speak above a whisper. Gen. [Robert] McCook's battery had taken possession of the town two weeks before we came. I will here state that these men are all from Kentucky, and although they wear the uniform of *Uncle Sam*, some of them are base traitors. The way they treated our colored people was *shameful*. We soon showed them that we came for justice. Justice we wanted, and justice we would have. The leading men of the rebellion showed signs of resistance, and ventured to look upon the nigger soldiers, as they

called us, but when Gen. McCook and staff came and witnessed
our dress parade, and remarked that our men were well drilled,
and in fact looked as well as any soldier he ever saw, they changed
colors, and every day after 5 o'clock, P.M., the parade ground was
covered with spectators. We had to keep a guard to keep off the
crowd. When we left, many remarked that they were sorry we had
to leave, and many colored families followed.

Lake City is the next place that we will inspect. The town is
small, and you can ride around it in two hours time. The inhabitants were inclined to be civil and most of them did all they could
for me. One particular and interesting feature in Lake City: the
road about a mile from town, where the rebels drove the Blacks
into, in the summer of '64, to keep our scouts from bring them to
our lines. Many lost their lives in this way; but thank God they had
their time, and now comes ours. By good behavior, we will show
them that we are men, and able to fill any position in life that we
are placed in. There is only one thing I want; that is my vote; let us
see what time will do.

LETTER 74

(H. S. Harmon [Herman?], [Private,] Co. B. 3d USCI, Gainesville,
Florida, [October 1865]; *CR*, October 21, 1865) Private Harmon,
like many other African-American soldiers, discovered that when
the shooting ended, his white officers revealed their racism. When
the war was still being fought, those officers had urged their men to
forget the old insults and oppressions and join the common struggle against the Confederacy. But now, with the war over for six
months, those white officers had more in common with the white
Southerners than with their own black soldiers.

. . . Since the surrender of the troops in Florida by General Samuel Jones and during the actual existence of the Rebellion, we have
been told by our commanding officers on the eve of battle to forget

old grudges and prejudices, and fight like men for a common cause, meaning for us not to let the unjust and cruel treatment of the officers to the men influence us to a disregard for our duty to our common country. But now there is nothing of the kind to fear, the officers feeling that they have nothing now to fear from stray bullets, are exercising all the arrogance and despotism that their power gives them, and what appeals has an enlisted man if he applies for redress to a superior officer? It can only be endorsed through the officer who is his worst enemy, whose endorsement will be, as a matter of course, the most detrimental to the interest of the soldier. Now we have the tying up by the thumbs of which Mr. Green speaks, on the public streets of the town, and what is called riding the horse, which is two upright posts set in the ground, fully seven feet high, and a three-cornered cross beam, on which the men are compelled to sit astride, and other punishment, which even these people, both white and black, are horrified at witnessing, used to slavery and its horrors as they all are. And for what? Because some of those stanch Union men, many of whom wear the uniform of the so-called Confederacy, and have not to this day taken the oath of allegiance: but their word is sufficient to condemn any amount of colored soldiers, or citizens, for even citizens feel the effect of that most prevalent and baleful disease, negrophobia. Negro citizens, although they have been the only true and avowed friends of the United States Government in this section of the country, are still compelled to feel that they are black, and the smooth oily tongue of the white planter is enough to condemn any number of them to a tying-up for twenty-four hours, or two hours up and one down.

Such, my friends, is what we endure or witness, and if the United States Government ever gets five-year men she will not get them from the veteran 3d Regt. U.S.C.T., until she is compelled to give us officers of our own choice, who will be officers and gentlemen. Officers who can sympathize with the enlisted man without regard to color; men who will take into consideration a man's former conduct, before punishment. . . .

SOUTH CAROLINA

LETTER 75

(Benjamin M. Bond, [Private,] Co. B, 54th Massachusetts Infantry, Charleston, South Carolina, July 3, 1865; *WAA*, July 22, 1865). Now that slavery had ended, both blacks and whites in the South struggled to define new economic, political, and social relationships. Private Benjamin M. Bond of Bel Air, Maryland, was offended by the segregation he found in a Charleston church.

. . . I disdain the idea of absenting myself from the 1st-M[ethodist] E[piscopal] Church on account of caste, and would cordially fellowship our white brethren without distinction or prejudice, and would beg to state that we, the Anglo-African race, as far as I understand, do not object to equality, neither are we wholly prejudiced to social intercourse, but we reject such distinction as set forth in the resolutions at the reorganization of the M.E. Church in Charleston – the separation of the blacks from the whites is sufficient ground for an objection; the setting apart of separate seats is unworthy of the name of Christian. If we are Christians we must be loving Christians, as we all promise that we are the true children of God, and joint heirs with Christ, we cannot refuse the acceptance of each other's Christian and social fellowship, but the separation of a society on account of caste is entirely obnoxious to the Christian faith, and contrary to the teachings of Christ and the Gospel. We cannot be true Christians without fellowship with each other, and that combines all the endearing ties of brotherhood, and when we are treated without distinction we have no objection to give them the hand of fellowship, and will feel no desire to separate; but if we are held as inferiors and unfit for equal and social religious privileges we must stand on our dignity and absent ourselves from their fraternity, and make every possible effort to evaluate our race, and show by our zeal and energy that we may secure a standing in the Christian Community.

LETTER 76

(B. J. Butler, [Private,] Co. I, 55th Massachusetts Infantry, Orangeburg, South Carolina, July 29, 1865; *WAA*, August 12, 1865) Private Benjamin J. Butler of Vincennes, Indiana, watched with interest as South Carolina blacks and whites tried to work out new labor arrangements. He wrote that the freed slaves still lived and worked under grim conditions.

. . . Mr. Editor, I wish to inform your readers what was expressed by a Southern planter to brevet Brig. Gen. A[lfred] S. Hartwell – I was the adjutant's orderly and was present. The gentleman first complained about the contract between him and his laborers, because he could not drive them, and that they would go and work for themselves. He said that he gave them plenty to eat and clothing and a smart person could do the task that he gave them in half a day, and all the remainder of the time they could work for themselves, and that he would buy all the poultry and produce and given them as good a price as he was giving them heretofore.

The General said the old price was two cents per dozen for eggs and six and a fourth cents for chickens. This was the price of the majority. The gentleman then said that he had lost about twenty thousand dollars worth since the war, and all this he had made by his ten fingers out at sea and running the rivers. Hard work he was used to, but his brothers at home, he was sorry for them, for they never worked any in their lifetime. Then, said the General, let them take hold and work and they will get along. I was exceedingly glad to hear that he had to go to work.

I wish to inform you and all your readers as to what provision is found for the colored laborers that are at work in the Orangeburg District and Columbia District. The colored people inform me that the majority of them get four quarts of meal or corn for one week, and nothing else, and that their task is one acre of ground to work over in a day. If some of the soldiers did not give them meat to eat they would not get any, and if they kill a hog they are arrested for stealing. If any of them are sick and send for a doctor, he will say let them die or go to work. This is very hard for me to hear. I saw a very old man who told me that he had not had a pair of shoes for five years, only as he worked by night and could buy them.

If ever we expect to become a people we must try and educate ourselves and our children, and rise out of degradation and press onward. This is what our people need in this state. School teachers are wanted here, and ministers are wanted to preach the Gospel.

LETTER 77

(B. J. Butler [Private,] Co. I, 55th Massachusetts Infantry, Fort Motte, South Carolina, August 1, 1865; *CR*, August 12, 1865) African-American soldiers did what they could to help the freed slaves find new lives after emancipation. The freedmen at Fort Motte, South Carolina, asked Private Benjamin J. Butler to visit their town and preach in their church. White and black together heard him preach a new message of freedom.

I have a matter of much importance to write to you and all true Christians at home. My subject is the freedmen of this part of South Carolina. They inform me that a great many who desire to assemble themselves in a body for social worship are deprived because they have no elder to minister to them. They have a few

exhorters, who labor for them, but the greater portion of the professors [of religion] appear to be on the barren mountains, desiring
a pastor and finding none.

They want colored ministers to establish a church and preach
the gospel to them. They informed me that it has been a long time
since they heard the truth of the gospel, preached to them. Bro.
Fralem came to camp, and requested me to try and pay them one
visit in the settlements. They were in a very lonely situation, and
desired some one to come and expound the great mysteries of
salvation, and the wonderful works of God.

After a few days had expired, I consulted with the brother, and
told him I would go for the comfort of the children of God.

The commanding officer of the post gave me permission to go
and assemble at the Bethel Station Church, near Fort Motte Station. I was accompanied by three other soldiers of my company. On
reaching the Church, we found a large number of members belonging to different churches, and also a number of other spectators. They were seated in good order. There was a number of
white persons present. They did not think that colored men could
expound the true gospel of Christ.

Never, there, were colored men admitted to the pulpit to preach
before. On July 11th, a 1 o'clock, I took my place in the pulpit, and
ministered to my beloved brethren and sisters. They all seemed to
be fed from the Holy Spirit of God, and greatly rejoiced in the
deep mysteries of Christ. I was truly happy to find them in such
good spirits, and I contended for the faith once delivered to the
saints. It was very interesting to myself, and I think it would have
been much more so to my beloved brethren and friends at home, to
see how

> God moves in a mysterious way,
> His wonders to perform

Because it is the power of God unto salvation to every one that believeth in Him. May the great God be with you all. "Come over and help us."

KENTUCKY

LETTER 78

(William A. Warfield, Sergeant, Co. D, 119th USCI, Camp Nelson, Kentucky, July 7, 1865; *WAA*, July 22, 1865) Even though Kentucky did not leave the Union, when the war ended several thousand black soldiers stayed there to help the government emancipate and protect the slaves. Sergeant William A. Warfield, stationed at Fort Nelson, near Lexington, describes the African-American celebration on July 4, 1865.

This is an age of wonders, and not the least among them is the celebration of the Fourth of July at Camp Nelson, Ky., by the colored people. To see so many thousands, who a year ago were slaves, congregate in the heart of a slave State and celebrate the day sacred to the cause of freedom, "with none to molest or make afraid," was a grand spectacle. It was the first time we have ever been permitted to celebrate the Nation's Day.

The celebration was under the management of Capt. [T. E.] Hall, and Rev. J. G. Fee. These men deserve much credit for their zeal and untiring activity in the cause of our race.

The people gathered in from far and near. With several regiments of colored soldiers, with the thousands at the Refugee Home, and with the many from different parts of the country, the numbers swelled to many thousands. Such an assemblage of colored people on the "sacred soil of Kentucky" was never before beheld.

The exercises consisted in martial music, songs, speeches, and declamations, with an interlude of a good dinner. The first part of the exercises were performed by the colored people themselves. The school-girls took an active part in the singing and recitations. Speeches, pointed and witty, were made by several colored speakers. In the afternoon, toasts were given and responded to in well-timed and effective remarks. Almost boundless enthusiasm prevailed throughout.

In the forenoon, a review of the troops in this camp was held. Of all the regiments on review, ours seemed to take the banner for its soldier-like appearance.

Through the kindness of the Lexington ladies, numbers of us have been receiving your excellent paper, for which we feel grateful. I would suggest to my friends in Lexington that they are behind in their efforts for the race. Other sections are sending up petitions and representatives to secure the rights of the colored people; but, either from fear or want of zeal, there is no special movement being made in that direction in my native city. If we would obtain our just privileges, we must *strive* for them. We must be willing to pay the same price that other people have always been compelled to pay. By laboring for our own cause we show, in the first place, that we understand and appreciate what our rights are; in the second place, that we have the courage and manhood to ask for them; in the third place, that we are determined, sooner or later, to have them.

We need not expect those who have held us as slaves, and regarded us as incapable of an honorable position in government and society, to grant us that which we are indisposed to labor for. . . .

LETTER 79

(George Thomas, [Corporal,] Battery L, 12th USCHA, Fort Smith, Bowling Green, Kentucky, July 18, 1865; *WAA*, August 12, 1865) Corporal George Thomas was a slave until he enlisted in the army in 1864. In this letter he sketches his life as a slave and his current duties guarding a railroad.

. . . I was born in Nelson County, Kentucky, and lived there until I was eighteen years of age, at which time I went to Louisville, and was in that city when the late horrid rebellion broke out.

I enlisted in the 12th U.S. Colored Heavy Artillery in the Fall of 1864, and my only sorrow is that I did not enlist sooner. I left a home such as would have made a slave happy, as long as there was a grain of happiness to be found in slavery. While living in Nelson county I indeed thought that it was right that all colored people should be slaves, and I was far from being the only one having the same opinion; but oh, how different now! There were five or six colored people in the county who could read, and they were disliked very much by the white people on that account; so you see, although we were capable of being taught, the fear of our masters and mistresses kept us bound in the frontiers of ignorance. A man could not visit his wife, living a mile from him, scarcely once a week, and the infringement of any rule was followed by at least a hundred lashes; but, thanks be to God, those terrible days have passed away forever. At that time those cruel practices were not strange to me, neither did I think the masters cruel until I was, by the providence of God, partly released from ignorance by learning to read; then I saw that slavery was contrary to the laws of God and debasing to man. Things like this caused me to look forward, hoping and praying for the time at which these things must end – and behold, the time has come, and I see, as it were, a nation born in a day – men and women coming forth from slavery's dark dungeons to the noonday sunshine of the greatest of God's gifts – Liberty.

Our wives are now cared for by our government, homes for them being already prepared at Camp Nelson, and we feel like men, and are determined to be men, and do our duty to our government honestly and faithfully, as good soldiers ought to do. . . .

Our regiment now numbers nearly seventeen hundred men, and is stationed all along the Louisville and Nashville railroad, from Louisville to this place. The first battalion is stationed here doing garrison duty; almost too easy for soldiers, me thinks. We have dress parade downtown in the public square, and as we are drilled *very well*, the former slaveholders open their eyes, astonished that their former Kentucky *working stock* are capable of being on an equal footing with them at last.

LOUISIANA

LETTER 80

(William P. Green, [Private,] 11th USCHA, Donaldsonville, Louisiana, August 8, 1865; *CR,* September 9, 1865) Private William P. Green of Washington, Pennsylvania, complains bitterly about how white officers treated their black soldiers in postwar Louisiana. The prejudice, he writes, went all the way to the military commander of the district, General Thomas W. Sherman.

I would beg leave to insert a reply in your valuable paper to a question that has been asked me for the information of all who feel disposed to inquire the same. The question is: "Were we (soldiers in this department) satisfied and contented with our soldier's duty now that peace has been declared?" I answer, "No!" and shall not be backward in giving my reason for such frankness in the reply.

Since peace has been declared between the Federal Government and the so-called Confederate States, our task has become more laborious, our treatment more severe, and, to be brief in our remarks, we will say that it is more than we can bear, without letting the world see how they (U.S. officers) reciprocate the sacrifices that men have made in becoming soldiers, and always were ready to offer up their lives for them when called upon, as well as for the Government of the United States.

Officers who heretofore have been furnishing substitutes for drafted men, and recruiting to fill vacancies in colored regiments, have used as inducements to recruits, words to the effect that since colored troops received the same pay that white troops receive, they were all willing to enlist in the regular service for five years; but they are very much mistaken in their views on this subject. Never have I witnessed such lack of confidence as is beginning to dawn here with us, and if there ever was a time that we felt like exterminating our old oppressors from the face of the earth, it is at the present time. The overthrow of the rebellion is consigning us to perpetual misery and distraction.

The animosity existing between the United States colored troops and the conquered Southerners is so great that they cannot ever expect to live in peace together. Several soldiers of this command have been severely punished for chastising citizens or returned Confederate soldiers for their insulting remarks whilst passing along the streets.

A report from any white citizen against one of our men, whether it be credible or not, is sufficient to punish the accused. We might say that the whole battalion suffers by the doubling of the guard, and not allowing to pass to an enlisted man until the Major commanding the battery sees fit to examine into the report, and then it generally proves in favor of the plaintiff.

Yesterday evening, on dress parade, we were astonished by the reading of a General Order from Department Headquarters, referring to reports that had reached Gen. [Thomas W.] Sherman about the misbehavior of colored soldiers in this Department. The General says no doubt the fault is on both sides, but he does not say that the punishment shall be equally divided. His instructions to commanders of posts are that they will be held responsible for the regularity of their commands, but means that he shall punish to the extent of their laws any colored soldier that fights his own battles with citizens.

The origination of this Order arises from the above mentioned stratagem that the poor whites take for revenge. It surely grieves me to think that our officers do not place the confidence in us that they did when we were expecting an attack every minute from the same persons, only they were in a different station of life.

Think for a moment of the treachery in the people of Louisiana! In the year 1862 it was impossible for a Union soldier to make his appearance one mile from the reserves on picket duty without being captured or brutally murdered, and when a thorough search would immediately be made, there could not be a rebel soldier found within the limits of ten miles of the place where the murder was committed. Gunboats in the United States service were fired into from Donaldsonville, although no persons were found to bear arms against the Government, they being, as they (the citizens) said, loyal to the Government of the United States.

Now there being no gunboats to fire into, nor rebel forces to seek protection from, they dare not boldly attack a soldier in the United States service. But they take advantage of the protection shown to them by the United States Government and seek to annoy the soldiers by repeatedly entering complaints against them, or us, and I am sorry to say that their complaints are more or less effective.

I will here digress by summarily stating to you the modes of punishment that I have witnessed since our arrival at this post, the effects of the above-mentioned circumstances. It makes me shudder not only when a witness of such transactions, but when my thoughts run thither. Men have been bucked and gagged in their company streets, exposed to the derision of the majority of the officers, who seem to take delight in witnessing their misery, and are kept there from morning until tattoo at night. I have also seen men tied up by their thumbs, so that they could only stand on their toes, until they have fainted after being released from punishment. But the most cruel of all the punishments is a box, five feet in height, two feet in breadth, and two feet in width, with an inch auger hole bored in the top of it to let in air. This is called a sweat box.

The victim for punishment is confined in this place of torment until the Battalion Commander feels disposed to order his release, which depends altogether upon the state of his sobriety. I will therefore ask the question, Do you, Mr. Editor, think that any one who ever knew the definition of the word freeman should endure such treatment and feel contented? Surely any rational man will answer, "No!"

In conclusion, I would advise all persons who wish to know how colored troops like the service to refer to Northern men in this department, and some of them will give them details of transactions that have occurred, which I dare not at present make known.

LETTER 81

(Richard T. Henry, [Corporal,] Co. H, 11th USCHA, Donaldsonville, Louisiana, August 15, 1865; *WAA*, September 16, 1865) Richard T. Henry of Plattsburg, New York, paid close attention to how the ex-slaves got along. White popular opinion held that they could not work unsupervised, could not learn, and could not be useful citizens. Corporal Henry reports that the freedmen were doing better than many of the whites.

I take the liberty of writing to you a few facts that have come under my observation respecting the freedmen. In looking over the various journals that come to us, I see statements of the condition of the freedmen that are prejudicial to them. The papers that we get are mostly Southern, and consequently we get nothing very flattering as to their moral condition. We are in a parish of Louisiana where the hand of slavery pressed the hardest and where oppression, in all of its bitterness, held sway over the slave. I take every opportunity to glean information from those who have been the

victims of slavery, and from the narrations of personal suffering. It
is a wonder to me that the mind is not so dwarfed and deadened as
to be past restoring to mental life, but thank God it is not. The
enemy of emancipation cries that the negroes will not work, that
the government will have to support them, or they will become
pests to the country, and that they cannot be educated either to
usefulness or knowledge sufficient for them to become citizens
capable of enjoying all the privileges that belong to the free man. I
believe that that cry is false – false as slavery. Any one who has
been where he can observe the working of emancipation can see
the fallacy of such cant. Through the parishes where I have been I
think I never saw the laboring class more industrious. Many seem
to vie one with each other in making a living, and saving something
for a future day. There are those who have to receive something
from the Government on account of old age and sickness, and
others that are compelled to leave their homes to escape cruelties
worse than the savages would inflict on their victims. Those who
feel so badly because the Government feeds a few negroes should
be with me on ration day and see their white brethren and sisters,
those who for the last four years have been trying to destroy the
nation, come for their food that the Government has to give to save
them from starving; and these same persons hate the Government
as bitterly as they ever did. And these whites will not work for fear
that it will destroy their respectability! So far as the capacity of the
freedmen to receive education, I never saw any class of people
North who were more anxious to learn, or learned more quickly
than these crushed and abused brethren of ours.

I might state fact upon fact to prove that the freedmen are self-
sustaining, and capable of becoming as good citizens as any other
people in the land, but time compels me to close.

LETTER 82

(George W. LeVere, Chaplain, 20th USCI, Milliken's Bend, Louisiana, August 30, 1865; *WAA*, November 4, 1865) Milliken's Bend
had been the site of a battle in June 1863; black soldiers had fought
well there and won the approval of white troops and generals.

When the war ended, a New York regiment of black troops went there to serve as military police. Chaplain George W. LeVere, a black Congregational minister from Brooklyn, New York, writes about affairs in the wake of war.

This section of the country presents a vivid picture of the desolating effects of the "Slaveholders' Rebellion." Extensive tracts of land that were formerly plantations, owned by those who would be lords of the earth, have been abandoned, the dwellings and sugar houses knocked down, leaving only their huge chimneys standing, cotton gins gutted, slave quarters ventilated, and here and there you can see a Freedman or woman, or a returned rebel on a half-starved horse or mule, riding in great agony through what is at present an over-grown weed field.

We have been endeavoring to find out for which of our many sins we have been sent here to be punished.

It is going on the third week since we landed here, and we have yet to get the first mouthful of fresh meat. The rebs, when they went to Texas, did not only drive their slaves with them, but everything else that could be driven. Consequently, they stripped the place of horses, mules, cattle, sheep, hogs, &c., and now they have the impudence to be sneaking back to look for what is left and to lay claim to it.

But thank God there is one fact demonstrated here, "The Freedmen can take care of themselves," notwithstanding the desolate and barren condition of this God-forsaken section of the country.

The Freedmen are industriously and perseveringly engaged in the cultivation of small portions of lands, raising for themselves and their families what they need to subsist upon [*missing*] rations. Let the enemies of the [Freedmen put] that in their pipes and smoke it. [*Missing*] slaves can make industrious Freedmen [*missing*] others. Give them "Fair play". [*Missing*]

I am in hope the children – there are quite a number now – may have some way provided for their education. The benefits of General [Nathanael] Banks' system have not reached here, consequently they are ignorant of letters.[6] In other respects they appear quite bright, and should be looked after. I am doing all for them that my leisure time will permit.

There is no church nearer than Vicksburg, which is twenty-five miles from here.

The people hold meetings in their quarters in their old plantation style. I propose to preach to them at least once each Sabbath. I desire the prayers of the faithful that my labors among them may not be in vain. . . .

TEXAS

LETTER 83

(S. H. Smothers, [Private,] 45th USCI, Santiago, Texas, June 24, 1865; *CR*, July 15, 1865) Shortly after the fall of Richmond, in April 1865, several regiments of black soldiers that had been part of the Army of the James were sent to occupy southern Texas. The trip by sea was tedious and marred by serious sickness. But Private Samuel Smothers, a teacher from Troy, Ohio, tells of his pleasant visit to New Orleans and his arrival at Brazos Santiago, near the mouth of the Rio Grande.

. . . During the latter part of May and the beginning of June, the Twenty-fifth Army Corps, General [Godfrey] Weitzel commanding, of which my regiment (the 45th) formed a part, embarked at City Point, Va., for Texas. The writer came with the corps head

6. Banks instituted a rigid system of work and education for freed slaves in Louisiana.

quarters. We embarked on the 5th of June, on the steamers Crescent and Governor Chase. We had a very pleasant voyage, the weather being fine and the sea smooth and calm. We arrived at New Orleans on the evening of the 16th, and remained there until the evening of the 17th. . . .

I called at the office of the "Black Republican" newspaper, No. 6, Carondolet street, and had a very pleasant interview with its publisher, Captain Jordan B. Noble. Mr. Noble is a colored man, and his paper is the organ of the colored people of Louisiana. The Captain's military history is very interesting indeed. He is an old soldier. He was a soldier in the war of 1812, and participated in the memorable battle of New Orleans. He was also engaged in the Florida and Mexican wars, and in the present war he went out as Captain in one of the regiments of the Louisiana Native Guards. There were two of these regiments, both of which were raised in New Orleans, composed of free colored men, and the line officers were all colored men. They took a prominent part in the battle of Port Hudson, but soon after that bloody struggle, and when they had been in the service only three months, the prejudice among the white officers against the colored officer became so strong that the latter, to avoid having their commissions taken from them, resigned.

A portion of the troops landed on this island a week ago, but the corps headquarters did not land until three days ago. Most of the regiments have now landed. The island is sandy and desolate-looking. We are put to considerable inconvenience about water; we have to use condensed water altogether, which is issued to us boiling hot, at the rate of three pints per day.

The health of the men is generally good. We will probably not remain here long. The first division is already moving up the Rio Grande.

LETTER 84

("Rufus," 25th Corps Headquarters, Indianola, Texas, July 15, 1865; *WAA*, August 12, 1865) The mission to Texas was not well planned, and the men found shortages of water, fresh food, and other supplies. "Rufus" complains about conditions and tells of meeting German-speaking Texans.

The whole of the 1st Division, and two Brigades (2d and 3d) of the 2d Division, disembarked from the 23d to 30th of June at Brazos de Santiago, Texas, a place made famous in our war history by the landing of Gen. Taylor's forces in 1846, and a more God-forsaken spot does not [exist] in the wide world; entirely without fresh water, and little or no facilities for making it; not a bush or a tuft of grass or a particle of vegetation within its entire area of twelve miles.

After enjoying (?) the comforts of the spot called Brazos for several days, someone discovered that the condensing machine could not supply water to more than 3,000 men, and that all over that number depending on it must suffer for the want of that necessary article. Consequently the 1st Division and 3d Brigade of the 2d Division were ordered above the mouth of the Rio Grande River for the enjoyment of its fresh water. This water is good when you have not tasted any for 50 hours, but I would prefer Croton [New York], if only for the appearance of the thing. The water of the Mississippi is crystal compared to it, and what is worse, is that all the sediment seems to be alive.

We were there on the 7th, and arrived here on the 9th, and found the 1st Brigade, Col. James Shaw, 7th USCT commanding post. Troops doing provost duty all around. One regiment in Victoria, three companies at Metta Gordo, four at Port Lavaca, and the balance "lying around loose."

This place is very little better than Brazos, and the people are not worth speaking of. They are all Germans, of recent importation, and if they are a part of the Texan desperadoes of whom we have heard, I do not think we will have any trouble in teaching them their true level. Though they do not understand our language, we *speak* a tongue, in case of necessity, which they will readily comprehend. . . .

LETTER 85

(Henry Carpenter Hoyle, [Private,] Co. F, 43d USCI, Brownsville, Texas, August 28, 1865; *CR*, September 25, 1865) Occupation duty in Texas gave the soldiers time to think about the changes that had come in the past two years: emancipation, enlistment, and fighting for the Union. It also gave Private Henry Hoyle an opportunity to think about what he wanted next: the right to vote and a trip home to Philadelphia.

The question has often been asked, What benefit has the colored soldier been to the Government? I will try, if possible, to answer this question. In the first place, there have been few deserters and bounty-jumpers among them. Second, the colored troops can stand more fatigue than the others. Third, they can make more desperate charges, build breastworks more briskly, and stand heavier assaults than white troops. We are sorry to say that we have seen several [whites] who called themselves old veterans skulking and hiding in the woods, when they ought to have been with their regiment, fighting for the country. Nothing is more contemptible than to see a soldier shrinking from duty in the hour of danger.

And such men we find ready to condemn the colored troops. But we know of what value we have been to the Government, and I guess our officers know our bravery, and of what metal we are. And we defy any one to dispute our rights as soldiers and men.

I hope, when the colored soldiers arrive at home, they will disappoint the expectations of the copperheads, who predict that they will be riotous. But may we be an honor to our race, and may our future conduct be such as to please a most noble and generous public. We want the right of suffrage, that we may be free and equal as other men.

It is reasonable to suppose that the same God who made the white man made the African. We have proved true and trustworthy to the Government. We have, it is true, been subjected to some cruel treatment at the hands of some of our officers, but, as Gen. [Benjamin] Butler remarks, let by-gones be by-gones. Let us study our present and future condition, and not study to do any man harm, but let us strive to do good unto all men.

God has willed it, that he has taken our beloved father, Abraham Lincoln, from us. But although dead, yet he lives. He brought liberty to the slaves, both North and South, and gave us in the North the freedom of speech in a proper manner, and I have no doubt we will get our rights as men and citizens of the United States. Let us not care for man as long as God is on our side. He will be true to His promises. "Ethiopia shall stretch forth her hands unto God." She has partly done so already, and God has given liberty and freedom to the slave. Let her continue to call upon God, and He will raise us to our rightful and proper place among the nations of the earth.

Thank God! we are now free! No more will the torturing whip be inflicted on gray-headed fathers and mothers. No more will families be torn asunder and sold as cattle. Those dark days are past, and bright laurels attend us. May God grant us a safe return and bring us up out of Texas, for we have great trials and tribulations to go through. May we soon return to our quiet homes and enjoy the sweet comforts of life. God has brought us safely through the hottest of the raging battle, and He will stand by us while passing the scorching sun of Texas. . . .

LETTER 86

(Garland H. White, Chaplain, 28th USCI, Corpus Christi, Texas, September 19, 1865; *CR*, October 23, 1865) "Black Codes" were laws passed in 1865 by Southern states to adjust to their new status after slavery ended. Most of those laws seemed to the blacks little better than slavery itself. As Chaplain White bitterly notes, former rebels were getting the right to vote much faster than were blacks who had always been loyal to the Union.

... Some silly-minded men talk sometimes about home, and I have to quiet them by assuring them that all will come right in the end, at the same time feeling in my own heart that unless we are made equal before the law we have got no home.

Texas fever or no Texas fever, my hope is that I may never see Ohio again less than a man. What? Shall traitors and rebels, who waged war against the general Government be made legal voters at every ballot box, and we, the National Guard who by the General-in-Chief and War Department were selected to establish a new picket line on the Rio Grande, to look after the welfare of the whole nation, be deprived of the privilege?

While such is the case, I cannot believe that any set of Legislators will endorse what is already being done in some, if not all the Southern States.

My hope, politically speaking, is in the meeting of the next Congress, and I do sincerely invoke the special presence of Almighty God to guide them in their most trying deliberations, and bring them to such decisions as will reflect credit upon their country, release the down-trodden from their sufferings, and for ever wipe from our history this vexed question which has more than once convulsed our land from the Lakes to the Gulf.

The Government has a right to the services of men, when and where it [needs them] and we calmly submit to it. But we soldiers ask the nation to grant us the right to vote, that we may, by that bestowment, be enabled to protect our families from all the horrors that prey upon a disfranchised people.

I am glad to see that there are some, both white and colored, who think as we think, and are determined to do all they can to arouse the mind of the nation to a sense of its duty. May they continue to speak until the bonds of ignorance are riven – till dark oppression is driven from the earth – till from every land and every sea, one universal, triumphant song is heard, to hail the long-expected jubilee, when every bond is broken, and every slave at liberty.

And ye who possess the glorious power of eloquence to thrill the immortal soul, use not unwisely the priceless gift, but let your ambition be a name enshrined upon the scroll where generations yet unborn shall find the deathless deeds of those who fought and bled to free mankind; and we mean free in the broadest sense of the term.

No set of men in any country ever suffered more severely than we in Texas. Death has made festful gaps in every regiment. Going to the grave with the dead is as common to me as going to bed, for I also attend on such occasions in other regiments, rather than see men buried indecently. Chaplains are very scarce out here. It seems as though they only obtained commission to preach while around Washington and City Point, Va., as I have never seen but one besides myself in all Texas. . . .

I have spent a great portion of my time at the hospitals and I never witnessed such fearful mortality in all my life. I have not seen a lemon, peach, apple or pear, nor corn enough over all that part of the country through which we have passed, to fatten a six months' pig. How the people live another writer must describe, and not I. It may be better farther in the interior, but few are willing to search for it. . . .

LETTER 87

(Thomas Boswell, Sergeant-Major, 116th USCI, Roma, Texas, November 6, 1865; *WAA*, December 23, 1865) Some black regiments were left in Texas after most had been mustered out and sent home. Sergeant-Major Boswell thought he knew why his Kentucky unit remained: It was from a slave state; the regiments from the free states had gone home first. Boswell's regiment would not be mustered out until 1867.

. . . The weather has been truly enchanting for the last three days; and the boys have just completed their winter quarters. Though not as good as those we had last year in Virginia, still they are preferable.

This day one year ago was a rather warm day for our regiment at White House, Va., but you know all about that, so I shall say no more.

Roma is a very nice little village, situated on a high bluff, and is kept very clean. There are but two or three Americans in the place. If our regiment stays here any length of time we will all speak Spanish, as we are learning very fast.

We were in high hopes of being mustered out soon, but it seems that they have slighted us. Our Corps is pretty much all gone home; but it is said that we are to be retained because we are "slave State troops." Is this a good reason for our retention? No. We earnestly hope that the Government will not be guilty of this great wrong toward us, as we have tried to do our duty.

We are Kentucky boys, and there is no regiment in the field that ever fought better. We can boast of being the heroes of eight hard-fought battles, and this we deem a sufficient recommendation for our discharge. . . .

6

For the Rights of Citizens

JAMES HENRY HALL enlisted in the 54th Massachusetts Infantry at his first opportunity. When a recruiter came to his city in February 1863, he left his job as a barber in Philadelphia, even though he was thirty-eight years old, almost too old to be a soldier. With his regiment he fought at James Island, at Fort Wagner, and at Olustee; and he went without pay to protest the army's racism. By August 1864 he told newspaper readers why he was fighting: "If we fight to maintain a Republican Government, we want Republican privileges." He added, "We do not covet your wives nor your daughters, nor the position of political orator. All we ask is the proper enjoyment of the rights of citizenship, and a free title and acknowledged share in our own noble birthplace." Whatever else Hall and his fellow soldiers might be fighting for, they were fighting for their rights as Americans.[1]

1. J. H. Hall, Co. B, 54th Massachusetts Infantry, Morris Island, S.C., August 3, 1864; *CR*, August 27, 1864.

When the African-American soldiers of the Union Army thought about why they were fighting, American citizenship came first. Some wrote about their desire to free the slaves, and probably all of them wanted to see their brothers and sisters free from bondage. Many of them had been slaves themselves, and more had slave relatives; they knew from experience the pains of slavery. Those who had lived in the Northern states also wanted slavery abolished because it reinforced racism; whites could justify discrimination against free blacks by pointing out that slavery had made them inferior. But most soldiers' letters do not focus on emancipation. President Lincoln had already issued the Emancipation Proclamation before these soldiers had enlisted, so they had no need to argue for abolition. Instead, they argued that they were fighting to show that they deserved full equality and citizenship.

For the short term, they wanted equality in the army. Many soldiers resented the fact that they could not have black officers. The black officers of the colored militia regiments in Louisiana were forced to resign. All the officers appointed to lead the United States Colored Troops were white. The enlisted men resented the fact that, while many white soldiers were promoted to officer ranks as a reward for their skill and bravery in battle, blacks were not allowed to lead, no matter how excellent they might be. The army commissioned a few African-American chaplains and doctors, but the key positions of leadership were closed. A month before the fighting stopped, to help recruit new men, Dr. Martin R. Delany was made a major. Only after the fighting had stopped and the soldiers were being discharged did a few battle-tested men win promotion to lieutenant. But through most of the war, commissions were off-limits to black soldiers. Fighting for equality in the army, they wanted their own officers.

For the longer term, African-American soldiers fought for full citizenship in the United States. Even most Northern states put restrictions on free blacks. Some prohibited them from even moving into the state. Other states would not let them serve on juries or testify in court. And some would not let them attend public schools. In Philadelphia and Washington, D.C., they could not ride the streetcars. President Lincoln and many other whites had urged them to leave the country and settle in Liberia or Haiti. And the Supreme Court had ruled in 1857 that they were not citizens of the United States, that they had no rights that white men must respect. Although many Republican politicians said that African Americans were indeed citizens, the matter would not be finally settled until after the war. The black soldiers were eager to fight for the Union to show whites that they deserved full citizenship rights.

The most important of those rights was the right to vote. With political power, blacks could work for equality in other areas. Only six of the Northern states allowed African Americans to vote, and in some of those states that right was restricted to those who owned property. Free blacks in general and black soldiers in particular resented the fact that immigrants from Europe could vote soon after their arrival, while blacks who had lived here all their lives could not. Many of those immigrants voted for the Democratic party and against the war policy of President Lincoln. These "Copperheads" urged peace with the Confederacy and rioted when asked to fight for freedom for the slaves. This outraged black soldiers who strongly endorsed Lincoln's goal of freeing the slaves and who risked their lives to defeat the Confederacy. When disloyal whites had the franchise, why shouldn't loyal blacks vote?

Under the leadership of Frederick Douglass, a "National Convention of Colored Men" met in Syracuse, New York, in October 1864. Several of the delegates were army men. The flag on the platform was the battle flag of the First Louisiana Native Guards, who had proven their valor at Port Hudson, the first major battle for black troops. "We want the elective franchise in all the states," read the convention's address to the American people. Whites had once argued that blacks should not vote, because they were not required to serve in the military. Now, they served willingly on many fronts. "Are we good enough to use bullets, and not good enough to use ballots? May we defend rights in time of war, and yet be denied the exercise of those rights in time of peace?" Through the letters from African-American soldiers ran echoes of this question, this call for the right to vote.

The letters selected for this chapter focus on the call for equality, for the rights of citizens. The soldiers demanded suffrage, justice in the courts, equal access to schools, street-cars, and jobs, and they wanted black officers. They had earned these things, not only for themselves but for their race.[2]

LETTER 88

(J. H. B. P., [Corporal,] 55th Massachusetts Infantry, Morris Island, South Carolina, May 24, 1864; *CR*, June 11, 1864) This letter was written by Corporal John H. B. Payne, a thirty-year-old schoolteacher from Bellefontaine, Ohio. He claimed that even though the promises of freedom and civil rights had been broken in the past, at least the pay of white and black troops had been equal. But more important than equal pay, he wanted the right to vote and be voted for.

. . . I am not willing to fight for anything less than the white man fights for. If the white man cannot support his family on seven dollars per month, I cannot support mine on the same amount.

And I am not willing to fight for this Government for money alone. Give me my rights, the rights that this Government owes me, the same rights that the white man has. I would be willing to fight three years for this Government without one cent of the mighty dollar. Then I would have something to fight for. Now I am

2. *Proceedings of the National Convention of Colored Men Held in the City of Syracuse, N.Y., October 4, 5, 6, and 7, 1864* (Boston, Rand & Avery, 1864), 12–13, 55–58. Mary Frances Berry, *Military Necessity and Civil Rights Policy: Black Citizenship and the Constitution, 1861–1868* (Port Washington, N.Y., Kennikat, 1977) passim.

fighting for the rights of white men. White men have never given me the rights that they are bound to respect. God has not made one man better than another; therefore, one man's rights are no better than another's. They assert that because a large proportion of our race is in bondage we have a right to help free them. I want to know if it was not the white man that put them in bondage? How can they hold us responsible for their evils? And how can they expect that we should do more to blot it out than they are willing to do themselves? If every slave in the United States were emancipated at once, they would not be free yet. If the white man is not willing to respect my rights, I am not willing to respect his wrongs. Our rights have always been limited in the United States. It is true that in some places a colored man, if he can prove himself to be half-white, can vote. Vote for whom? The white man. What good do such rights ever do us – to be compelled always to be voting for the white man and never to be voted for?

Now, the white man declares that this is not our country, and that we have no right to it. They say that Africa is our country. I claim this as my native country – the country that gave me birth. I wish to know one thing, and that is this: Who is the most entitled to his rights in a country – a native of the country or the foreigner? This question can be very easily answered. Now there are foreigners who have flooded our shores. They bring nothing with them but antagonistic feelings to rule and order, and they are without the rudiments of education, and yet they can train their children to be law-abiding citizens. In their own country mis-rule reigns. Generally very poor, they have no leisure for the cultivation of their hearts' best feelings; for in their case, poverty degrades human nature. In this country their social influence is much greater than in their own. Here every avenue to distinction is open to them. The foreigner, when he enters this country, enters into life in an age full of a progressive spirit in the elective franchise. Such persons are the first to take up an offensive position against the Government, instead of marching under the banner of the Prince of Peace. Such people have ruled this country too long already.

The ignorant Irish can come to this country and have free access to all the rights. After they have gained their rights, they cannot appreciate them. They then want to bully the Government. They soon get tired of living under the laws of the country and commence to mutiny, riot, ransack cities, murder colored children, and burn down orphan asylums, as was done in New York.[3] Is the power to be given to such men to direct and govern the affairs of the Union, on which the weal or woe of the nation depends? This is productive of moral degradation and becomes one of the fruitful sources of evil in our land, from which we shall suffer most severely unless some plan is specially adopted to check its onward course. How can this nation ever expect to prosper? I wonder that God does not bring on them present deluge and disaster. I do not wonder at the conduct and disaster that transpired at Fort Pillow. I wonder that we have not had more New York riots and Fort Pillow massacres.

Liberty is what I am struggling for; and what pulse does not beat high at the very mention of the name? Each of us, with fidelity, has already discharged the duties devolving on us as men and as soldier. The very fact of such a union on grounds so commonly and deeply interesting to all, undoubtedly cannot always fail, by the blessing of God, to exert a hallowed influence over society, well fitted to break up alike the extremes of aristocratic and social feeling, which too often predominate in society, and to beget unity, love, brotherly kindness, and charity. . . .

LETTER 89

("Sergeant," 54th Massachusetts Infantry, Morris Island, South Carolina, August 26, 1864; *The Liberator,* October 4, 1864) Although the 54th Massachusetts Regiment had many officers who were abolitionists and competent military leaders, the simple fact that they were white created problems for the black soldiers. This

3. The New York riots occurred in July 1863.

regiment had earned glory in the charge on Fort Wagner in July 1863, and its officers earned fame for their devotion to the cause of abolition. But, as "Sergeant" writes here, that was not good enough: The men wanted officers of their own color and the possibility of commissions for themselves.

Charleston is not ours yet, but no doubt will soon be. And why? Because the country needs an important victory, and somehow it is a religious or superstitious belief with me that this country will be saved to us (black men) yet. I say I believe this; but it is not a mere blind belief. I know that we shall have to labor hard, and put up with a great deal before we are allowed to participate in the government of this country. I am aware that we in the army have done about all we can do, and that to you civilians at home falls the duty of speaking out for all – as we have done the fighting and marching, and suffered cold, heat, and hunger for you and all of us.

My friend, we want black commissioned officers; and only because we want men we can understand and who can understand us. We want men whose hearts are truly loyal to the rights of man. We want to be represented in courts martial, where so many of us are liable to be tried and sentenced. We want to demonstrate our ability to rule, as we have demonstrated our willingness to obey. In short, we want simple justice. I will try to be plainer: There are men here who were made sergeants at Camp Meigs, (Readville,)[4] who have had command of their companies for months. Can these men feel contented when they see others, who came into the regiment as second lieutenants, promoted to captaincy, and a crowd of incompetent civilians and non-commissioned officers of other regiments sent here to take their places? Can they have confidence in officers who read the Boston *Courier* and talk about "Niggers"? . . .

4. Camp Meigs, in Readville, was the place near Boston where the Massachusetts regiments trained before going south.

LETTER 90

("Africano," Regimental Hospital, Point Lookout, Maryland, September 2, 1864; *WAA*, September 24, 1864) In the summer of 1864, the Democratic party met in Chicago to nominate General George B. McClellan to run against Republican Abraham Lincoln for the presidency of the Union. McClellan opposed Lincoln's policies on the war and emancipation. "Africano," probably a member of the 5th Massachusetts Cavalry, predicted that the election of McClellan would reverse all the gains made under Lincoln's Emancipation Proclamation. Although Lincoln and his proclamation had their faults, according to Africano, they were much better than the Democrats and McClellan.

. . . McClellan and his party have ever been the chief instruments in giving aid and assistance to the common enemy of the country, inaugurators of this bloody conflict for the erection of the temple of Slavery on the rightful domains of Freedom. Is this the people's candidate? – McClellan, the secret advocate of dissension, disloyalty, treason, and the ardent lover of human slavery?

When Mr. Lincoln stabbed slavery, had he followed up his political victory by stabbing the monster to death, and eternally hiding its foul stain, by immediately eradicating it from the entire country, today it would have been dead, buried, and grown out of the memory even of those who fostered, idolized and made it the center of their affections; and the Union would have been restored, the chivalry made to repent of their audaciousness, and the *beloved institution* would have perished without having found so many thousands of "poor white trash" to rally in her defense, to the detriment of the pride and glory of this great country, seeing that the foundation of the political fabric of the so-called Confederacy had crumbled to ruin. In this, as in many other things, Mr. Lincoln has shown his inefficiency as a statesman, and though we abhor him when we consider the many injustices he has allowed to be practiced on colored men, we cannot but think him a better object than George B. McClellan. We do not in the least pretend to be a Lincolnite, for these reasons: 1st, Mr Lincoln's unjust policy towards the negro soldiers in not enforcing upon the rebel authorities the necessity of acknowledging and treating them as prisoners of war. 2d, His partial freedom and his colonization scheme. 3d, His ordering the enlistment of slaves and paying the bounty to their so-called masters, under pretense of being loyal men, thereby recognizing, to a certain extent, the right of property in man. 4th, His protecting disloyal Kentucky and parts of greater disloyal States from the liberating influence of his double-sided instrument; but for the time being we shall carefully avoid intermingling him with baser coin, and come more closely to the subject under consideration. . . .

Where is the man to be found on this broad continent, who is more desirous of seeing the South achieve her independence with human slavery for its cornerstone than George B. McClellan, nominee of the Chicago Convention, vehement partisan of Jeff Davis and his crew? Nowhere! nowhere! . . .

LETTER 91

(Charles W. Singer, Sergeant, Co. A, 107th USCI, Louisville, Kentucky, September 18, 1864; *CR*, October 8, 1864) Sergeant Singer makes clear in this letter the close link between freedom for the slaves and citizenship for the free African Americans of the North. He believes the Union government the best hope for true freedom, and he calls on all black men to join the war against the Confederacy.

. . . Freedom! What a glorious word to commence with! I place it above all others except my God. I never was a slave; but my imag-

ination furnishes to me a picture, which must approximate somewhat to the reality of that miserable condition. I sincerely and
candidly think that every man in the North should, to the fullest
extent of his abilities, aid and further the cause of freeing the slaves
now held in bondage by Southern tyrants.

To this appeal some may answer: "What do we want to fight for
the slaves for? Let them win their own freedom." To all such I
would say, make an imaginary exchange of conditions with those
poor, down-trodden and degraded slaves at the South, and then
would you not think it very hard for others to tell you to help
yourself, and get out of it the best way you can? Most assuredly you
would.

We should not forget the fact that the free colored man's elevation is at issue, as well as the slave's. Suppose the rebel army was as
far North as the Union Army is South; what would be the result? I
will tell you. Our homes would have been burned to the ground,
and our aged and defenseless parents barbarously treated. Rather
than have such outrages perpetrated, I would remain in the army
the rest of my life. . . .

I wish for nothing but to breathe, in this land with my fellow
subjects, the air of liberty. I have no ambition, unless it be to break
the chain and exclaim: "Freedom to all!" I never will be satisfied so
long as the meanest slave in the South has a link of chain clinging
to his leg. He may be naked, but he shall not be in irons. Remember, soldiers, we are fighting a great battle for the benefit not
only of the country, but for ourselves and the whole of mankind.
The eyes of the world are upon us, and on the result depends our
future happiness. One portion is gazing with contempt, jealousy,
and envy; the other with hope and confidence. Do you expect to
execute this high trust by allowing yourselves to be trampled down
by your enemies in the North? No, we can battle against both; at
least, we can try. . . .

It is not merely that I am grateful for the protection and citizenship that I may hope for; but I recognize in the stability of this
Government a source of strength to other nations. While this Gov-

ernment stands, there is hope for the most abject, disabled, and helpless of mankind. Our race may, at some future day, become an independent nation. Should we ask the protection of the United States Government, we could not, with consistency, be refused if we do our best to aid it in this, its time of danger. . . .

The question has frequently been asked: What will be gained by the present war? I ask, in return: What will you not lose by a mongrel state of peace? We would lose the best opportunity that has ever been afforded to us to show the whole world that we are willing to fight for our rights. . . .

LETTER 92

(Joseph H. Barquet, [Sergeant,] 54th Massachusetts Infantry, Morris Island, South Carolina, [October 1864]; *WAA*, November 5, 1864) The National Convention of Colored Men, held in Syracuse, N.Y., in October 1864, got the attention of African-American soldiers, even though most could not attend. Sergeant Joseph H. Barquet wrote this open letter to the Convention, encouraging its delegates to work for the economic rights of blacks. He believed that hard work, especially in Southern agriculture, and sound education would be necessary for the race to take advantage of the changes brought on by the war.

GENTLEMEN: . . .

There are many points of vital importance that ought to claim your undivided attention. I will not arrogate to myself to mention to you what these are, but remember education, and force this on the people. This I mention because my present position brings it more plainly and painfully to my view. By education, and that alone, scarcely aided by wealth (can ignorance ignore this?) must we assume a new position; and education alone can enable us to maintain the same.

New fields of operation will from this time forth open up themselves to view, and we must not stand idle because no man has need of us, but [we] must follow our white brethren holding him by the heel, and securing to ourselves and posterity a part of a common heritage. There be now places to fill that laboring colored men at the North could secure in the service of government where good wages could be awarded, and a spirit of independence at once schooled for future usefulness.

Agriculture, where negro labor is the dominant motor or power, should call your divided capital into one or several strong central funds. Though secession has, for a time dethroned the monarch Cotton, yet the time is not distant when under the full sway of freedom he will once more ascend his throne, and sway his scepter with more potency than ever. Generations, at least one, must pass after a peace before this member of the family of the soil will cease to pay a large dividend on capital. You need not be cited to the risk that our Northern men are now running to obtain even an uncertain footing. I need not state what you well know, that the southern agricultural labor is of us.

Next, the possession of land by our people either individually or collectively, or having a body for the residence of the soul – a foothold that will give us the claim of home; and no life gives to a people that spirit of independence as the tillage of the soil; the primitive occupation of man; the product that brings in market the same value as that produced by others. . . .

Brethren, let us join hands. Let us by a common cause now made holy by our blood, raise ourselves from the mire. Let us be men. May heaven smile on your doings. . . .

LETTER 93

(Thomas B. Wester, Orderly Sergeant, Co. I, 43rd USCI, Bermuda Hundred, Virginia, [December 1864]; *CR*, January 7, 1865) By the end of 1864, Confederate leaders grew desperate for more soldiers; they considered using blacks, including slaves. Sergeant

Thomas B. Wester, of Princeton, N.J., believed that Southern blacks would never fight for the Confederacy, because their Northern brothers were already helping win freedom for the slaves. Soon, he thought, black soldiers would win equal rights for all.

. . . What have [the rebels] to fight for? They have nothing. They cause bloodshed when there is no necessity for it. They cause their families to suffer and be driven from their homes, and their children to cry for bread. Their homes are levelled to the ground; but their hearts are like Pharaoh's, in the days of old. When God went to him seven different times, to let the children of Israel go, he refused until he was compelled to submit.

It is just so with the rebellious foe. They have been offered peace or war; but they preferred war and now they have it. They will have to succumb shortly, or like Pharaoh, be overthrown.

They have exhausted the material to organize new white armies, and they now, as a last resource, call upon the black men of the South – the poor, despised, down-trodden slaves – to fight against the glorious Union. They ask those, who in days gone by, and indeed, at the present time, are not considered as human beings by them – who are fit for nothing but to be bought and sold like horses and mules – whose sacred ties of husband and wife are to be set at naught – whose families can, at any time, be torn asunder, the father sold to one master, the son to another, the daughter to another, and the wife and little ones to yet another – whose chief duty is to enrich Southerners, at the cost of his own infamy and degradation – yes, they call upon the black men to do what they themselves have not been able to do.

But will the slave fight against us? Will he fight against his own father, son, or brother, now in arms for universal liberty and the preservation of this glorious Union? No, never! He will turn his back upon the traitors, and leave them to their ignominious fate. They will flee to our lines for protection.

Have they been taught to hate us? Yes, they have been told many an untruth concerning the Yankees – that we would kill them, and commit other atrocities. But they have detected the *lie.* Some of them are now in our army, fighting side-by-side with the white men. The bones of the black man are at the present time whitening the battle-fields, while their blood simultaneously with the white man's oozes into the soil of his former home.

Have they not fought bravely at Port Hudson, Fort Pillow, Fort Pulaski, and on the bloody fields of Virginia and Georgia, besides many other places? Yet, notwithstanding all the gallantry displayed by colored soldiers, there are a few men in our Northern cities, who do not want to give the colored man his equal rights. But these men do not rule Congress. I hope that the day is not far distant when we shall see the colored man enjoying the same rights and privileges as those of the white man of this country.

We are fighting as hard to restore the Union as the white man is. Why, then, should we not have equal rights with a foreigner, who comes to this country to fight for the preservation of the Government? . . .

LETTER 94

(Henry Carpenter Hoyle, [Private,] Co. F, 43d USCI, near Richmond, Virginia, February 18, 1865; *CR*, March 18, 1865) Streetcar companies in Philadelphia offended African Americans by refusing to let them ride on the cars. After protests and challenges, the decision was finally reversed. News of this reached men in the army, and Private Henry C. Hoyle wrote to congratulate his friends in Philadelphia.

In looking over the columns of the "Philadelphia Inquirer" a few days ago, my eyes fell upon an advertisement which gave a great deal of pleasure to myself and those of my companions who were at that time with me. It is the success which the people of this country are fast gaining over the once too popular prejudice against our race. The advertisement alluded to is from the Fifth and Sixth Street Passenger Railway Company, announcing their intention of allowing colored people to ride the cars of their line. This is indeed another progressive stride, which redounds to the credit of the Quaker City and her liberal-minded citizens. The great Giver of all good is slowly but surely opening the eyes of the white man to the injustice which they have long practiced upon the negro. That He may continue this great reformation should be the prayer of every Christian.

I cannot see why we should still be kept from exercising the full rights of citizenship. We are taxed and required to conform to all the laws of the community in which we live, and are even included among that class of white citizens who owe their allegiance and service to the government, (I mean, subject to the draft and the call of the President, when soldiers are wanted to defend the rights and institutions of the country) and yet we are not allowed to exercise those rights for which we may, at any time, be called upon to lay down our lives. I do not mean to grumble, but merely to show how inconsistent it is to require us to battle for privileges which we are not allowed to enjoy. But God, in His own good time, will batter down this barrier to our advancement in the human scale, and open the hearts of the people to the justness of our claim. Already has He worked wonders through the agency of this rebellion. He has struck the chains of bondage from nearly half a million of our race, and given new strength and vigor to the doctrine of Universal Freedom and Equal Rights.

It behooves every loyal black man to shoulder his musket and do battle in this great war for human liberty. . . .

LETTER 95

(George S. Massey, [Sergeant-Major,] 43d USCI, near Richmond, Virginia, March 27, 1865; *CR*, April 8, 1865) Civil rights were important, according to Sergeant-Major George S. Massey, a barber from Pittsburgh, but just as important or more so was economic independence. In this letter he urges his people to get practical education that will prepare them to make money.

. . . The subject of making money is one which should engage the most profound attention of every man of color in the United States; notwithstanding its great importance, it is one which rarely excites discussion among us, therefore we consider that it is to a great degree neglected. All of us, who have had any experience whatever in society, must be aware of the great influence wielded by the mighty dollar, and for this reason it becomes us, as a distinct portion of society, to be wide awake to our interests. We can gain nothing by our industry which will tend more to give us respectable positions in society, than homes and property, real and personal.

In order to thus situate ourselves it is necessary that we should take hold of every respectable and profitable occupation that is in our reach, and follow it with earnestness, and make it our effort to bring those who are out of our reach within it. But we hear it argued that we are few in number, and cannot get the general patronage of the public. I do admit that these are serious difficulties, but most of them are difficulties that can be overlooked. We are not so weak as to be unable to accomplish much, if we will only persevere.

A million of men using proper efforts cannot be overlooked in a nation like this, and as American Slavery is to be abolished as the friends of freedom shortly hope, and its enemies fear, then our population will be sufficiently great to set at defiance every attempt to crowd us out of respectable employment, and to compel those who would succeed in business to court our patronage.

We call for equality before the law, but while we justly make this call, we should remember that equality in this respect will do but comparatively little towards elevating our race or condition when we are wanting in every other respect. While we have to look to others for equality before the law, we must depend entirely on our own hands and heads for equality in financial resources.

I am happy to know that some are laboring with good results for our elevation in science and literature, but these qualifications alone will not enable us to perform all the duties of independent and good citizens. Our education needs to be practical, such as will profit us and our families, and the rest of mankind. Let no one harbor a thought that, because he is not permitted to occupy the most prominent position in society, there is nothing left worthy of his attention. We need farmers and mechanics as well as statesmen, lawyers, and doctors. We should not be discouraged because we are poor and have to live by our labor, for a large portion of the capitalists, and a great many business men of the West once knew how to labor with their hands. . . . Cultivate industrious habits, practice strict economy, and proportion your expenditures to your income; take pleasure in your daily avocations, and look with contempt on all extravagant nonsense which some are pleased to call taking pleasure: what you lack in advantage to make, try to supply by saving; never go about spending money to show people that you have it, for such notions will only impress the idea on the minds of thinking people that you are not accustomed to having money.

LETTER 96

(Martin R. Delany, Major, 104th USCI, Charleston, South Carolina, April 20, 1865; *CR*, May 20, 1865) Whatever complaints black soldiers may have had about President Lincoln's slow progress in emancipating the slaves and granting equality to African Americans, they disappeared when he was killed on April 13, 1865. With anguish fully equal to that of white Americans, blacks mourned the death of Lincoln. Martin R. Delany, who had recently been commissioned an army major, wrote this open letter urging all blacks throughout the nation, no matter how poor, to contribute toward a memorial for the president.

A calamity such as the world never before witnessed – a calamity, the most heart-rending, caused by the perpetration of a deed at the hands of a wretch, the most infamous and atrocious – a calamity as humiliating to America as it is infamous and atrocious – has suddenly brought our country to mourning by the untimely death of the humane, the benevolent, the philanthropic, the generous, the beloved, the able, the wise, great, and good man, the President of the United States, Abraham Lincoln, the Just. In his fall, a mighty chieftain and statesman has passed away. God, in his inscrutable providence, has suffered this, and we bow with meek and humble resignation to his Divine will, because He does all things well. God's will be done!

I suggest that, as a just and appropriate tribute of respect and lasting gratitude from the colored people of the United States to the memory of President Lincoln, the Father of American Liberty, every individual of our race contribute one cent, as this will enable each member of every family to contribute, parents paying for every child, allowing all who are able to subscribe any sum they please above this, to such national monument as may hereafter be decided upon by the American people. I hope it may be in Illinois, near his own family residence. . . .

LETTER 97

(William P. Woodlin, Musician, 8th USCI, Petersburg, Virginia, April 28, 1865; *CR*, July 22, 1865) Education clearly had a priority among African Americans. Because many white public schools kept out blacks, they started their own schools wherever possible.

In 1863, the African Methodist Episcopal Church (which published the *Christian Recorder*) took over Wilberforce College, in Ohio, the first college to be run by African Americans. The Church issued an urgent appeal for money to keep Wilberforce open. As this letter from Virginia shows, black soldiers responded openly to support the black college.

The appeal of the Trustees of the Wilberforce University for aid, in the columns of the *Recorder*, suggested the idea to a friend of our race of the following collection; and I, as the agent, am happy to state that the men of the regiment representing at least ten different States, have responded to my solicitations with alacrity, and I am enabled to present you, as the result of my labors, the sum of $241, which, if too late for a redemption fund, we desire to be placed in the endowment. The great changes which are now so rapidly molding the public mind have brought us to realize the necessity of intellectual improvement to a much greater degree than ever before. We wish, therefore, to show our interest practically now, so that in days to come posterity may enjoy it. It may be of some interest to you to know that this money was collected on the march after General Lee, from Petersburg to Appomattox Court House, and some of it the day after his surrender. . . .

LETTER 98

(William Gibson, Corporal, 28th USCI, City Point, Virginia, May 18, 1865; *CR*, May 27, 1865) When the war ended, optimism about civil rights was high. But when the soldiers returned home, many found that the old prejudices and the old laws had not changed, despite heroic service by the men. Corporal William Gibson visited his home in Indiana and discovered that the whites there were not interested in removing the restrictive "black laws" from the books.

It is the first time in the history of my life that one so humble as myself ever attempted to write anything for publication through the columns of your most worthy journal; and it is with great reluctance that I attempt it on the present occasion, owing to my short stay at home in Park Co[ounty], Ind[iana], on a furlough, where I found many friends to rejoice over, and many disadvantages upon the part of the colored people to mourn over. It seems very strange to me that the people of Indiana are so very indifferent about removing from their statute books those Black Laws, which are a curse to them in the eyes of God and man, and above all things in life, the most grievous to be borne by any people.

Shall the history of the old 28th [USCI], which was raised in that State, stand upon the great record of the American army second to none? Shall these brave sons return home after periling their lives for several years in the storm of battle for the restoration of the Union and to vindicate the honor and dignity of that fair Western State which is classed among the best composing this great nation, but to be treated as slaves? Shall it be said by the nations of the earth that any portion of the United States treated her brave defenders thus? I hope never to see the day; yet it is fast approaching.

Have we no friends at home among the whites to look this great injustice in the face, and bid its sin-cursed waves forever leave? Have we no colored friends at home who feel tired of the burden and are willing to pray to the thinking public to lighten it? As for us, we have done our duty and are willing to do it whenever the State and country call us; but after responding, are you not willing to pay the laborer for his hire? It is to be seen in all past history that when men fought for their country and returned home, they always enjoyed the rights and privileges due to other citizens.

We ask to be made equal before the law; grant us this and we ask no more. Let the friends of freedom canvass the country on this subject. Let the sound go into all the earth. . . .

LETTER 99

(W. A. Freeman, 22nd USCI, [Virginia, May 1865]; *CR*, May 27, 1865) The old idea of forcing African Americans out of the United States had a revival during the Civil War years. President Lincoln suggested emigration to Haiti or Central America; others suggested they go to South America, and the American Colonization Society wanted them in Liberia. When the war ended, such ideas were raised again. After serving with valor in the war to preserve the Union, black soldiers, such as W. A. Freeman, proclaimed vigorously that they had earned their right not only to stay in the United States but also to have equality with whites.

. . . Colored soldiers are opposed to Colonization; too long have we procrastinated; too frequently has this subject been discussed, and those in favor of it have been defeated. The problem has been solved. No longer is the question asked, "What shall we do with the colored man?"

I believe that the same God who created the white man created the black; and am also convinced of the all-important fact that God in his wisdom designed that the colored man should be a man on this continent. After four years of incessant toil, suffering, blood-shed, and carnage, we have been released from a worse-than-Egyptian bondage, not that we might colonize Liberia nor migrate to Mexico, but that we might engage in the great struggle and assist in making this a Republic. And shall we forfeit all claim to those rights which God has in his wisdom, designed for us at home! No, never! Justice to that God who has delivered us forbids! Manhood itself, and justice to our race forbids! Justice to that martyr for liberty, who died by the hand of the assassin, forbids! The blood of our comrades who have fallen upon the fields of battle, while assisting to plant the tree of liberty; the tears of our widows and mothers, which have watered the tree of liberty; the prayers of our ancestors who have died in oppression, and whose pious ejaculations have ascended to the throne of God like incense and sweet perfume, forbids; for this liberty and equality have been purchased at too great a sacrifice. . . .

LETTER 100

("A Citizen of Geneva, now a Soldier" to "The Colored Citizens of Geneva," Co. E, 11th USCHA, [Louisiana, July 1865]; *WAA*, July 22, 1865) During the summer of 1865, President Andrew Johnson pardoned most of the men who had served in the Confederate Army; they were now ready to return to the Union and vote. Black soldiers watched with alarm as these former "traitors" were again citizens, while the black defenders of the Union were not yet voters. This "Citizen of Geneva" urges the folks at home to work hard for their rights.

. . . Are there young ladies capable of teaching schools, or young men capable of becoming lawyers or statesmen? If there are, that is what we want to hear. We want school teachers here at the South, and we want men at home that are not afraid to battle against any argument that any white man may produce, to show that we ought not to have the rights of franchise. We are a people who have just been relieved of the yoke of a cursed oppression, and the whites argue that we are not capable of taking care of ourselves, and that we will make vagabonds and won't work for wages. But I deny all of this. Is it possible that we, who even in bondage supplied the nation with cotton, sugar, tobacco and other products too numerous to mention, and have made the United States rich by the sweat of our brows, are not capable of taking care of ourselves? I say *that we are, and we have proved it.*

Citizens of Geneva: As the war is very near to a close, and soldiers, both white and black, are about to be discharged, what are we to do with the blacks? Are we to disband them as supernumeraries or as citizens? And shall it be that these paroled rebels, that have caused the nation to mourn the loss of a second Moses, and a father of a second nation, to become citizens of these United States? And shall these damnable traitors have the same privileges that they have heretofore had? If so be the case, what will become of us as a people? We must walk uprightly and honestly, and educate those who have been kept in bonds, and educate our children, and fit them for the field; and we must battle against prejudice, and continue to do so until we have redeemed our race. . . .

LETTER 101

(N. B. Sterrett, [Sergeant,] 39th USCI, Caroline City, North Carolina, August 19, 1865; *CR*, August 26, 1865) In the old slave states such as Maryland, racial prejudice died slowly. As soldiers returned home, they found the social climate still harsh. Sergeant Norman B. Sterrett has discovered that in Baltimore the old attitudes still prevailed. He predicts that as soon as all the black soldiers have returned, they will reform Baltimore's prejudice.

. . . It was no little joy to me to think, when starting, that I was about to return to my home after an absence of fifteen months. After sailing over the briny ocean for three days, I found myself happily seated with my family at home, in Baltimore, Md.

Now, I do assure you it was a great gratification for me to know that although when I left home I left a slave State, with laws existing as black as the nocturnal regions, on returning I found it free and every slave at liberty. But I also find that this good work is only begun, not finished. There are many characters still living in Maryland who have no better breeding than to offer insults to colored ladies and gentlemen, while walking the streets, and I am sorry to say, that I saw these diabolical acts perpetrated by those who in past days would have classed themselves with ladies, but, in my estimation, they are no more than fiends.

I became perfectly exasperated at first, and then a new idea struck me, that every filthy, rusty article needed a great deal of rubbing to make it bright. And I do assure you, when three or four thousand brave colored soldiers, who have endured privation and suffering to crush the wicked rebellion, return to their homes in Maryland, it will be rubbed so bright that respectable colored people will be able to walk the streets without being insulted.

. . . The fact is this; we have been in Egypt, and from the plague of death they have been obliged to let God's people go. And God has placed President Andrew Johnson, (like Joshua of old) to lead His people into perfect liberty. We are entitled to equal rights and privileges, and with the assistance of God we mean to obtain them.

7

The Struggle for
Equal Pay

SERGEANT WILLIAM WALKER, an escaped slave, marched with others of his company to the tent of their commander. Lieutenant Colonel Augustus G. Bennett, of the Third South Carolina Infantry (Colored), watched as the black men stacked their rifles and ammunition belts. "What does all this mean?" he asked. Sergeant Walker replied that he and his men were "not willing to be soldiers for seven dollars per month," about half what white privates were paid. He called them "an assemblage who only contemplated a peaceful demand for the rights and benefits that had been guaranteed them." The colonel told them that what they were doing was against army regulations; they should pick up their arms and return quietly to their quarters. But the men disobeyed his order, returning to their tents *without* their rifles, and Sergeant Walker, their leader, was charged with inciting a mutiny. He was court-martialed, convicted, and sentenced to die. A firing squad shot him on February 29, 1864, for wanting equal pay.[1]

Sergeant Walker carried his protest beyond legal limits, and he paid an extreme penalty for it. Many other African-American soldiers, especially the free men from the North, also resented their inferior pay – but instead of refusing duty, they protested by declining *any* pay at all until they would be paid the same as white soldiers. They also wrote letters complaining that they had been promised a soldier's pay and would not accept "a laborer's pay."

The pay question arose because the government had no clear idea of what rights black soldiers should have. The racist ideas of the time convinced most Americans that the black soldiers were simply not worth as much as the whites. The hodgepodge of wartime Federal laws that dealt with African Americans stipulated that the army could use blacks as laborers and pay them ten dollars, minus three dollars for clothing, a total of seven dollars a month. When the first black regiments were organized, it was not clear whether they should be paid the same as white soldiers or the same as black laborers. Secretary of War Edwin M. Stanton had to make a clear decision; he asked his chief lawyer, William Whiting, for a legal opinion based on the confusing laws already passed by Congress. Reluctantly, in June 1863, Whiting said the law made all blacks in the army equal only to one another – no African-American soldier of any rank could be paid more than seven dollars a month.

This decision shows the racism of the time, but it also went directly against what the soldiers themselves had been told when they enlisted. The secretary of war had promised full army pay to the South Carolina regiments, and Governor John A. Andrew of Massachusetts had told the men in his regiments that they would

---

1. Otto Friedrich, "We Will Not Do Duty Any Longer for Seven Dollars per Month," *American Heritage*, 39:1 (February 1988) 64–73. Harold C. Westwood, "The Cause and Consequence of a Union Black Soldier's Mutiny and Execution," *Civil War History*, 31 (1985) 222–236.

be paid the same as all other troops. When the Federal government announced its decision for seven dollars, black soldiers and many of their white officers protested. First, the low pay was an insult; they believed they were just as good soldiers as the whites. Second, it was a financial hardship, especially for the men who had families back home. Third, it hurt morale and discipline because black corporals, sergeants, and even chaplains were paid less than white privates. Many black soldiers simply refused to accept any money at all until they got equal pay.

Equal pay did not finally come until August 1864 for the men who had been free before the war. Not until March 1865 did the South Carolina regiments and other units made up of ex-slaves get full back pay from the date of their enlistment.

During these long months while Congress and the War Department debated about how much to pay black soldiers, most of the men went about their army duties faithfully, if not happily. Most understood that they must obey orders or risk the same fate as Sergeant Walker. Furthermore, they knew that the rest of the nation was watching them to see how they behaved: Any act that could be seen as disloyal, unpatriotic, or unmilitary would harm their claim to civil rights and equality.

To make the public aware of their feelings, many of the men wrote letters to the newspapers. They explained their point of view, told of their hardships, and replied to their critics. (Some black soldiers criticized the protesters for complaining instead of fighting.) But their steadfast refusal to take any money until they got equal pay played a major role in persuading Congress to change. When the paymaster finally arrived and the African-American soldiers got their back pay at full value, they could celebrate a major victory in the long struggle for their rights.[2]

2. Herman Belz, "Law, Politics, and Race in the Struggle for Equal Pay During the Civil War," *Civil War History* 22 (September 1976) 197–213. Ira Berlin et al. "Fighting on Two Fronts: The Struggle for Equal Pay," *Prologue* 14 (Fall 1982) 131–139.

LETTER 102

(G. E. S., [Sergeant,] 54th Massachusetts Infantry, Morris Island, South Carolina, September 2, 1863; *WAA*, September 19, 1863) "G. E. S." was probably George E. Stephens. This letter was written about six weeks after the 54th fought its famous battle at Fort Wagner, where the regiment charged the fort bravely and lost many killed, wounded, and captured. Massachusetts Governor John A. Andrew had promised the black troops fully equal pay and treatment; now his promise has been reversed by the Federal government. Stephens questions the need for a special law for paying African-American soldiers.

... The question of our pay continues to be the topic of conversation and correspondence. Numerous letters have reached us from distinguished friends in the State of Massachusetts, all expressing the utmost confidence that we will receive all of our pay, and have secured to us every right that other Massachusetts soldiers enjoy. His Excellency Gov. Andrew, in a letter dated, "Executive Department, Boston, August 24th," and addressed to Mr. Frederick Johnson, an officer in the regiment, says:

"I have this day received your letter of the 10th of August, and in reply desire, in the first place, to express to you the lively interest with which I have watched every step of the fifty-fourth Regiment since it left Massachusetts, and the feelings of pride and admiration with which I have learned and read of the accounts of the heroic conduct of the regiment in the attack upon Fort Wagner, when you and your brave soldiers so well proved their manhood, and showed themselves to be true soldiers of Massachusetts. As to the matter inquired about in your letter, you may rest assured that I shall not rest until you have secured all of your rights, and that I have no doubt whatever of ultimate success. I have no doubt, by law, you are entitled to the same pay as other soldiers, and on the authority of the Secretary of War, I promised that you should be paid and treated in all respects like other soldiers of Massachusetts. Till this is done I feel that my promise is dishonored by the government. The whole difficulty arises from a misapprehension, the correction of which will no doubt be made as soon as I can get the subject fully examined by the Secretary of War. I have the honor to be your obedient servant,

JOHN A. ANDREW, Governor of Massachusetts."

The trouble seems to be something like this: The Paymaster General, whoever that may be, has directed the paymasters to pay all negro troops of African descent, $10 per month, the pay allowed to contrabands by statute when employed in the Commissary or Quartermaster's Department. There seems to have been no provision made to pay colored soldiers. There may be some reason for making a distinction between armed and unarmed men in the service of the government, but when the nationality of a man takes away his title to pay it become another thing. Suppose a regiment of Spaniards should be mustered into the service of the United States, would Congress have to pass a special law to pay Spaniards? Or, suppose, a regiment of Sandwich Islanders should do duty as soldiers of the United States, would it be necessary to pass a law to pay Sandwich Islanders? Does not the deed of muster secure the services and even life of the man mustered into the service to the government? And does not this same deed of muster give a man title to all pay and bounties awarded to soldiers bearing arms? I believe that, "by law, we are entitled to the same pay as other soldiers," and "misapprehension arises" from this: The Paymaster General will not have the colored soldiers paid under the law which pay[s] white soldiers, and virtually creates in his own mind the necessity for the passage of a special law authorizing them to be paid. Is there a special law on the statute books of the National Legislature touching the payment of colored men employed in the naval service? . . .

("Massachusetts Soldier," 54th Massachusetts Infantry, Morris Island, South Carolina, December 1863; quoted in a letter from Theodore Tilton to *Boston Journal*, ca. December 15, 1863, from the Fifty-fourth Regiment Papers, Massachusetts Historical Society) Governor Andrew of Massachusetts worked diligently to get equal pay for his black soldiers. If the Federal government would not pay them properly, he would get the Massachusetts legislature to pay them the difference. But in this letter written to Theodore Tilton an anonymous soldier points out that the main issue is not so much the money itself as the principle of equality.

"A strange misapprehension" . . . "exists as to the matter of pay; and it pains us deeply. We came forward at the call of Gov. Andrew, in which call he distinctly told us that we were to be subsisted, *clothed, paid,* and treated in *all* respects the same as other Massachusetts soldiers. Again, on the presentation of flags to the regiment, at Camp Meigs, the Governor reiterated this promise, on the strength of which we marched through Boston, holding our heads high, as men and as soldiers. Nor did we grumble because we were not paid the portion of United States bounty paid to other volunteer regiments in advance.

"Now that we have gained some reputation as soldiers, we claim the right to be heard.

"Three times have we been mustered in for pay. Twice have we swallowed the insult offered us by the United States paymaster, contenting ourselves with a simple refusal to acknowledge ourselves, in this matter, different from other Massachusetts soldiers. Once, in the face of insult and intimidation, such as no body of men and soldiers were ever subjected to before, we quietly refused, and continued to do our duty.

"For four months we've been steadily working, night and day, under fire. And such work! Up to our knees in mud half the time – causing the tearing and wearing out of more than the volunteer's yearly allowance of clothing – denied time to repair and wash (what we might by that means have saved), denied time to drill and perfect ourselves in soldierly quality, denied the privilege of burying our dead decently! All this we've borne patiently, waiting for justice.

"Imagine our surprise and disappointment, on the receipt by the last mail of the Governor's Address to the General Court, to find him making a proposition to them to pay this regiment the difference between what the United States Government offers us and what they are legally bound to pay us, which, in effect, advertises us to the world as holding out for *money* and not from *principle* – that we sink our manhood in consideration of a few more dollars. How has this come about? What false friend has been misrepresenting us to the Governor, to make him think that our necessities outweigh our self-respect? I am sure no representation of *ours* ever impelled him to this action."

LETTER 104

("Wolverine," 55th Massachusetts Infantry, Folly Island, South Carolina, December 1863; *CR*, January 2, 1864) Like the 54th, the 55th Massachusetts refused to accept either the reduced Federal pay or the supplement offered by the governor of Massachusetts. In this letter "Wolverine" answers critics who have said that the black soldiers were not properly grateful for what Massachusetts offered. "Liberty and Equality" is his motto.

. . . We don't wish you to look upon us as being inclined to be a little stubborn; we were told that we would be accepted by the U.S. Government on the same terms as her other Regiments, and do you call the same terms reducing pay, and receiving part pay from

Mass., and a part from the government of the same? If you look at
it in that way, you don't look at it as we do. Massachusetts has
always been first to open the door to the poor colored man; was
first to send two colored regiments in the field to extinguish the last
spark of a most infamous rebellion – one that will figure largely in
the annals of history for centuries to come. You sit at your firesides
and just study a little what the poor soldier is suffering. You have no
idea, and just you fight and slay the rebels that are at our backs, or
we will fight them that are in front of us, or fight in Congress for
our rights, and we will fight here for yours. I feel proud, and so
does every other man that belongs to the 55th, to think that they
stand so well upon the principles which they came here to fight for.
Our pride has won us a name amongst the white regiments around
us; they call us the Independent Colored Regiment, and say to us,
You do the work that we ought to share in, and they don't want to
pay you anything for it. Do you want to break that spirit of pride! I
hope not; and as you say that we have proved ourselves worthy of
approbation, don't put our principle upon the grindstone. We love
this government, and will sacrifice our lives to maintain it. Just
think for a moment, reflect deeply, that there is good for you to gain
by it; our lives we value just as highly as you do yours; but without a
stimulant, our exertions would not be worth anything. Let our
faces be black, but our hearts be true, you will find us true and
loyal and obedient, and all qualities pertaining to a soldier. A true
and rather singular idea for a colored man to wish to be placed on
equal footing with a white man! Why not? Can't we fight just as
well? We showed our qualities at Port Gibson and Wagner. Now, if
there is not pluck, just fall in some big hole, and we will guarantee
to pull you out without blacking your hands; fall down and we will
pick you up; we won't pass by and perhaps give you a kick or a cuff,
but pick you up, carry you home to your good wife, and won't ask of
you your daughter for compensation; all the compensation that we
ask is to give us our rights, and don't be dodging around every
corner as if you owed us something, and your conscience is getting
the upper hand of you. . . . Our motto: "Liberty and Equality."

LETTER 105

("Bought and Sold," 6th USCI, Yorktown, Virginia, February 8, 1864; *CR*, February 20, 1864) If the black soldiers felt insulted by their low pay, the people who suffered most were their families back home. "Bought and Sold" had been drafted and served in a regiment from Pennsylvania; his letter shows his despair at his inability to provide for his wife and children.

I am a soldier, or at least that is what I was drafted for in the 6th USCT; have been in the service since Aug., last. I could not afford to get a substitute, or I would not be here now and my poor wife at home almost starving. When I was at home I could make a living for her and my two little ones; but now that I am a soldier they must do the best they can or starve. It almost tempts me to desert and run a chance of getting shot, when I read her letters, hoping that I would come to her relief. But what am I to do? It is a shame the way they treat us; our officers tell me now that we are not soldiers; that if we were we would get the same pay as the white men; that the government just called us out to dig and drudge, that we are to get but $7.00 per month. Really I thought I was a soldier, and it made me feel somewhat proud to think that I had a right to fight for Uncle Sam. When I was at Chelton Hill I felt very patriotic; but my wife's letters have brought my patriotism down to the freezing point, and I don't think it will ever rise again; and it is the case all through the regiment. Men having families at home, and they looking to them for support, and they not being able to send them one penny. . . .

LETTER 106

(R. H. B., [Sergeant,] 3rd USCI, Jacksonville, Florida, June 30, 1864; *CR*, August 6, 1864) Richard H. Black had been a seaman from Philadelphia before enlisting in the army. In this letter, he points out that because black soldiers had to pay for their uniforms, and because many had to work long hours digging trenches, ruining their clothes, some of them actually owed money to the government on payday. At this time Congress was debating the pay question, and rumors had spread that equal pay was a fact. But the men were disappointed and angry.

. . . Local newspapers and periodicals have been teeming with reports for some time that Congress had passed bills equalizing the pay of colored soldiers. We had all been expecting to receive [with] the next payment, equal pay. The most skeptical mind had become reconciled, believing the reports to be true. But we were doomed to disappointment. The Paymaster did not hesitate to tell us that he had received no official notice to pay us any more than the usual amount, meaning the insignificant sum of seven dollars. The surplus of clothing that the men have drawn was charged to their account, leaving the majority of them now in debt to the Government.

This latter could have been avoided, and it was thought by those who sympathized with us that there was no necessity of having this surplus of clothes charged on the payroll at this time; but those who have it in charge were fearful lest a man should die, and then be charged with the amount due.

To attempt to describe the feelings of the men would be impossible; they can scarcely be imagined. The case, as it now stands, is more embarrassing than before, as our families and the public are induced to believe by current reports that we receive the pay. Hence they expect what we do not receive. . . .

LETTER 107

("Wild Jack," Sergeant, 5th USCI, near Petersburg, Virginia, July 28, 1864; *CR*, August 6, 1864) The letters and protests, especially from the Massachusetts regiments, did not please every black soldier. "Wild Jack," a sergeant in an Ohio regiment fighting in Virginia, writes that they should keep their complaints to themselves. Apparently, the army paymasters in Virginia were paying the black troops the same as whites. "Wild Jack" also points out that some "army correspondents" glorified their own regiments at the expense of others that did most of the fighting.

. . . Now, I believe in justice, and justice I will show to those who deserve it. I also see letters from the 54th and 55th. This would be a great rebellion if we allowed ourselves to be shot down when we can erect breast works. They also think they are neglected and commence to grumble. . . .

Now, I ask you Mr. Editor, if that is acting like soldiers? I will answer, No! And yet their cry is when shall we be paid?

I have a loving wife at home, as well as a good many of the 54th and 55th. I have hope, and as long as I can hope, I shall.

They call themselves veterans; now I don't call them so. Perhaps you and also they want to know why. Well, I will tell you. Old staid men will never find fault, and a still tongue makes a wise head. They can never accomplish any thing with a clamor. I believe we all see now. Time will tell its tale.

So far, we receive our pay now the same as white soldiers. We got paid from the first of January to the 1st of May, at $13 per month, and after the 1st of May, $16. We cannot make Congress do any thing, but we must always wait the result before we try to kick.

I know they are a brave set of men, but there is just as brave a set in the field as they are.

The charge on Fort Wagner was a good one, on the [James] Island was another, but the charge before Petersburg was as good as any. Of course we did not lose as many men, but our corps was handled as if we were soldiers, and every regiment participated in the charge. I say, neither one of the veterans need cast up their bravery any more. . . .

To hear a regiment all the time after money, goes to show that they only came after money; but a regiment who keeps her grievances to herself is more to my eyes, and I believe to the public, the most thought of. . . .

LETTER 108

("Bellefonte," 55th Massachusetts Infantry, Folly Island, South Carolina, August 19, 1864; *CR*, September 3, 1864) "Wild Jack" had criticized the Massachusetts men, and they were prompt to reply and justify their protests. "Bellefonte" points out that those who refused to accept seven dollars per month were actually working for "Wild Jack's" benefit by "contending manfully for our rights."

. . . I notice an article in the columns of your truly important paper which has a tendency to occasion bickering and contention among the soldiers now in the service of the United States. We, as soldiers, writing for the inspection of the public eye, should be very careful not to assert anything that does not meet the hearty concurrence of our comrades engaged in the same cause. . . .

Perhaps "Wild Jack" was not impressed with thoughts like the above, or he would not have written so scathingly of the 54th and 55th Massachusetts Volunteers. He should remember that our contending manfully for our rights as volunteers is his gain.

The reason why we refused to receive the pay offered us was on account of its not being according to our enlistment. Consequently, we refused to take it. After which, we were assured that Congress, when in session, would settle the matter of pay.

We agreed to await the action of Congress, willingly and uncomplainingly doing our duty as soldiers and men. After the session of Congress was over, we found ourselves no better off than we were before, that body having done nothing for us. "Wild Jack" must have been ignorant of this, or he would have spoken differently.

I desire the public to remember that we were not allured into the service of the Government by money, as some have thought. We were enlisted as a part of the quota of Massachusetts. We were promised the same clothing, rations, pay and treatment that other soldiers from the Old Bay State received. The Governor of Massachusetts assured us that he did not think any thing would occur to occasion faction among the soldiers composing the 54th and 55th regiments.

We have had a holy and sacred object in view, not for the sake of having the name of soldier, but for the sole purpose of striking the fatal blow to slavery, that the oppressed may be set free. . . .

LETTER 109

(John C. Brock, Commissary Sergeant, 43rd USCI, near Petersburg, Virginia, August 13, 1864; *CR*, August 20, 1864) When Congress finally passed an equal-pay law in July 1864, it gave back pay only to January 1, 1864, except for blacks who had been "free" before enlisting; those men would get full back pay from the date of their enlistment. Furthermore, the pay was raised to sixteen dollars per month for all privates, black and white. When the paymaster began in August 1864 to pay them, there was great joy among the men, as Sergeant Brock writes in this letter from the trenches near Petersburg.

I again take my pen in hand to inform you how we are coming on. Yesterday was a joyful day in our brigade on account of the presence of the Paymaster. We have been expecting him for some time, and at last he came, with greenbacks in abundance. He commenced immediately to pay us off – that is, early the next morning after he arrived on the ground.

The boys fell in the ranks with more alacrity than they ever did on any other occasion. They were paid at the rate of sixteen dollars a month, that is the privates were, while the non-commissioned officers were paid more according to their rank.

The boys had heard a great deal of talk about seven dollars a month, but they never believed that they would be offered such wages. So the Paymaster told us. He said that we received the same pay as any other soldier since the 1st of January; and as none of our regiment was enlisted before that time, we all received the full complement of Government pay. Every regiment had a Paymaster. Consequently our brigade was paid off very quickly. . . .

LETTER 110

("Fort Green," [54th Massachusetts Infantry,] Folly Island, South Carolina, August 21, 1864; *CR*, September 24, 1864) The Massachusetts regiments finally got their pay in August 1864. The new law required the men to take an oath that they were "free" on April 19, 1861, the day when the Union first called up the state regiments. This requirement offended some black soldiers because they had been born in free states and their freedom had never been challenged before; others were upset because they had indeed been escaped slaves. The solution, drawn up by Colonel Edward N. Hallowell of the 54th Massachusetts Infantry, was to have each man swear that in April 1861 "no man had the right to demand unrequited labor of you." This "Quaker oath" could apply to *any* black soldier who believed slavery was wrong. "Fort Green" tells in this letter about payday, the oath, and the continuing problem of racism in the regiment.

. . . We were mustered this morning according to custom, for pay, and our Colonel administered the oath prescribed by the recent law concerning persons of African descent, in the military service of the United States; and touching the law of 1861, concerning free, able-bodied citizens from that time forward. The reason given for administering the oath is, in order to procure the just wages of a soldier. It looks like going a step backward, to be obliged to swear that we are free in order to get our just dues, having been born in the states where our right to freedom was not questioned. But we had no right to doubt the veracity of our gallant Colonel, and we consented in our company to a man; and we now have our names enrolled with the promise of our just pay, for once in seventeen months: that is better than never.

If we should not be again deceived, our distressed wives and children will hail the happy moment to be relieved from suffering and they may with glad hearts offer up prayers and tears for the speedy end of this great rebellion, and the enjoyment of our firesides in peace and happiness. In the promise of our pay, we were not promised promotion. I will say something about the prejudice in our own regiment when we returned from Olustee to Jacksonville. One of our captains was sick, and there was no doctor there excepting our hospital steward, who administered medicines and effected a cure; he was a colored man, Dr. [Theodore] Becker, and a competent physician, and through the exertions of this recovered Captain, there was a petition got up for his promotion. All the officers signed the petition but three, Captain [Charles] Briggs, and two lieutenants; they admitted he was a smart man and understood medicine, but he was a negro, and they did not want a negro Doctor, neither did they want negro officers. The Colonel, seeing so much prejudice among his officers, destroyed the document; therefore the negro is not yet acknowledged.

Notwithstanding all these grievances, we prefer the Union rather than the rebel government, and will sustain the Union if the United States will give us our rights. We will calmly submit to white officers, though some of them are not so well acquainted with military matters as our orderly sergeants, and some of the officers have gone so far as to say that a negro stunk under their noses. This is not very pleasant, but we must give the officers of Company

B, of the 54th Massachusetts regiment, their just dues; they generally show us the respect due to soldiers, and scorn any attempt to treat us otherwise. . . .

LETTER III

(F. S., [Sergeant,] 55th Massachusetts Infantry, Folly Island, South Carolina, October 14, 1864; *CR*, November 12, 1864) This letter was probably written by Sergeant John F. Shorter, who was elected one of the secretaries of a committee to organize a celebration of the successful drive for equal pay. The affair was a grand success, with speeches, toasts, music, and a splendid banquet. Shorter was one of the handful of black men in the Massachusetts regiments who would later be made commissioned officers because of their battlefield leadership.

Doubtless you will have heard before this reaches you that the Fifty-fourth and Fifty-fifth Massachusetts regiments have been paid. The Paymaster "filed his appearance" with us on Friday, September 30th, commencing operations with Company B, at present doing provost duty.

There was some little delay before he got fairly to work the other companies; but in the course of a week from the time it began, the paying off of the Fifty-fifth was among the accomplished facts. It came at last, after we have been kept out of it for nearly a year. You can imagine how we all felt. We felt overjoyed, and at the same time thankful to God for the successful termination of our suit.

Now, don't be surprised at what follows. We resolved to have a celebration. It was thought by the wise ones that an event of so much importance to us and ours deserved it. A meeting was, therefore, called at which a Committee was appointed to prepare for the occasion a programme, and resolutions expressive of the sentiments of the regiment. The Committee, with a promptness as commendable as it is rare in such bodies, submitted in a short time everything "cut and dried" to the next meeting, which was large and enthusiastic. Their report was unanimously accepted.

Monday, the 10th, was the day selected for the celebration. It came, and at precisely 3 o'clock, the assembly was sounded. Each company issued forth from its street in charge of a non-commissioned officer, and was formed in line by acting Sergeant Major [Charles] Mitchell, Marshal of the day, and Sergeant George Bazil, Assistant Marshal.

The procession, headed by the band, marched by the right flank in two wings, with space between, which was occupied by the speakers and officers of the day. After marching a short distance beyond the camp, the procession turned and proceeded directly to the place of meeting, in front of the Colonel's quarters. We were saved the trouble of erecting a platform, as there was a piece of rising ground, just the right thing, and in the right place. On top of this seats were arranged for the officers of the regiment, officers of the meeting, and the band. . . .

Programme
Prayer by the Chaplain [John Bowles]
Opening Address by the President Sergt. P[eter] R. Laws
Music by the Band
Speech by Sergt. H[enry W.] Johnson, Co. F
Music by the Band
Speech by 1st Sergt. I[saiah H.] Welch, Co. C
Music by the Band
Speech by Sergt. [Richard] White, Non-com Staff
Reading of resolutions by Sec'y Shorter
Music by the Band
Speech by Sergt. G[abriel] P. Iverson, Co. D
Song – "Vive l'America"

A few comments on the above, and we are done. It was a most impressive scene – a regiment of brave men celebrating, in the midst of war, one of the triumphs of peace, without arms, in the presence of their officers – a band of veteran warriors doing honor by solemn ceremonies, to the recognition by Government of their citizenship and equality.

President Laws's opening address was appropriate and eloquent. He stated the object of the celebration to be the triumph of freedom and equality over despotism and prejudice. The Sergeant not only spoke well, but presided throughout the day with great dignity.

Sergeant H. Johnson of Co. F was very brief; but his speech was *multum in parvo.* . . . Sergeant Welch spoke with touching earnestness. . . .

Sergeant White gave one of those solid and manly speeches that Western men know so well how to make. . . .

Sergeant Iverson was introduced by the President as orator of the day. I wish that I could give you his speech. We all felt proud of him as he stood there describing in the most beautiful language our triumph, its legal bearing, the slave power, the past sufferings of our race, and "the bright future which awaits it as the reward of its wisdom, patriotism, and valor." It was plain to see his legal culture in his style of speaking. Although limited in time, he nevertheless managed by skillful reasoning and lucid expression to make perfectly clear every point he took up. He was enthusiastically cheered.

Our splendid Regimental Band played a number of popular airs. There could be nothing finer than their performance. . . .

The management of the processions and the entire arrangements of the day reflected the highest credit upon the abilities of Sergeants Mitchell and Bazil, showing them worthy of the high opinion in which they are held by their comrades.

Finally, Mr. Editor, I must tell you about the Supper. In the evening the gentlemen of the Committee and officers of the day sat down to an elegant supper. The usual events took place – speeches, toasts, songs, and cheers. Gentlemen sang that night who were never known to sing before. The supper was gotten up in Mr. Lee's best style, and I think it deserved the justice which it received; in other words, both the supper and the eating were admirable. The whole affair passed off with much *eclat.*

(Gabriel P. Iverson, Sergeant, 55th Massachusetts Infantry, Folly Island, South Carolina, October 14, 1864; *CR*, November 12, 1864) Sergeant Iverson was responsible for drawing up the resolutions that were adopted by the men of the 55th Massachusetts at the celebration of October 10, 1864. The men renewed their commitment to the Union and their race, forgave those who had criticized them for protesting their low pay, and thanked their friends at home who had worked for equality.

Whereas, the just claims of the 55th Regt. Mass. Vol., on the pay question, having been admitted on the basis of equality, and whereas, we, the non-commissioned officers and privates of the Regiment, anxious to take advantage of this and every opportunity of giving expression to our loyalty to cause and country, especially when we behold that country in the midst of perils, rising to the dignity of giving freedom and knowledge to an unfortunate race, and bestowing upon it the rights of citizenship, therefore,

Resolved, That we stand now, as ever, ready to do our duty whenever and wherever our country requires it, in the work of crushing this wicked rebellion and preserving the national unity.

Resolved, That we are determined to make it our first duty as soldiers, by promptitude, obedience, and soldierly bearing; to prove ourselves worthy of the responsible position assigned us by Providence, in this the grandest struggle of the world's history, between freedom and slavery, and our first duty as men, by every means possible to contradict the slanders of our enemies, and prove to be true to our fitness for liberty and citizenship in the new order of things now arising in this our native land.

Resolved, That while it deeply grieved us to find many who should have understood and appreciated our motives, in connection with the pay question, failing to give us support and sympathy, sometimes even going so far as to condemn, thereby, unconsciously giving aid and comfort to the enemy – nevertheless, we have no hard feelings against such, being convinced, that, ere long, if not already, they will see the error of their way, and discern the wisdom of our acts, as surely as they are to enjoy the benefit of our successes.

Resolved, That even as the founders of our Republic resisted the British tax on tea on the ground of principle, so did we claim equal pay with other volunteers, because we believed our military and civil equality at issue – and independently of the fact that such pay was actually promised; and not because we regulated our patriotism and love of race by any given sum of money.

Resolved, That we do most sincerely thank those of our friends at home who have stood by us throughout our trials and privations, and whose sympathy and practical kindness went far toward soothing the rigors of our condition. Especially are our thanks due to William L. Garrison, Wendell Phillips, Gov. [John] Andrew, Senators [Charles] Sumner and [Henry] Wilson, those heroic champions of liberty, for their untiring and successful efforts in our behalf.

8

Racism in the Army

LIEUTENANT ROBERT H. ISABELLE resigned
as one of the black officers of the Second Louisiana Native
Guards. With other free black men from New Orleans, he
had volunteered to serve the Union soon after Federal troops took
that city in 1862. He had been elected an officer by the men, many
of whom were well educated, some of whom were wealthy, some of
whom had served in the War of 1812. His was one of the only three
black regiments to be led by men of color. But Lieutenant Isabelle
resigned, and the other black officers soon followed. The reason
was racism: "I joined the United States Army . . . with the sole
object of laboring for the good of our Country," he wrote, "but
after five or six months experience I am convinced that the same
prejudice still exist[s] and prevents that cordial harmony among
officers which is indispensable for the success of the army." Racism
drove him out of the service.[1]

1. Second Lieutenant R. H. Isabelle to Captain Wickham Hoffman, March 3,
   1863, carded service record of Robert H. Isabelle, 74th USCI, Record Group
   94, United States Archives.

Racism pervaded the United States, North and South. In the Southern states it went hand in hand with economics to support slavery. It gave slaveowners a convenient reason for keeping their laborers in permanent bondage. Other whites, no matter how poor, liked to think that all blacks, slave or free, were less worthy than any whites. In the North most whites felt the same way about blacks: Even some abolitionists, who wanted a quick end to slavery, believed blacks were not as good as whites. Restrictions, insults, and unfair treatment plagued the everyday lives of African Americans. In the North they resisted such treatment as best the could, but when they joined the army, they were not strangers to racism.

Racial prejudice surrounded the black soldiers in every part of their army lives. When African Americans first tried to enlist, they were told that it was "a white man's war; no blacks need apply." When the war went on longer than anyone had expected, and when the army needed more men to hold down the Confederacy, blacks were at first allowed to enlist, then drafted and compelled to serve. Even though some officers worked hard for the well-being of their men, most white soldiers, whether officers or enlisted men, thought the blacks were inferior, and they showed that attitude in many ways. Officers in some black units treated their men badly – striking them, ridiculing them, neglecting their needs, and assigning them harsh duty. Other soldiers insulted them. Most white civilians, whether on city streets, in railway cars, in recruiting offices, or in service organizations such as the Sanitary Commission, showed their dislike for black troops. Civilians in the occupied South demonstrated their racism by violence and complaints to sympathetic Union officers. The few blacks who became commissioned officers particularly drew the ire of white racists.

Army regulations limited what soldiers could do to protest their treatment. One Louisiana black regiment mutinied against its sadistic colonel and forced his removal, but that was a risky rebellion. Most soldiers knew they could be severely punished for open protest against officers or civilians; instead, some wrote letters to black newspapers. They told readers their complaints, detailed their experiences, and called for justice. Because their letters could get them into trouble, some soldiers did not sign their own names; others left out the names of the white officers. Complaints about racism showed up in many soldiers' letters, but the ones selected for this section focus sharply on the mistreatment African Americans got because of their race.[2]

LETTER 113

(Robert H. Isabelle, Lieutenant, 2nd Louisiana Native Guards [74th USCI,] New Orleans, Louisiana, February 25, 1863; *WAA*, March 14, 1863) Lieutenant Isabelle, one of the first African Americans to become a commissioned officer, reports the resignation of the black officers of the 3rd Louisiana Native Guards. He and his fellow officers in the 1st and 2nd Native Guards would do the same within a month. Although he was a well-educated and cultured man who had passed an examination demonstrating his military knowledge, he would be forced out of his leadership position by racism.

. . . The 1st Reg. La. Vols. (Native Guards) are at the English Turn, a few miles below the city, where they are building a fort. Seven companies of the 2nd are at Ship Island, fortifying the place. The 3rd regiment is at Baton Rouge, the capital of the State, fortifying that town. I am sorry to announce that seventeen of the colored commissioned officers of the 3rd have resigned, owing to some disagreement between them and Col. [John A.] Nelson. One mistake is made by the northern soldiers and officers: they think that all the colored population in New Orleans are contrabands. They have not been made aware that several thousands of this class are free-born, well educated property-holders, who have always enjoyed all the respect and privileges, with the exception of voting,

---

2. Fred Harvey Harrington, "The Fort Jackson Mutiny," *Journal of Negro History*, 27 (1942) 420–431. Berlin, Reidy, and Rowland, *The Black Military Experience*, 303–516. Glatthaar, *Forged in Battle*, 169–206.

of other citizens. Hundreds of them have graduated in Europe, are licensed to practice all kinds of professions, are doctors, dentists, &c. Silversmiths, portrait-painters, architects, brick-layers, plasterers, carpenters, tailors, cigar-makers, &c – all responded to the call of Gen. [Benjamin] Butler, closed up their establishments and enlisted as privates in the regiments of Native Guards to fight for the Union. Nearly four thousand of those brave and patriotic colored sons of Louisiana have enrolled themselves for three years or during the war to defend the flag of their country and keep Louisiana in the Union. Some of the regiments have been nearly six months mustered in the service, without receiving bounty or pay, but still are serving don't care for Davis' proclamation;[3] we are ready to march on Mobile, Vicksburg, Richmond, Charleston, or wherever we may be ordered. . . .

LETTER 114

(Alexander T. Augusta, Surgeon, United States Volunteers, Washington, D.C., May 14, 1863; to the [*National*] *Republican*, reprinted in *CR*, May 30, 1863) Dr. Augusta earned his medical degree in Canada, passed an army examination, and was appointed to the rank of surgeon. His appearance in public wearing the uniform of an army officer enraged some who saw him, and the result was violence. Later, white assistant surgeons would refuse to serve under him because of his race. In this letter, Dr. Augusta gives details of the attacks on him by civilians in Baltimore.

Inasmuch as many misstatements relative to the assault upon me in Baltimore have been made, I deem it necessary in justice to myself,

---

3. Confederate President Jefferson Davis, on learning that the Union would enlist African Americans, ordered his generals to treat any captured black soldiers as runaway slaves rather than as prisoners of war. Davis considered the officers of colored regiments "robbers and criminals deserving death."

as well as to all parties concerned, to give the public a true statement of the facts as they occurred.

I started from my lodgings in Mulberry Street, near Pine, about a quarter past nine o'clock, on the morning of the 1st inst., in order to take the 10 A.M. train for Philadelphia. I went down Mulberry Street to Howard, Howard to Baltimore, Baltimore to Gay, Gay to Pratt, Pratt to President, and thence to the depot. No one interfered with me during the whole route. I obtained my ticket from the agent, without the usual bond required of colored persons wishing to proceed North, and took my seat in the car – little expecting any one to make an attack on me then.

After remaining in my seat about five minutes, I heard some one conversing behind me, but paid no attention to what they were talking about, when of a sudden a boy about fifteen years of age, who appeared to be employed about the depot came up behind me, and swearing at me, caught hold of my right shoulder strap, and pulled it off. I jumped up, and turning toward him, found a man standing by his side who had directed me which car to get in, and while I was remonstrating with the boy for what he had done, he pulled the other one off; while at the same time the boy threatened to strike me with a club he held in his hand. I then turned toward the door of the car near where I was standing, and found I was surrounded by about eight or ten roughs; and knowing that should I [touch?] one of them all the rest would pounce upon me, I thought it best to take my seat and await what further issue might take place.

Shortly after I had taken my seat, the parties who had assaulted me left the car, and a policeman came in and stood near me. A person standing by asked him if he intended to interfere. He answered him by saying it depended upon circumstances. I then turned toward him, and said to him, "If you are a policeman, I claim your protection as a United States officer, who has been assaulted without cause." Just about that time I was informed that the provost guards were in the car, and that I had better apply to them for protection. I called to the guards, and told them I was a

United States officer; that I had been assaulted and my shoulder straps torn off by employees of the road, and that I claimed their protection. Having satisfied them of my connection with the service, they assured me of their protection. I might have gone on in that train, but I was determined to stop back, so as to have the parties punished, knowing full well that the same thing might occur again, unless a stop was put to it at once. I therefore went to the Provost Marshall's office with one of the guard, and reported the facts to Lieut. Col. Fish, the Provost Marshall.

He examined my commission, and finding it was all right, said he did not care who it was, so he was a United States officer, and claimed his protection, he should have it to the fullest extent. He then deputed Lieut. Morris to accompany me to the depot and arrest the parties. The Lieut. told me I was as much authorized as an officer to arrest them as he was; and that I had better go ahead of him and the guard, fearing that if the parties saw them they would get out of the way. He directed me, at the same time, that when I saw any one of the parties to go up to him and place my hand upon his shoulder and claim him as my prisoner, and he would be on hand to take him in charge. I knew this was an extraordinary step for me to take in Baltimore, but I told him I would do it. I accordingly went down to the depot, and when near it I recognized one of the parties crossing the street; I went up to him, and while accusing him of taking off my straps, put my hand on his shoulder and claimed him as my prisoner. I then ordered the guard to take him into custody, which he did. I then hunted around the depot for the boy, but could not find him.

The Lieutenant having come up by this time, we started for the Provost Marshal's office, and when opposite Marsh market, on Baltimore Street, Lieut. Morris, the guard, the prisoner, being on the opposite side of the street, a man, whom I learned afterwards to be named Hancock, emerged from the market and assaulted me. I called the guard across, and had him taken into custody. We then proceeded to the office unmolested, where I remained until about half-past twelve o'clock, when Lieut. Morris told me it was time to start for the depot, to take the one o'clock train. I got ready, and we proceeded together, and every step we took after leaving the office, the crowd which was standing around the door increased. No one, however, interfered with me until we arrived at the corner of Pratt and President Streets, when a man, whose name I since learned to be Dunn, was standing in our way, and as soon as I reached him he dealt me a severe blow in the face, which stunned me for a moment and caused the blood to flow from my nose very freely. In an instant, Lieut. Morris seized him by the collar and held him fast; and I not knowing there was anyone else in the crowd to protect me, made for the first door I saw open. When I reached it, a woman was standing there and pushed me back to prevent me from entering. In the meantime I looked back and saw a person with my cap and revolver in his hand. He told me to stand still, that I was protected. I came down the steps, and proceeded between two guards with revolvers drawn until we reached the depot.

Upon our arrival, Lieut. Morris put the prisoner upon a settee, and placed a guard over him, with orders to shoot him if he dared to stir from the spot. A short time after we arrived, two other persons were identified as having been engaged in the last assault upon me, and were arrested. I washed the blood from my face and prepared to take my seat in the cars, when an officer, whom I subsequently learned to be Major Robertson, of Maj. Gen. [Joseph] Hooker's staff, having learned the facts of the case from Lieut. Morris, came up to me, and told me he was going to Phila-delphia, and offered to protect me at the risk of his own life. The guard surrounded me with drawn revolvers, conducted me to the cars, and remained with me until the train started. During the time we were waiting for the train to start, I learned from the guard that when I was struck by Dunn, they were in the crowd dressed in citizen's clothes, and were just about to shoot him when Lieut. Morris ordered them not to shoot as he had the prisoner safe.

When the train was about to start, Lieut. Morris, in addition to Major Robertson, who had volunteered to protect me, sent on two armed cavalry to guard me to Philadelphia, or as long as I might want them. I, however, did not consider it necessary to detain them after we arrived, and accordingly discharged them from any further attendance upon me. Since my return to Washington, I have learned that some of the parties have been tried and sent to Fort McHenry. . . .

The question has no doubt been frequently asked, What has been gained in this transaction? I will answer. It has proved that even in *rowdy Baltimore* colored men have rights that white men are bound to respect. For I was told by a gentleman since I returned, whom I saw in the crowd at Baltimore, that when Dunn was taken to the Provost Marshall's office, the Marshall reprimanded the officer who had him in charge for not shooting him when he struck me; and told him if a case of the kind occurs again, and the officer in charge does not shoot the aggressor, his commission shall be broken. . . .

LETTER 115

(George W. Hatton, Orderly Sergeant, 1st USCI, Hampton [Virginia] Hospital, July 1, 1864; *CR*, July 16, 1864) Racism could show up in any place where there were black soldiers. Hospitals were no exception; life there was difficult enough for any wounded soldier, but when doctors let their racism govern their actions, African Americans suffered more. In this letter, Sergeant Hatton tells what happened when he tried to go home to recover from wounds received during the attack on Petersburg, Virginia.

I have been silent for a long time, but today I must speak, for it is a day long to be remembered by me, a wounded soldier of the U.S. Army.

I was wounded at the battle of Petersburg on the 15th of June last, and arrived at the Hampton Hospital on the 20th. On my arrival there, I wrote to my father, stating that I was wounded and would like him to come and see me, and if possible, take me home, where I should have the attendance of my kind and loving mother. My father complied with my request, and arrived at Fortress Monroe on the 30th. I was overjoyed to see him.

Today, he departed with a hung-down head, leaving me with an aching heart. I must here state the cause of my trouble. It is as follows:

On my father's arrival at the hospital he stated the object of his visit to the doctor in charge, who, very short and snappish, referred him to Dr. White, one of the head surgeons. Father immediately proceeded to Dr. White's office, where he expected to receive a little satisfaction, but to his heart-rending surprise, received none. After making every exertion in his power to get a furlough, he failed in so doing, without receiving the slightest shadow of satisfaction.

All of this I was willing to stand, as I had discharged my duty as a soldier from the first of May, 1863, up to the time I was wounded, for the low United States' degrading sum of $7 per month, that no man but the poor, down-trodden, uneducated, patriotic black man would be willing to fight for. Yes, I stand all this; but the great wound I received at the hospital was this: A white man, whose name I did not learn, came from Washington with my father for the same purpose, to see his son and carry him home. His success needs no comment; let it suffice to say that he was white, and he carried his son home.

Such deception as that I thought was crucified at the battle of Fort Wagner [July 18, 1863]; buried at Milliken's Bend [June 7, 1863]; rose the third day, and descended into everlasting forgetfulness in the Appomattox River at the battle of Petersburg.

Mr. Editor, when, oh! when can one of my color, and in my position, at this time, find a comforter? When will my people be a nation? I fear, never on the American soil; though we may crush this cursed rebellion.

LETTER 116

(B. W., [Private,] 32nd USCI, Morris Island, South Carolina, July 8, 1864; *CR*, July 30, 1864) Some units were especially oppressed by racist officers. The 32nd USCI was one of these. Even after complaints about heavy duty and hard conditions are discounted as the usual "soldier gripes," it is clear that the men of the 32nd were badly treated because of their race. In addition, the officers seemed generally incompetent in military matters. Several soldiers from the 32nd USCI wrote letters that gave a consistent picture of mistreatment by officers who objected to any efforts of the men to assert their pride. This letter is probably from Benjamin Williams, a nineteen-year-old private from Philadelphia, who at the time this was written was under arrest for unknown charges but was still in camp with his regiment.

. . . We arrived at Sea Brook, eight miles up the creek, west of Hilton Head [South Carolina]. There we were ordered to encamp. We stayed there one week. We had nothing to eat but oysters and five hard tacks a day, that we picked up along the shore. As usual, after we had fixed up our camp so nicely, order came for us to strike tents and march, which was promptly executed. We marched back to Hilton Head and took the steamer Cosmopolitan, and reported at Folly Island, and marched to Morris Island, where we are still in camp near Fort Shaw. We are encamped on the old hospital ground, where they buried all their dead. We had to dig wells in the graveyard, and drink the water off the putrid bodies, and it is killing our men.

The health of the men in general, is as well as can be expected. We have lost ten men since our departure, and among the brave hearts was that of Jesse Dexter, the Quartermaster Sergeant, who leaves a wife and child to mourn his loss.

The paymaster has made us a visit, and offered us seven dollars a month, which all of the men refused, except a few in the left wing, who sneaked up at night and signed the pay roll; but the majority of the men would sooner stay their time out and do without the seven dollars. Our officers seem very much put out, and beg the men to take it. They said that the next day we would get all that is coming to us, and said, "Boys, we think that you had better take the money." But we told them that it was a big thing on ice, but we could not see it; and, after the officers found out that the men would not take the seven dollars, they began to treat those men like dogs. The least thing that the men would do, they were bucked and gagged, and put on knapsack drill, and made to stand in the hot, broiling sun for four hours at a stretch; in consequence of which, a few of the men got sunstruck.

We have drills and dress-parades and battalion drills, which none of our officers know anything about. When they are ordered by a command, they don't know how to do it. One night we went out on picket duty. Every thing went on well all through the night, and in the morning, when the pickets were taken off, the rebels began to shell and cross-fire. Our brave officers sent the men on ahead and they stayed behind, because they were afraid of the rebels' shells, and, when they came down to camp they were under arrest for their cowardice. The officer in command told them that they had not as much heart as their men had, and that the regiment would be better drilled if they had the officers to command them, but they had not an officer in the regiment that knew his business and knew how to do his duty, and that the regiment was hardly worth the rations that they drew. And there is our drum-corps, that we brought with us from Philadelphia. They have not got their uniforms yet, and they are the worst corps on the island. They are laughed at and sneered at by all the other regiments. We know it is not the fault of the drum-major. It is the fault of the commanding officers. The General says that if we were to go into the field with such officers as we now have, we would all get cut to pieces, and that there is no use taking us into action until our officers have learned a little more.

Mr. Editor, it looks hard that a party of men should treat colored men in this way. There is our gentlemanly doctor. He is a very nice man, indeed. He has not got any medicine fit to give the men. If they get very sick in their quarters, the doctor will order them brought to the hospital where they will not be more than twenty-four hours before they are dead. That is the way the men are served. Dr. [Charles] Wight growls and snaps at the men as if they were dogs, and he says, if the men are not fit for duty, send them to him and he will soon get them out of the way, for he says it is no harm to kill a nigger.

When the regiment first encamped here, we were treated more like soldiers; but as soon as we refused to take seven dollars a month, they commenced to treat us like dogs. Before the Paymaster came around, there was not anything like bucking and gagging; but as soon as we refused to take the pay, they commenced. They even bucked and gagged a boy because he happened not to have the seat of his pants sewed up for inspection. It was impossible for him to sew them up, as he had no money to buy a needle and thread with.

Now, Mr. Editor, don't you think this is bad treatment for a Pennsylvania regiment to get? I think it is ridiculous and a shame before God and man. There was not a group that left Camp William Penn with such a set of officers as the Thirty-second United States Colored Troops. Look at the Forty-third Regiment United States Colored Troops, which was raised after we were. They have been brigaded and are now acting as rear-guard over the baggage train of the Army of the Potomac, whilst we are not fit for anything but to do all of the picket duty and drudgery work on the island; and we don't get our rations as we ought to. All the rations that are condemned by the white troops are sent to our regiment. You ought to see the hard tack that we have to eat. They are moldy and musty and full of worms, and not fit for a dog to eat, and the rice and beans and peas are musty and the salt horse (the salt beef, I mean) is so salt that, after it is cooked, we can't eat it. Some days the men are sent on fatigue in the hot sun, and when they come home to dinner, there is nothing to eat but rotten hard tack and flat coffee, without sugar in it.

Now, Mr. Editor, if this is not killing men, I don't know what is. There is one thing that I had almost forgotten. It is concerning the Sergeant-Major of the regiment. He made his boasts and went around bragging to the men in camp that he would not take seven dollars a month; and before he would take it he would stay out his three years and do without it, and he hoped that no man in the regiment would take it. But when the paymaster came, he changed his tune, and signed his name to the pay roll, and took the seven dollars. The next day he looked like a man that had done some great deed. Only look at it, he holding the highest non-commissioned office that a colored man can hold. We would not think so hard of it if he had been a private. He is one of your Philadelphia sports, and bears the title of Sergeant-Major George W. Clemens. . . .

LETTER 117

("Private," 43rd USCI, Bermuda Hundred, Virginia, December 23, 1864; *CR*, January 28, 1864) Even when the black regiments were on the front lines, racism haunted them. "Private" reports that it was usually the officers who had once been enlisted men who treated the black soldiers worst.

. . . The conduct of the officers toward the soldiers is good only at times. Some of them do things which I think they have no right to do. They strike the men with their swords, and jog and punch them in their side to show them how to drill. And I will here say, that if it be not soon stopped, I will report such conduct to the public, by giving their names. I do not think it right that soldiers should be cuffed and knocked around so by their officers, especially as we colored soldiers are. It is not consistent with either the laws of nature or of humanity, and is a base and cowardly act to do so.

Some of these men who do these base things are not overgifted with spunk. If I understand military tactics aright, it says no officer has a right to strike or misuse a private in any way. I know it is inconsistent with military rules, but I don't like to find fault with my officers, although some of them richly deserve it. . . . Our officers must stop beating their men across the head and back with their swords, or I fear there will be trouble with some of us. There are men in this regiment who were born free, and have been brought up as well as any officer in the 43d, and will not stand being punched with swords and driven around like a dog. I guess some of the 43d's officers have been privates in their time, and I suppose they know what it is for the officers of Co. F to gain the ill-will of the privates. But, I hope we will be able, someday or other, to vindicate our cause.

Such is the usage we get for our conduct as soldiers and men. Some of our friends have attempted to write to you concerning our marching, hardships, trials, the country, &c., but they don't let you know how we are treated. No, that is kept dark. But I hope some of our friends will see about this matter, as I consider it of the utmost importance. Our friends should arouse themselves, and be ready to do something for those who are down in Dixie suffering and fighting for the Union, and get no thanks but – "No negro shall be a citizen of the United States."

LETTER 118

(Thomas J. Griffin, Sergeant Major, 29th Connecticut Infantry, Virginia, March 15, 1865; *WAA*, March 25, 1865) The Sanitary Commission was a civilian organization set up at the beginning of the war to help Union soldiers maintain their health and comfort. It raised money across the North to supply bandages, transportation, nursing care, reading material, and other aid. African Americans supported the Sanitary Commission in their hometowns, holding fund-raising fairs and donating supplies. But as Sergeant-Major Thomas J. Griffin of Philadelphia reports in this letter, racism determined how those supplies would be handed out to the black soldiers. He was told by the clerk to wait until all the white soldiers had been served. "It is to these persons," he wrote, "a lesson must be taught."

Knowing that the Sanitary Commission of our land is held in high and just appreciation by our fellow-countrymen, and by none more so than the soldiers of "our army," I would not speak a word depreciating its worth, or against those connected with it without sufficient cause.

It fell my lot recently to be passing through the capital city of "Free Maryland" viz.: Annapolis, and while there I saw a large number of *white* soldiers procuring handkerchiefs from a branch office of the United States Sanitary Commission.

I, being greatly in need of the article above mentioned, thought the opportunity presented a fitting one to obtain the same, and accordingly entered the house with the crowd.

On arriving at the point from which the different articles were dispensed, I was directed to "fall back and wait" until the *white* men had been waited upon.

In my opinion this was unnecessary, and I desired to know the reason why I should fall back and wait? I was answered by the clerk, "because I desired it."

I asked, why so?

"Because," said he, "I make a distinction, and want you to wait." I replied that I was sorry a distinction should be made by one having or filling a position which none but gentlemen were entitled to.

I am a soldier in the United States service; he, a civilian. Now I would ask, which is most entitled to the right of discrimination?

In this instance I had gained an inkling of the principle and dispositions of not one alone, but many of these persons in the employ of true, patriotic, self-denying citizens.

The conduct of these clerks in this, as in many other instances,

is I am well aware, unknown to those of our citizens who are daily,
aye, hourly contributing to the wants and comforts of those men,
who, as soldiers, have gone forth to battle against the enemies of
our common country.

The name of the clerk, as I afterward learned, is Philip
Swearer. . . .

LETTER 119

("Observer," 22nd USCI, Chapel Point, Maryland, May 13, 1865;
CR, May 27, 1865) General Benjamin Butler of Massachusetts
was one of the first generals to employ black soldiers for combat.
He believed they were brave fighters, and he gave them every
opportunity to show their qualities in the fighting around Petersburg and Richmond, Virginia, in 1864. Butler was dismissed from
his command, however, when he failed to attack vigorously in December 1864. Black soldiers were sorry to see him leave, because
he had helped them struggle against racism. In this letter, "Observer" describes the harsh treatment given a black soldier who
tried to march in the funeral parade for Abraham Lincoln. If General Butler had been in charge, "Observer" writes, such incidents
would not have happened.

Allow me, through the columns of your most worthy paper, to
address you in behalf of wronged and mistreated men – men who,
for the love of God and their country, have sacrificed the pleasures
of home and friends, and have met the enemy face to face, and
driven them from their strongholds – men who have charged up to
the very mouths of cannon that were incessantly belching from
their iron stomachs a perfect shower of grape and canister, sweep-
ing down whole platoons at every discharge, and scattering death
and destruction around broadcast, as the sower cast the bright
grain around him!

Let me ask you, patriotic people of America, should such men as these be beaten to the ground with swords in the hands of foul-hearted, craven, red-taped humbugs? They deserve not the name of officers.

Private Burke, Co. D, of this regiment, who has been sick for some time in the Hospital, after leaving that Institution, was detached from this command, where he remained until we were all ordered to Washington to participate in the funeral-procession of our late lamented President, by way of respect to the memory of the illustrious departed.

Not being properly drilled, and being perhaps a little awkward in his movements, this devoted soldier of the United States army was struck senseless and bleeding to the ground with a tremendous blow from a sword in the hand of an arrant coward and brute, his Company commander. How long is this to be endured? How long must the Government strain at gnats and swallow camels? How we long for the presence of that noble patriot and true soldier, who, for no other reason than his unwillingness to sacrifice the lives of hundreds of his true and trusty followers, was relieved of his command – bold and faithful BEN. BUTLER, who never shrank from a soldier's duty, and always avoided useless slaughter.

With such a man for commander, brutality like that which we have described would find instantaneous redress, and the perpetrator be fitly punished. To complain in the present instance would be deemed insubordination. How inconsistent to laud the brave soldier as a hero, and yet kick him like a dog! Butler's name will ever live in the hearts of his countrymen.

LETTER 120

(Richard McDaniel, [Private,] Co. G, 11th USCHA, Donaldson-ville, Louisiana, June 25, 1865; *WAA*, July 26, 1865) After the war ended, racism continued. Black soldiers had enlisted hoping that brave, loyal service would prove their right to be treated equally. Instead, whites continued to treat them as inferiors who were useful in an emergency but must be constantly reminded of their inferiority. Richard McDaniel of Indiana tells in this letter how racism had kept him out of the army when he had first tried to enlist, and how white soldiers later took advantage of their race.

. . . In the year 1861, when the President called on the citizens of the United States to volunteer and stop the Southern rebellion, I was one among the first of my township to rally to the stand and offer my services; but what was the reply of Capt. Menray, of Knightstown, Ind.? His answer to me was, "Stand back, my young fellow; I will give you the berth of cooking for my mess or attending to my horse."

Well, I stepped back and looked on my young playmates step up and enter their names on the enlistment roll, and in a day or two I looked at them take leave of their friends in old Rush Co., Ind., and started for camp at Indianapolis. The last word I remember hearing was from a particular friend – as I thought. As he started he shook his head and bellowed back at me, and what was his parting address? "Why," said he, "you niggers are the cause of my having to leave my home. If it had not been for the negroes this war would never have been."

Well, of course, I did not like to be branded with such a crime as that, but I said nothing, thinking that they were excited. In a short time I entered into conversation with another white gentleman, and was speaking to him concerning the number of colored men that I knew were ready and willing to enlist at a moment's notice. I said that I was willing to take my chances with the rest if ever called on, and what do you think was his reply? He said, "You need never be afraid of having to fight, because this is not a negro's war, and the rebels will have to spill the blood of all the white men in the North before a nigger can take up arms. They don't know anything, and what would they do if they were armed? It would only cause the greater portion of the white men in the field to throw down their arms and rebel."

He went on to say that before he would stand by the side of a black man and fight, he would be shot in the back.

I found out that there was no chance for me to be a soldier, so I gave it up till the Fall of 1863, and thought part of the time that I never would enlist at all. But it happened that Rhode Island sent out her recruiting officers just at the right time to strike my patriotism. I came to that State and enlisted, and have been a soldier ever since. I am a member of the 11th USCHA, formerly the 14th R.I. [Heavy Artillery]. I have now been in the service one year and nine months, and where is our honor? What honor have we gained? The black men fight well and make good soldiers, but the Union is safe; and let us go to work and decide what we shall do with the colored men, and make provision for them before their time is out in the army, so that we shall not be plagued with them in the Northern States. Well, what is the first proposition? It is to colonize the negroes because we can't all stay together any longer; the negroes are getting too much sense. Another sends in a bill to have the Union as it was, and leave the negro question until the present sore gets well. I hope it may never heal, because if it gets well to easy there will be one, in the course of the year, much worse than at present. So I think it is best to keep the old sore running till all the corruption runs out, then heal it up so that it may not scar. This war has been useful while the Union was in danger, and there was no hope, only the black man.

We could see officers around the villages; we could see them around the country in the school houses, and we could see them going with their body-guard from plantation to plantation, both begging and compelling the colored men, North and South, to go and enter their names on the enlistment roll. For what was it? Because they wanted to free the men? That is what they would tell them, but that you can all see was a lie from its foundation. To prove this I will simply ask, can you point out one of those men that is saying a word in favor of giving even the free colored men of the North the rights of suffrage? If you can, have it put in some Southern paper so that we can see it. . . .

It puts me in mind of an affray which I chanced to witness, and which took place between a party of drunken Irish and a few colored men. They were all together in the same hotel, drank and ate together, and appeared as loving as brethren, until the Irish got what they wanted to eat and drink and the colored men had paid the bill, then Pat could begin to bellow out, "D — n the black soul of you, you must get out or we will give you the shillaleh," and the men who had paid all the expenses had to leave, there being more than twice their number of Irish.

It is just so with the United States. The colored men have fought their battles, achieved their victories, and saved the Union. Now they say that we can't all live on the same soil, and we will have to make some provision to dispense with the negro! Now, it will not do for our people to let this thing go on without opposition, and I hope that all who see this will arouse to a sense of their duty, and look forward to see what it is going to bring about, and find out if they are allowed the right to school funds, or allowed to poll a vote in favor of candidates for state offices.

9

The Navy

JOHN LAWSON knew that August 5, 1864, would be a day of hard fighting, danger, and death. With the other sailors on board the U.S.S. *Hartford*, he awoke at two in the morning, drank a cup or two of hot coffee, and prepared to attack. Mobile Bay was the target, the last Confederate port on the Gulf of Mexico, and a place where blockade runners took out cotton and brought in cannons, ammunition, medicine, and other supplies needed by the rebels. Lawson, an African American from Pennsylvania, had been through battle before; he had been wounded when the U.S.S. *Cayuga* had helped capture New Orleans in 1862. Now he prepared his heavy gun on the berth deck of the *Hartford* for one of the great naval battles of the Civil War.

At 5:30 A.M., Admiral David Farragut had himself tied to the upper mast of the *Hartford* and ordered the fleet to attack. There were four major obstacles: Fort Morgan, which guarded the entrance to the bay; some Confederate gunboats inside the bay; the

269

monster ironclad *Tennessee;* and three lines of mines, or as they were called then, "torpedoes." The Confederate ships and forts fired away at Farragut's eighteen-ship fleet. In the smoke and confusion of battle, the ship ahead of him stopped, so the admiral had to send the *Hartford* around it, straight into the minefield. When the crew pointed out that they were heading for the mines, Farragut shouted from his perch high above the deck, "Damn the torpedoes! Full speed ahead!" Only one ship sank owing to the mines, and the rest of the fleet steamed on to fight the rebel gunners.

On the gun deck of the *Hartford,* John Lawson fired away at Fort Morgan, and the guns of the fort fired back. Solid shot and explosive shells from the fort did serious damage; dead bodies were lined up on the far side of the ship, and the wounded were tended by the surgeons below decks. One shell from the shore hit the shell-whip where Lawson and five other men were loading and firing. It exploded, killing or wounding all six men. Lawson was struck in the leg and thrown across the deck against the side of the ship, badly stunned. He was told by his officers to go below to get help from the doctors. But he returned to his post and continued firing away. Other shells tore off men's arms, legs, and heads, but Lawson stayed at his post until the fleet had passed the fort and the minefield, sunk most of the rebel gunboats and captured the ironclad *Tennessee.* By ten o'clock, the great battle ended, and Lawson could get care for his wounds. The next day, the captain of the *Hartford* commended him for his bravery in action; for his heroism, he received the Congressional Medal of Honor.[1]

John Lawson was one of almost ten thousand African Americans who served in the Union Navy during the war. Unlike the soldiers, black sailors were welcomed into the service almost from the beginning, probably because there had always been some black men in the navy and because many of them already had a career at

1. Quarles, *The Negro in the Civil War,* 231–232. Herbert Aptheker, "Negroes in the Union Navy," in Aptheker, *To Be Free* (New York, International Publishers, 1968) 128, 229n. Foote, *The Civil War: Red River to Appomattox,* 492–508.

sea. It is difficult to know exactly how many such men served in the navy, because many of the records simply make no distinction between white and black. Some letters and diaries show that on some of the ships, most of the crew were black. Although there were some restrictions on how far blacks could advance in rank, there seems to have been no discrimination in pay or in duties. They served in large ships and small, wooden and ironclad, riverine and oceangoing. John Lawson and four other African-American sailors earned Medals of Honor for their heroism.[2]

The Union Navy had four basic functions during the Civil War. First, on the high seas, it tried to protect Union ships from Confederate raiders. Those ships attacked, captured, and burned the North's merchant ships and did great damage all around the world. (The Union Navy eventually sank the raider *Alabama* off Cherbourg, France. It captured the *Florida* in South America. But the *Shenandoah* was between Japan and Alaska, destroying Union whaling ships, when the war ended.) The second function of the navy was to attack Confederate ports, such as New Orleans and Port Royal, both of which were captured much as Mobile Bay was taken by Admiral Farragut. The third function was to operate the blockade against ships that carried goods between the Confederacy and the rest of the world. That duty required many ships and men, who put in long, boring hours outside rebel ports waiting for the fast smugglers, who usually outran the Union ships. The fourth function of the navy was to operate in the rivers as a support for nearby army units. Union gunboats served as waterborne artillery to protect army bases and to cover the movement of troops. They also raided Confederate positions and harassed the enemy along the riverbanks. Black sailors, who served on ships in all these roles, wrote few letters to the newspapers. Only five have been discovered, and all five are included here.

2. Aptheker, *To Be Free*, 113–135. Berlin, Reidy, and Rowland, *The Black Military Experience*, 14n.

LETTER 121

(George W. Reed, Drummer, U.S.S. *Commodore Reed,* Potomac
Flotilla, May [14], 1864; *CR,* May 21, 1864) George W. Reed
served on a gunboat that had many African-American sailors in its
mixed crew. The vessel operated not only in the Potomac River
near Washington, D.C., but also in nearby Chesapeake Bay and the
rivers that flowed into it. The Rappahannock River separated the
Union Army from the Confederate Army upstream near Fredericksburg. On May 4, 1864, General Ulysses S Grant crossed the
river at the "Wilderness" and launched his great Virginia offensive
against General Robert E. Lee. The gunboats downstream rescued
wounded Union troops and escorted rebel prisoners, but their
raids on the shore were more exciting.

Sir, having been engaged in the naval service nearly six years, I
have never before witnessed what I now see on board this ship. Our
crew are principally colored; and a braver set of men never trod the
deck of an American ship. We have been on several expeditions
recently. On the 15th of April our ship and other gunboats proceeded up the Rappahannock River for some distance, and finding
no rebel batteries to oppose us, we concluded to land the men from
the different boats and make a raid. I was ordered by the Commodore to beat the call for all parties to go on shore. No sooner
had I executed the order than every man was at his post, our own
color being first to land. At first there was a little prejudice against
our colored men going on shore, but it soon died away. We succeeded in capturing 3 fine horses, 6 cows, 5 hogs, 6 sheep, 3 calves,
an abundance of chickens, 600 pounds of pork, 300 bushels of
corn, and succeeded in liberating from the horrible pit of bondage
10 men, 6 women, and 8 children. The principal part of the men
have enlisted on this ship. The next day we started further up the
river, when the gunboat in advance struck a torpedo, but did no

material damage. We landed our men again, and repulsed a band of rebels handsomely, and captured three prisoners. Going on a little further, we were surprised by 300 rebel cavalry, and repulsed, but retreated in good order, the gunboats covering our retreat. I regret to say that we had the misfortune to lose Samuel Turner (colored) in our retreat. He was instantly killed, and his body remains in the rebel hands. He being the fifer, I miss him very much as a friend and companion, as he was beloved by all on board. We also had four slightly wounded.

On the 28th of April we landed two boats' crew, armed and equipped, on the shore at Mathias Point, a distance of seventy-five miles from Washington, and captured 400 pounds of salt pork, corn, &c., and a rebel captain, who happened to be home on a furlough eating his dinner. He was very politely asked to march on board the ship, where we gave him a fine dinner of double irons, and bread and water.

On the 9th of May we landed three boats' crew on shore at night and captured a rebel signal company and two officers, and all their provisions. The Commodore Reed is the fighting ship of the Potomac Flotilla; and we are never idle.

On Thursday, the 12th inst., we were notified that wounded soldiers were drifting on rafts in the river near Aquia Creek, having been driven there by guerrillas in their retreat from the front. We have been lying here ever since – when there have been over 20,000 wounded brought here to be transported to Washington. I had the pleasure of conversing with some of the colored soldiers who were wounded in the late battles. I am told by them that their officers could not manage them, they were so eager to fight. Whenever they caught a rebel they cried out, "No quarter! Remember Fort Pillow! No quarter for rebs," &c. They distinguished themselves highly. They are doing as well here as can be expected, and are being properly cared for. They seem principally to belong to Burnside's division; and many who were slightly wounded have gone back to the front. They are all eager to go back to retaliate for the Fort Pillow massacre.

I must close now, as we are ordered to convoy a steamer loaded with rebel prisoners to Washington.

(George W. Reed, Drummer, [U.S.S. *Commodore Reed*,] Potomac Flotilla, July 4, 1864; *CR*, July 16, 1864) Becoming a prisoner of war was always a threat to black soldiers and sailors. Drummer Reed tells in this letter how he and his colleagues dealt with the problem.

I feel it essential for me to give you a synopsis of the life of a sailor, or the way we spend and celebrate the Day of Independence on board ship. As a general custom, we celebrate that day above all others by firing a national salute at daybreak and at 12 o'clock noon, besides a great display of colors; but, owing to our domestic troubles, we are deprived of all that pleasure, as all our time now is employed in watching the rebels, who infest this part of the country. The Potomac Flotilla is noted for its daring and successful raids, and we are a perfect terror to the rebel community. They fear us more than they do General Grant's great army, so they say themselves, and, as a proof of the same, I notice a piece in the Richmond Examiner of the 10th ult. – an order from Jefferson Davis, authorizing his troops in this vicinity, whenever they capture a tar or sailor belonging to the Potomac Flotilla, to hang him to the nearest tree, and take no prisoners. This created a great excitement here, and made the officers and men more eager to fight and destroy their property than ever. The captain concluded to try them, and the men were all anxious to take part.

We concluded to land our forces from the different boats, and made a raid on the night of the 3d of July. It proved successful. We destroyed a large amount of Confederate beef, corn, wheat, and grain of all descriptions and captured two prisoners. They succeeded in capturing three of our men belonging to the U.S. steamer Fuchia, who happened to stray off from us to get some poultry for a Fourth of July dinner. We followed in pursuit of them, but met with a larger force of rebels, and retreated to our gunboats safely.

After getting on board, we saw twenty or thirty rebels come down near the beach, when a shell from our 100-pound rifle exploded in their midst, and must have done great execution. Later in the day we observed a force of fifty rebel cavalry, with a flag of truce. We sent an armed boat's crew to learn their wants. It appeared that the two prisoners captured by us were their principal leaders, and they wanted an exchange. The boats returned, stating their wants, when our captain replied with his 100-pound rifle: "No exchange." We intend to hold them, in case they should hang our men. We intend, tonight, to endeavor to capture our men.

LETTER 123

(George W. Reed, [U.S.S. *Commodore Reed*,] Potomac Flotilla, September 6, 1864; *CR*, September 17, 1864). One function of the river gunboats was to spirit away pro-Union families from behind the lines. They also liberated slaves, but some slaves would not leave.

On the 28th of August we proceeded up the Rappahannock River for the purpose of getting a Union man's family away to go North. We were accompanied by the steamer Mercury. We reached our place of destination, and landed thirty men in small boats, for the purpose of bringing off the family and furniture, in consequence of there being a large force of rebels near.

No sooner had we reached our vessels than about fifty rebels made their appearance on the shore; but a well-directed shot from our 100-pounder made them leave. This is all very easy for us to go on shore after these families, but a great risk.

On the 4th of September we proceeded up the same river for the same purpose, only for another family. We landed as before, with the same number of men. After reaching shore, we met an old colored man, and asked him his name. He replied that his name was Abraham, and that he was going to Bertenham to carry some bacon and hams to Mrs. Kelly's house, who lived in Bertenham, three miles beyond Lawyer Cunningham's.

This may appear very silly to your readers, but it is true. It created a great deal of laughter amongst us. We proceeded to the house, and stationed our pickets, and began removing the family and furniture to the boats. Shortly after, our pickets were driven in, and we were all fired on and driven from the house by rebel cavalry or home-guards.

The order was given us to retreat at double-quick, as the rebel force was one-hundred strong, while ours only amounted to thirty men. We retreated in good order, and but for the gunboats shelling the rebels back, we would all have been captured or killed during our rapid retreat. Robert Jackson was accidentally wounded by a bayonet during our retreat. We were all anxious to get to the boats first, particularly myself, as I have but three weeks to remain in this service, and do not like the way they treat us after our capture.

Some time since, the rebels captured a colored man, and put twelve bullets in his body and left him in the road. This is the way they treat us when they take us prisoners.

We succeeded in bringing off the family, but had to abandon all the furniture and farming utensils. I am sorry to say that the colored people belonging to the family refused to come, for what reason, I am at a loss to say.

The rebels are getting very numerous in this vicinity, and they are making great preparations to capture the Commodore Reed some dark night. They will be rightly received when they come. We are watching for them, and whenever we see one of them on shore, we bid him good morning with a 100-pound shell, which soon makes him scamper away.

LETTER 124

(John B. Clark, U.S.S. *Monadnock,* Hampton Roads, Virginia, March 16, 1865; *WAA,* March 25, 1865) The famous battle between the *Monitor* and the *Merrimac* took place on March 9, 1862, in Hampton Roads, Virginia. It was, of course, the first head-to-head battle between ironclad ships, and it ended in a draw. The Union Navy was enthusiastic about its "cheesebox on a raft" and built sixty more of them. John B. Clark, an African-American sailor on one of those "monitors," tells in this letter of this ship's work.

We arrived at this place on the 14th inst., after a passage of sixty hours from Port Royal [South Carolina]. The Anglo was received on board here today, with great enthusiasm. The first intimation that I received of its arrival among us was of a goodly sized [package] striking me full in the face, and Johnny Buchanan cried: "Look out for them. They are Anglos and they have followed us all the way from Beaufort." Since leaving Beaufort [South Carolina], we have participated in the fight at Fort Fisher, where we received some honorable scars and we were also at Charleston when that place was evacuated by the rebels. Since then we have been to Warsaw Sound [North Carolina], and now we are on our way up James River, and I hope that within a fortnight I shall have the pleasure of writing my friends from Richmond.

When we left Port Royal the steamer Mohican came with us to convoy us to Hampton Roads, but before we got off Cape Hatteras she gave out; but as we did not like to delay, we took her in tow and towed her safely to Hampton Roads.

I think that it is truly a great feat for a monitor to take a heavy sloop of war in tow at sea, and tow her into port; but we did, and made seven miles an hour all the time.

LETTER 125

("Jack Halliards," U.S. Gunboat *Kennebec*, off Galveston, Texas, May 1, 1865; *WAA*, May 27, 1865.) After the surrender of General Robert E. Lee on April 9, 1865, the end of the Civil War was near. Rebel forces in Texas were last to surrender, and Galveston was one of the last Confederate seaports to fall. In this letter, "Jack Halliards" tells about blockade duty off Galveston in the days after the death of President Lincoln.

The news of the death of President Lincoln by the hand of the assassin cast a deep gloom over the hearts of many of Uncle Sam's tried sailors. In but one or two instances heard we a harsh word spoken of the honored dead, and these by persons entirely incapable of appreciating the worth of such a man. God forbid that it should be said of us or any other colored persons, that we spoke aught but love of the just, made perfect by his transformation. The nation cannot but feel or realize that we have lost in his sudden demise, a father of his country, a true and tried friend of the downtrodden and oppressed, and a Christian soldier of God's own choice. . . .

Surely in four years great changes have taken place. From the President's proclamation of the 1st of January [1863] up to the present, our progress has been onward and upward. In 1865 we are ably represented in the Supreme Court of the United States by the accomplished and unsurpassed lawyer, J[ohn] S. Rock of Boston. A little later, we behold on the floor of the Capitol that Christian gentleman and scholar, H[enry] H. Garnet, discoursing to those learned Senators and Representatives from the word of holy writ, utterly astonishing them with his thoughts and eloquence. And last, though not least, is the form of that spotless African and well tried veteran in the cause of right, Martin R. Delany, we have a

regularly commissioned Major in the U.S. Army. May his future be
of more pecuniary good than the past. Four years ago, a colored
man would not be allowed in the Capitol unless he had a dust-pan
and broom in his hand. The idea of a colored lawyer speaking in
the Supreme Court, would have been preposterous, or a colored
minister preaching in those halls, entirely out of the question. A
colored major in the regular army would have been hooted at, as it
would be placing him on too much of an equality. These, and
various other great advantages, too numerous for comment, have
been brought about by this glorious man. . . .

The Kennebec, when we last addressed you, was lying at anchor
off Calcassien, La., watching the movements of blockade runners.
You will observe, by the caption of this, that we have changed our
station to that of Galveston, Texas. Galveston is a very fine-looking
city of about 10,000 inhabitants, with a commodious harbor for
vessels. The approaches to the harbor are defended by one large
fort and two small batteries, garrisoned by about 9,000 Confederate soldiers. We have a fleet stationed here of some fifteen vessels
of all classes, under the command of Port Captain Sands, Flagship
Fort Jackson, keeping an eye on the rebel blockade runners, and
their fortifications. A flag of truce boat went ashore yesterday to
demand the surrender of the place. The rebel officers refused to
reply to the demand. Two deserters came in to-day to the Flagship.
They said the rebel officers will not surrender the place without a
severe battle; that Capt. [John N.] Maffit, of piratical notoriety,[3] has
gone to Red River to take command of the rebel ram, Webb, and
proposes coming to Galveston to destroy our wooden fleet. The
U.S. steamer Augusta Dinsmore arrived with late papers from
New Orleans today. Reports say the ram came out of Red River,
and ran by a portion of the fleet, but was finally sunk below New
Orleans. We would just say that the gunboat Kennebec chased the

3. Maffit had commanded the Confederate raider *Florida* and was a successful
   blockade runner.

rebel privateer Owl, Capt. Maffit commander, on the 15th of April, about two hours, with little success, she going sixteen knots an hour to our seven.

There is nothing of a spirited character transpiring here at present, but look out for breakers. You may expect to hear of a heavy battle soon or a bloodless victory. We are only awaiting the appearance of Rear Admiral [Henry K.] Thatcher to strike the blow that will make the Texans tremble.

10

War's End

SERGEANT PETER VOGELSANG, a member of a prominent Brooklyn, New York, family, had left his job as a clerk and enlisted in the 54th Massachusetts Infantry as soon as the recruiters had come his way in April 1863. Now, two years later, the war was over. He and his regiment had won glory in battle, and they had won their campaign for equal pay. They had finished their task, and they were ready to go home.

But Vogelsang and the others would not get back to Boston until late in August 1865. The four months between the end of the fighting and their triumphant return to the Boston Common were spent in and around Charleston, South Carolina, There they kept law and order and helped the liberated slaves deal with freedom. For many of the men, time seemed to drag, but not for Vogelsang. As Quartermaster Sergeant he kept busy getting supplies and distributing them to the scattered parts of the regiment. And because, at age forty-eight, he was one of the oldest men in the 54th, he was frequently asked to settle problems among the soldiers.

So widely respected was Sergeant Vogelsang at war's end that his commander, Colonel Edward N. Hallowell, nominated him to become a commissioned officer. He must have been quite pleased, because only one other black soldier, Sergeant Stephen Swails, had been commissioned in the 54th, and most people could not tell that Swails was "colored." Vogelsang, on the other hand, was visibly one of the blackest men in the regiment; the nomination rewarded his battle record and his leadership. Colonel Hallowell persuaded Governor John A. Andrew of Massachusetts to commission Vogelsang and another black sergeant, Frank Welch. The governor agreed, and he sent the papers to Charleston.

But Colonel Hallowell had not consulted with the other white officers of the regiment, and several rebelled, talking of resigning their commissions if Vogelsang and Welch became lieutenants. One wrote, "Most of us [old officers] will resign or be 'mustered out of service,' we consider it an outrage and an insult and do not propose to pass it by without notice."[1]

Despite tension in the regiment, Vogelsang was promoted. White officers in the 54th, like officers in many other units, longed to go home and get on with their lives; the prejudice of some against Vogelsang helped speed their resignations. One by one during the summer of 1865, half of them resigned. Lieutenant Vogelsang weathered the protests and became the regiment's quartermaster. His biggest job was to get all the supplies and records ready for the final accounting, because the army had decided to send the 54th home in August.

On August 20, all the outlying detachments of the regiment were brought into Charleston, where Lieutenant Vogelsang checked over the supplies and accounts. Then the 54th Massachu-

1. Edward B. Emerson to Luis F. Emilio, June 8, 1865; Fifty-fourth Regiment Papers, Massachusetts Historical Society. Quoted by permission.

setts was officially mustered out of Federal service. Next day, the men marched onto transport ships and headed home. They arrived in Boston a week later. Vogelsang made his final report to the chief quartermaster of the army, and the men were paid off.

On September 2, the regiment marched through Boston in its final parade. At the State House, Governor Andrew saluted it, and friends and admirers cheered, waved flags, and welcomed the "brave black regiment" home at last. Lieutenant Vogelsang, who had marched with these men down these same streets in May 1863 as a proud black soldier, now marched proudly as a seasoned veteran, a pioneer officer, and a citizen. He could claim equal rights as an American. He would soon be back in Brooklyn with his wife and children. The war had finally ended.[2]

Most black soldiers, of course, did not get the recognition Peter Vogelsang received. But they returned home with the same pride in having earned their right to live in America. Most of the black regiments from the North got heroes' welcomes from their government leaders and local communities – parades, banquets, celebrations of all kinds. All of these black veterans, whether from the South or the North, expected life to be better now that they had proved themselves. For many, there was the work of putting their lives back together after the ravages of the slave system; reuniting their families was harder than just going back home, especially if home was in a former slave state.

Even those veterans from the free states of the North found that their war service was not enough to gain them the rights of citizens. The struggle to get the right to vote started as soon as the men returned home. Most Northern states did not let blacks vote at all, and others had restrictions. Because of the war record of the black troops, Republican leaders in several states tried to get laws passed that would let black citizens vote, but race prejudice defeated those

2. Fifty-fourth Regiment Papers, Massachusetts Historical Society. Emilio, *History of the Fifty-fourth Regiment of the Massachusetts Volunteer Infantry, 1863–1865,* second edition, 310–325.

efforts in Connecticut and elsewhere in 1865. As the year ended, the men tried to be optimistic; but they learned that, although slavery was dead, racism still lived.

When the men returned home, their letters to the newspapers slowed to a trickle, then disappeared altogether. There were reunions and political rallies, but mostly the black army veterans were busy getting back to normal and making a living. Later they would join veterans' groups, such as regimental societies and the Grand Army of the Republic. But they would always remember how they had proved their manhood, their right to be citizens.[3]

LETTER 126

(Olmstead Massy, Sergeant, 76th USCI, New Orleans, Louisiana, [July 1865]; *CR*, August 5, 1865) As soon as the fighting stopped, newspapers began publishing letters from African Americans all over the nation inquiring about missing people. Most were from ex-slaves who tried to find relatives who had been sold away in slavery. Sergeant Olmstead Massy, who apparently had been sold from Virginia into the Deep South at age seventeen, wrote to find traces of his long-lost mother. Hundreds of similar letters appeared during the summer of 1865.

Information wanted of Mrs. Nancy Massy. She was born and raised in Goochland County, Va. She was owned about fifteen years ago by John Mickey [Massy?]. Her name before marriage was Nancy Brown. Any one who can give any information in regard to her is requested to address,

3. James M. McPherson, *The Struggle for Equality* (Princeton, N.J., Princeton University Press, 1964) 333–334. Lesley H. Fishel, "Northern Prejudice and Negro Suffrage, 1865–1870," *Journal of Negro History*, 39 (1954) 8–26. V. Jacque Voegeli, *Free but Not Equal* (Chicago, University of Chicago Press, 1967) 166–168.

Sergeant Olmstead Massy
76th USCT
via New Orleans

Who will thankfully receive it, never having heard from her since he was *sold*, about fifteen years ago.

LETTER 127

(A. H. Newton, [Quartermaster Sergeant,] 29th Connecticut Infantry, Hartford, Connecticut, November 25, 1865; *WAA*, December 16, 1865) Sooner or later, each black regiment returned home. The process of being mustered out, getting paid, saying good-bye, and traveling home could take several weeks, especially for the regiments that guarded the Rio Grande frontier. Sergeant Alex Newton of New Haven wrote this report on the homecoming of the 29th Connecticut, which had seen hard fighting in Virginia before going to Texas. The week before these men returned to Hartford, Connecticut voted down a law that would have given them the right to vote.

After long waiting and witnessing many days of depression, and receiving the full benefit of Old Sol along the banks of the Rio Grande, we at last received the order to prepare for our last muster, which order we quickly obeyed. Sure enough, bright and early Saturday morning, October 14, 1865, who should enter the camp but Capt. J. E. Lockwood, of the 110th USCI, and informed us that he had come prepared to muster us out of the United States service. Soon the order was given, "Fall in," when cheer after cheer echoed through the air as the boys marched up to the place where the work was to be accomplished. Monday morning, October the 16th, the boys commenced to say goodbye to hard tack, salt horse, and other delicacies known no where but in the army.

Soon the boys were in line and marched off by the right flank, entering the road leading to Brownsville, Texas, where they were joined by the 9th USCI, headed by the 43d USCI brass band, and escorted through the city of Brownsville, where flags were flying as a final greeting to the soldiers on their homeward march. Onward the joyous battalion marched, beseeching the Divine Father to spare them to reach their homes, where they might smile on the countenances of their loving friends once more.

On Friday, October 20th, we arrived at Brazos, Santiago, and rested for a day or two. Sunday, October 22nd, at 11 o'clock, a.m., we embarked on board the steamer Alabama, for New Orleans. Precisely at 4 p.m., we found ourselves steaming slowly down the stream, the boys singing, "Homeward Bound". . . . How rejoiced we were when we awoke on Wednesday morning, Nov. 22d, and found that we, in a manner of speaking, had reached "the promised land." About 9 o'clock a.m., we arrived at pier 46, north river, New York. We soon disembarked and made our way to the Battery Barracks, where we rested for the night.

On Thursday morning, Nov. 23d, about half-past 7 o'clock, we embarked on board the steamer Granite State for Hartford, where we were to be paid off and receive our discharge papers.

About 7 o'clock on the morning of the 24th we arrived in Hartford, and were received by the Mayor and a committee, which had been appointed for the occasion, and marched up to Central row, headed by Colt's brass band, where we stacked arms and unslung knapsacks, after which the battalion was formed in two ranks and marched to the City Hall and partook of a fine repast, which had been prepared by the white and colored citizens of Hartford for the occasion.

On entering the hall the first thing we discovered was the star-spangled banner extended across the hall, and in the centre a banner bearing the following inscriptions: "Welcome 29th C.V.," "Deep Bottom," "Strawberry Plains, Va.," "Siege of Petersburg," "New Market Heights," "Darby Town Road," "Chapin's Farm," and "Fair Oaks." Over the head of this banner was hung a beautiful wreath of evergreens, which had been prepared by the ladies. On the stand in front were busts of our late much-lamented President, Abraham Lincoln, and other noblemen. After partaking of all the good things which had been prepared for us, we were ordered to "cease firing," and fall in and counter march to Central row, and soon learned that the [C]ity of Hartford had arrived, bringing the 31st USCI, Colonel Henry C. Ward, Commander.[4]

The City Guard, numbering eighty-six men, Capt. Williams, and the Buckingham Rifles, fifty men, Capt. Prouty, with Colt's brass band, received them and escorted them to the State House Square, where muskets were stacked and knapsacks unslung. The 29th and 31st were then formed in a square, where they were welcomed to the city by Mayor Stillman, who in the midst of his remarks said – "We believe you have done your duty, and your whole duty, and for this we give you a cordial greeting." After a few more remarks he then introduced his Excellency, Governor [William] Buckingham, who, mounting the stand, received the boys with gladness. . . .

Colonel [William] Wooster, formerly in command of the 29th, followed with a few remarks. . . . General [Joseph] Hawley said: – Fellow soldiers – I can heartily endorse all that has been said in your praise, for I have seen what you can do. . . . Seeing these things he would say now and always that every man whom the Lord made should be entitled, according to his intelligence and his moral worth, to all the rights and privileges of a freeman.

Gen. Hawley was received with tremendous cheers, and the conclusion of his remarks met with hearty applause. . . .

The procession marched through the principal streets and then to camp. All along the route of the procession flags were flying, handkerchiefs waving – the boys receiving a hearty welcome home. Saturday, Nov. 25th, we were paid off, disbanded, and everybody advised by the paymaster to take care of their money, and return to

4. Half of the 31st USCI was recruited in Connecticut and was sometimes called the 30th Connecticut Volunteer Infantry.

their homes and live the life of peaceable citizens. Thus ends the
29th's military career.

LETTER 128

("Hannibal," [5th USCI,] Western Theological Seminary, Allegheny, Pennsylvania, October 27, 1865; *CR*, November 4, 1865)
"Hannibal" returned to school immediately after his Ohio regiment was discharged. He was proud of its war record, and he was
confident that the men had earned the right to vote. But when
Governor David Tod, who had originally opposed using black
troops, had addressed the disbanding regiment, he had opposed
giving them the vote. "Hannibal" recommended that the veterans
organize themselves to push for the franchise and to preserve the
spirit of wartime brotherhood.

One by one the veteran regiments of color have been mustered out
of the service of the United States and returned again to their
peaceful pursuits; the 54th Massachusetts leading off, the 55th
following, and shortly after, our own brave regiment, the Fifth
United States Colored Infantry.

Every one is more or less interested in the colored troops, for we
regard them as representing the men to which we belong, and
whatever befalls them, we share with them. Hence it would naturally follow that our sympathies should become entwined around
that regiment, which, braving all opposition, were the first to represent us in the field, as a body, from our own beautiful state [Ohio].

We will not enter into the details of the organization, nor speak
of the contumely heaped upon it by its enemies, nor how the brave
spirited men such as Johnston, Graham, and [Captain O. S. B.]
Wall labored at the bar, in the pulpit, and upon the stump to
disabuse the public mind of the unnatural prejudice against colored soldiers. Nor will we speak of the treatment received at the

hands of the Government, who in the dark hours of the rebellion, called upon the colored men to assist her in quelling the civil war, and when under its control, refused to recognize them as soldiers, offering them a pittance for support from the treasury of the Commonwealth, and by word and deed considering them only as menials suitable for labor in the trenches. We will only revert to these things as they are fresh in the memory of every member of that gallant band, the remembrances of which will cause many a bitter thought when contemplating the injustice and ingratitude of the American people toward them.

But we leave this for a nobler theme – that of sketching some of the many deeds of valor performed by the Fifth regiment, which many spots of Virginia soil will fully attend.

Our boys deserve to have their names engraved on the scroll of fame – this is all we can do for them. The Government does not do so much, but discharges them with the injunction, "Go home and behave yourselves!" – the Jacksonian *modus operandi*, only on a larger scale.[5]

But to return to the subject before us. Our soldiers, by their determined energy, have won for themselves undying fame, and woven wreaths of victory that are imperishable. That they fairly won these honors, no one will question who follows closely their history. They started right, thus laying the foundation for that regulation which they carried through their terms of service.

While in Ohio, even their enemies were forced to acknowledge that there existed a latent power in them which, if developed, would make them the best soldiers, and so it proved.

When first introduced into active military life in Gen. [Edward] Wild's famous raid into North Carolina, although only skirmishing, yet our soldiers evinced that determination for thoroughness which afterwards rendered them such invincibles in that part of the army.

When the regiment was about to be transferred from Norfolk to

5. General Andrew Jackson made similar remarks to black soldiers after the Battle of New Orleans, in 1815.

Yorktown, Va., General [Isaac J.] Wistar said to General Wild, "Have them march up from Old Point Comfort, as I should like to have them somewhat familiar with the hardships incident to the march."

"If that is all," Gen. Wild replied, "let them go on the boat, for they are veterans already in marching."

We need not add that their after conduct fully verified this statement.

We rapidly glide over their history from that time until the 15th of June, 1864,[6] the interim being spent in making occasional reconnaissances from Yorktown to Bottom Bridge.

On that day they fought their first battle, and proved victors. It was a proud, yet sad day for them. Many of their comrades lay clasped in the cold embrace of death; yet the consciousness of being in the right imparted a proud bearing to their manly forms.

How sublimely interesting to see them as the evening shades were closing around, grouped together, earnestly engaged in discussing the past effort and the probable fate of each other on the morrow. Certainly, it was a touching scene.

Becoming gradually accustomed to the horrors of war, and with it the loss of friends, their friendship became more affiliated, until a bond of union pervaded the entire ranks of the regiment.

Hastily glancing over the battle just fought we pass on to that ever memorable occasion, July 30, 1864,[7] when their presence saved the 9th Corps from demoralization, and assured victory to the Union arms, though purchased at a terrible cost; then to those long, dreary days and nights spent in the trenches, where their moral power did as much toward keeping the enemy at bay as their military prowess on the field of battle, the tedium being relieved by occasional brilliant displays of pyrotechnics gotten up at their expense by the enemy, though more ornamental than useful.

Our attention is directed to that preparatory attempt to capture

6. Date of the first attack on Petersburg, Virginia.
7. Date of the Battle of the Crater at Petersburg.

Richmond, Sept. 29th, 1864, where so many of your noble braves, my dear boys poured out their blood in devotion to their country. Your remember Moss, the life of the sharpshooters, and Tibbs, with his pleasant greeting for every one; and at that desperate assault upon Fort Gilmore, where our boys lay heaped upon each other, weltering in the terrible carnage of that day – a tear starts when we remember the proud, manly form of Hall, with his clear, ringing voice, cheering on his men – and Terrah, with his feminine appearance heightened by his glossy curls, yet withal, possessing a noble heart – these have all fallen, a sacrifice in behalf of their country.

Following the regiment to North Carolina, we find them engaged at Fort Fisher, Sugar Loaf, Fort Anderson, and Wilmington, N.C., where many of that fraternal band were slain, and whose blood is but another of the many evidences of the devotion and loyalty of the colored man to his country.

Here the war ended, so far as the 5th Regt. was concerned, but in its stead came a *moral* war, which was to test their power for enduring hardships without the excitement of war. The most prominent of these seemed to be jealousy of the domineering class, who upon the withdrawal of the largest portion of the troops insisted upon assuming their old relations with their peculiar institution. Opposition to this, together with the dangers encountered in the climate, rendering it necessary for them to bring into requisition all their moral energy; but we are happy to add that they discharged their duty in a manner which won the admiration of the whole enlightened world.

We do not attempt to give even a synopsis of what the regiment has been doing; that must be deferred for the pen of the historian. But in conclusion, we would direct attention to the last hours spent by the regiment as an organization. Although inadequate to the task, yet we will attempt to draw a faint outline. We will get a good position and watch them as they go through the manual of arms for the last time; and when discharged see them turn away with a sad, lingering gaze upon that old flag which they have borne so proudly upon so many battle-fields. True, it is all tattered and torn, but it has not been dishonored. Its bright colors have become tarnished by exposure, but in their stead are jewels of heroism of undying luster. Then, as the order is given to *break ranks*, see how eagerly they grasp the hand of their comrades in earnest friendship for the last time. A tear courses down their bronzed cheeks, as they hastily say the parting word in final *adieu* to that comrade who has with them passed through all dangers. They bestow a parting word upon those absent ones whose bones lie blanching on the battle-fields of the South, and who would have been present had not Providence willed otherwise.

Do not forget, dear boys, Sergeant Shorter, the flower of the regiment. There are others who feel that the vacant spot ought not to exist in the ranks; that they have been robbed of a dear one. That mother, brother, sister, or loved one who strain their eyes in vain to catch a glimpse of other missing ones will mingle their tears with you in remembrance of the dead. We leave this sad thought, that some gentle being may be reminded of her bereavement, for who is there in this broad land that has not lost a friend in this war? Great will be the judgment meted out to those Southern instigators of this unhallowed rebellion.

We now turn from these sad thoughts of mourning to the speech of Ex. Gov. Tod, on the reception of the regiment at the capital. It must be borne in mind that Gov. Tod promised this address when the regiment went South, and now, after having witnessed the undaunted bravery of those troops – their soldierly bearing and thorough discipline in a hundred instances, he very emphatically says, "I am opposed to giving the *elective franchise* to these men." These are the men whom he very willingly accepted as soldiers. Then they were good enough to go in the place of white men, and thus avoid having a draft. But according to the governor's theory, they are not good enough to vote with the white man.

What absurdity! There is a day of retribution coming when justice will be meted out to those dangerous and political aspirants. A Cromwell will be found who will secure eternal justice to our oppressed race.

We will not revert to these acts of oppression again. *Qui transtroitit sustinet.* We who have, of the last three years, been so closely connected as to have formed a seeming brotherhood, now, when these ties are about to be dissolved, are we not willing to continue this connection in some form, which may bring us together in something like the former organization? How pleasant it is to meet annually, if not as a body, then by representation. . . .

What a glorious reunion we would have, say, the 1st of August next. If formed, I hope this association will include all the colored soldiers who have gone out from Ohio in the different branches of the service. To the soldiers of these regiments we would say, we hope [for an] organization which will connect bonds of friendship and grace and luster to our future advancement in liberty and justice.

LETTER 129

(I. N. Triplett, Orderly Sergeant, 60th USCI, Davenport, Iowa, October 31, 1865; from the *Muscatine* (Iowa) *Journal,* November 6, 1865, reprinted in *CR,* November 18, 1865) The 60th USCI was made up of African Americans from Iowa. When they returned from the war in October, they agreed to meet together to push for their civil rights. They drew up resolutions that called for the state to change its constitution to permit them to vote. Because the Republican party had been swept into control of the state, these veterans were confident that their appeal to the people of Iowa would succeed. But it would not be until 1869, when the Fifteenth Amendment to the United States Constitution would be ratified, that blacks in the North as well as the South would be treated equally at the voting booth.

In accordance with the earnest desire of numerous members of the regiment, the enlisted men and non-commissioned officers of the

60th U.S. Infantry (colored regiment), numbering about 700 persons, met in mass convention at Camp McClellan, Davenport, on Thursday, Oct. 31st, 1865. The convention was organized by electing Alexander Clark, of Muscatine, President, and I. N. Triplett, Secretary. . . .

The convention also appointed a committee of ten, one sergeant from each company, to draw up a petition to be signed by each man in the regiment, and to be presented to the next Legislature of Iowa, asking for the extension of the right of suffrage, so far as the Legislature can act in the premises. Alexander Clark was appointed to convey such petition to the capital and secure its presentation to the Legislature at the next session.

The following resolutions, as reported by the committee, were unanimously adopted:

Resolved, That we, the soldiers of the 60th U.S. [Colored] Infantry, formerly the Iowa African First, having returned home from the battlefield, and feeling conscious that we have discharged our duty as soldiers in the defense of our country, respectfully urge that it is the duty of Iowa to allow us the use of our votes at the polls; believing, as we do and must, that he who is worthy to be trusted with the musket can and ought to be trusted with the ballot.

Resolved, That we recommend our colored friends all over the State to prepare and cause to be presented to our next Legislature petitions asking of that body the action necessary to initiate the amendment to the State Constitution, by the adoption of which the right we desire will be secured.

Resolved, That we recommend to our people throughout the country that patient pursuit of education, industry and thrift, which will certainly be rewarded with increasing intelligence and wealth.

Resolved, That we recommend our people every where to abstain from the use of intoxicating drink, and from frequenting saloons.

Resolved, That we still have confidence in the President and the Republican administration; and rest in the hope that they will do all that can be done to secure us our rights, and protect our friends in the South from wrong and oppression.

Resolved, That we mourn, as we ever must, the sad fate of the martyr-President, Abraham Lincoln, the great Emancipator, and devoted friend of our race, yet rejoice that the great work which God appointed him to perform has been so nearly accomplished that the wrath of the oppressor is utterly powerless to prevent a full and glorious consummation. . . .

The Address of the Convention of Colored Soldiers to the People of Iowa.
FELLOW COUNTRYMEN: – We wish we could truthfully address you as "fellow citizens." – Having established our claim to the proud title of American soldiers, and shared in the glories won by the deeds of the true men of our own color, will you not hear and heed our appeal? We appeal to the justice of the people and of the Legislature of our State, for those rights of citizenship without which our well-earned freedom is but a shadow; we ask you to recognize our claims to manhood by giving to us that right without which we have no power to defend ourselves from unjust legislation, and no voice in the Government we have endeavored to preserve. Being men, we claim to be of that number comprehended in the Declaration of Independence, and who are entitled, not only to life, but to equal rights in the pursuit and securing of happiness – in the choice of those who are to rule over us.

We appeal to your magnanimity, to your good faith, to your sense of justice. We ask no privilege, we simply ask for our own rights, long denied by the misguided and now-conquered South, and withheld from us at the North in obedience to the political teachings and demands of a slaveholding public opinion. We will not believe but that the people of Iowa will be the first to do full justice to the men of color, as they have been among the foremost in upholding the flag of our country.

We rejoice in the fact and congratulate the people of our own color in every part of the land that in the recent election for Governor the gallant [William] Stone, who marched as bravely up to the manhood suffrage issue, as he was wont to do on the field of battle against the enemies of the country in arms, has been again chosen to the Gubernatorial chair, by the handsome majority of more than 15,000 votes. In this fact the colored citizens of Iowa take courage, and are the more incited to show our white friends, that if we do not get our rights as citizens and voters it is not because we do not deserve and have not fairly earned them, but only because prejudice and wrong still triumph over Truth and Righteousness. Seeing what our eyes have already beheld during the past four years, we know that the day of full triumph is coming as surely as the Omnipotent reigneth. We patiently wait our time, desiring ever to prove faithful to God and our country, and hoping that suffering humanity now contending for equal Rights and Justice, will, ere long, be made to rejoice in the hearty sympathy and aid of all good and true men every where.

Trusting that this our appeal will receive a candid consideration from the people of Iowa, we subscribe ourselves on behalf of our brothers and race. [Signed by one civilian and ten sergeants of the regiment.]

Index

297

Books in the series: